Toto, I Don't Think We're In Golders Green Anymore!

Five Butt-Clenching-Nail-Biting-Hysteria-Inducing Years in Israel

Andrew Reid

Bloomington, IN  Milton Keynes, UK

AuthorHouse™
1663 Liberty Drive, Suite 200
Bloomington, IN 47403
www.authorhouse.com
Phone: 1-800-839-8640

AuthorHouse™ *UK Ltd.*
500 Avebury Boulevard
Central Milton Keynes, MK9 2BE
www.authorhouse.co.uk
Phone: 08001974150

© *2006 Andrew Reid. All rights reserved.*

No part of this book may be reproduced, stored in a retrieval system, or transmitted by any means without the written permission of the author.

First published by AuthorHouse 12/14/2006

ISBN: 978-1-4259-7852-5 (sc)

Printed in the United States of America
Bloomington, Indiana

This book is printed on acid-free paper.

This book is dedicated to the kind and hospitable people of Israel who found a place for me in their nation.

I wish to thank Avi for his input and for jogging
my memory whilst writing this book.

I want to thank Carl Monk, Rachel Vieira, Jenny Mills, Chris
Maynard and Jane Carnall for their help with this project.

I want to thank my civil partner Carl Monk for his
love, support, patience and practical help.

"A tall, decaf, skinny cup of mud to go please"

I hadn't planned to stay for five years. In fact I was only going to stay for three months. It was spring 1992. I was young, foolish and gay. As in homosexual. Not as in happy. Which I wasn't. My journey had begun in Edinburgh a few months earlier when I realised I had had enough. I was tired of my job, tired of the murky grey, breath-freezing winters and rainy summers. I had had my fill of the snobby aloofness of Edinburgh, and of the feeling that life was happening elsewhere. I wanted to become a Jew and that was not going to happen in Edinburgh. After a long application process I had been accepted as a police officer with Sussex Police and an exciting new life in Brighton beckoned. I packed up my belongings into cardboard boxes and gave away the rest. March turned to April and the time came for me to head off to a kibbutz in Israel, where I planned to fulfil a teenage ambition before joining the police. Life felt good. After two years in a rut I was on the move.

It was dark when I arrived at Heathrow's Terminal One. I joined the long queue of Israelis for enhanced security, clutching my passport, ticket and a 'welcome pack' from the kibbutz. When my turn came a young security man interviewed me and asked me if I was carrying any bombs. When I replied that I was not, he began telling me lurid stories about all the beautiful women I would meet on the kibbutz. I smiled politely in the dignified but aloof manner of a gay man listening to a straight man engaging in heterosexual banter. Little did he realise I was more interested in what he had to offer rather than what he had to say. I wanted to run my hands through his thick, dark hair. We would kiss passionately, our love for one another growing stronger by the second, our lives entwined and …….

"Oh man, Israeli girls are so hot" he continued, leaning over my luggage.

"Mmmm. Yeah. Whatever" I replied politely.

The BBC programme *Airport* once featured the El Al team as part of their bloody-hell-look-how-stressful-life-at-Heathrow-is fly on the wall documentary. I think they filmed it on a quiet day. It was seriously nuts. The noise level was deafening, almost as if every single person in the entire world had decided to scream all at once after taking speed. The passengers in the check-in queue fascinated me. Male Orthodox Jews in black suits and white shirts, open at the neck, rocked gently in silent prayer. Studious and bespectacled, and at the same time self-assured and determined, they clutched their blue Israeli passports. A couple of years later I would have one too. An Israeli passport that is. Not an Orthodox Jew. Obviously. I didn't know it then. If I had, I might have turned heel and got the next train to Brighton. I might have saved myself a lot of bother. But then I would never have written this book. Other passengers were secular, some of them clutching huge boxes with electronic equipment, cuddly toys or duty free bags, bursting at the seams with expensive treats. Or all of the above. Hey why not? You don't travel to London everyday, right? A screaming, obnoxious child was wearing a plastic English policeman's helmet and had snot running down his chubby cheeks. "*Imaaaaaaaaa. Imaaaaaaaaa!*" he roared, roughly translated as "Mother, do you think I might have some attention please. Thanks awfully."

In the departure lounge I looked out the window at the enormous El Al jumbo jet, and felt excitement and a weird sense of familiarity. Soon we were airborne, dinner was served and the noise level subsided to deafening as 350 Israelis settled down to eat. It was my first ever flight with El Al. Down below England faded away. I had heard mixed reports about the level of service on El Al. One joke described a woman on a flight being asked if she would like a meal.

"What are my choices?" asked the passenger.

"Yes, or no" came the answer.

The service was fine, and the food delicious. I was sat next to an emergency exit and was amused to watch two elderly and very

Orthodox British ladies who had come to stretch in the gap. One of them decided to sit on the ridge formed by the emergency chute. They smiled pleasantly at me and resumed their chat. A furious stewardess appeared and told them to stand up. "Oh my, that's us told isn't it?" they tittered mischievously. Five hours later the seat belt signs came on and the captain made an announcement in Hebrew. At first I thought someone was coughing over the intercom until I made out the words Tel Aviv and *nechita*, the Hebrew word for landing. It was dawn and I got a glimpse of grey sea. Minutes later the long straight coast came upon us and we flew low over a hazy Tel Aviv, waking up to another frantic day. The wide roads stretched through the city like arteries. Then came miles of orange groves. As the plane touched down the passengers erupted into applause. I didn't join in. I am firmly of the school of thought that says if a captain needs applause for a safe landing, then he or she probably shouldn't be flying a plane.

Flying Instructor: "Well done Moshe, that was great, now let's try it again but this time let's put the wheels down first. Oh, and let's aim for that bit of concrete called the runway too. Come on everyone; let's tell him what a good boy he's been!"

As soon as I emerged onto the movable steps I was hit by the incredibly intoxicating smell of orange blossom and by the humidity. Everything felt damp to touch and I could feel the heat building up. I took off my jacket. I was here! I was toying with the idea of kissing the tarmac *à la Jean Paul II* when I felt a bony, sharp nudge.

"Hey you! Move!" said a woman so small she looked like a horribly aged toddler in jogging wear. The terminal was frantic as travel-wise passengers rushed towards the growing passport queues. A constant thump thump thump echoed from the booths, as young female police officers in smart blue shirts impassively checked passports. I gazed at the huge neon advertising hoardings in Hebrew. I was in Israel all right. Soon I imagined I would be clearing swamps, shaking hands with Golda Meir and dancing the *Hora*.

On the 222 bus into Tel Aviv I sat back and relaxed, content to enjoy the view of palm trees and orange groves by the side of the dual carriageway. The radio was on, and I recognised a song by the 1970s iconic singer Ilanit called *Kan ipol Hacochav Sheli* or *Here My Star Falls*. I was embarking on something big. Only days before, I had been working out my notice in a smart office in Edinburgh's Melville Street and now I was alone in Israel. If I had had an American travel companion I would have started saying things like 'wooooooo yeah' and doing high fives. As I was English and alone, I was content to hum quietly to myself. We arrived at the bus station thirty minutes later at eight in the morning. The *Tachana Merkazit* or Central Bus Station was in those days a piss stinking hive of streets and platforms, built up around an old market. All around were decaying Bauhaus buildings, the concrete eaten away by the sea air to reveal strips of metal. Vendors sold pretzels, covered with salt and flies, along with packets of cigarettes and bottles of soft drinks in buckets filled with iced water. Cheek by jowl, music vendors were hawking pirated tapes of *Mizrachi*, Jewish Oriental music. It was still early, but Boy, was it getting hot! I took a few minutes to get my bearings and grab a can of thick, cool apricot cectar before making my way to the biblical port of Jaffa by bus. This involved dragging my rucksack down the length of the crowded vehicle as dozens of passengers yelled "*'allo! 'allo!*" At first I thought they were saying *hello*, a trifle brusquely perhaps, but one did so have to make allowances for foreigners. Then I cottoned on that "*'allo! 'allo!*" was in fact Hebrew for "Oy! Fuck face! Look where you're going."

Once I had emerged from the hellish ordeal of the bus I sat on the ramparts and gazed over Tel Aviv. Along the coast were tower blocks and large hotels which were way beyond my means. No luxurious marble bathroom and fluffy towels awaited me. There would be no mini-bars and 24 hour room service where I was going. No sireee, there would not. I was again struck by the slimyness of everything. Feeling clammy, I took off my Scotland rugby shirt. Still carrying my rucksack, I walked around the Arab quarter. I passed a carved and ornate doorway that led into an ancient mosque. I wanted to go in but a picture of an infidel with a big line through it indicated that my presence was not wished for. Fair enough. At a small, tatty kiosk I bought yoghurt and some pitta for breakfast then returned to the bus station. Here I was to catch an Egged bus to Kfar Saba, literally meaning *Granddad's Village*. I impressed everyone at the ticket booth with my command of the Hebrew language, making lots of new chums. I could tell they liked me by the way they sucked their teeth and spoke by nodding their head. It was almost as though we had a strange tantric connection, that words somehow no longer mattered. Either that or the morose bastard was too lazy or too important to open his pinched, puckered mouth and speak to a paying customer. An indeterminate hissing noise indicated that the transaction was over. On the Intercity Egged coach I again settled back to enjoy the drive and noted the huge motorway signs with Biblical names. Most striking of all was the name Jerusalem which was written in Hebrew, Arabic and English. Jerusalem. I said it a few times to myself.

We arrived at Kfar Saba, a pleasant commuter town on the border with the West Bank, located at Israel's narrowest point. By now I was exhausted, never having learned the art of sleeping on planes. I was sticky, hungry and nervous. I jumped straight onto a local bus service and was soon travelling through the pretty Israeli countryside. On both sides were tall Cypress trees and lush orange groves. A couldn't-give-a-shit-clicking-of-teeth-accompanied-by-a-vague-nod-of-the-head from the driver indicated I should get off. The bus pulled away, leaving a cloud of dust in its trail. Then I was alone with the sound of birds and crickets. Flies buzzed round my head as I walked up to the gates of the Kibbutz. I noted the pretty display of 'conceptual art' in a small garden. It looked as if a bored Israeli geriatric with a creative impulse but no talent and way too much free time had somehow welded together bits of iron in the shape of a huge tit.

Kibbutznik: "Oh Christ! Has *Savta* got hold of the welding iron again?"

Granny with artistic leanings: "I'm 92 you know."

I carried my rucksack past the gatehouse and arrived at a collection of shabby 1930s buildings.

"Shalom" said a wizened woman with a devil-may-care approach to skin care. Like nearly all *Kibbutznikim,* the concept of smiling appeared alien to her. She nodded towards an office on the ground floor of another 1930s block. Inside sat an old lady with one of the longest ponytails I'd ever seen. She peered at me from behind half-moon glasses, making me feel uncomfortable.

"*Nu*, we were expecting you yesterday," she said by way of greeting. I was handed some blue overalls, shorts and a blue shirt along with some canvas boots and a bag for my underwear to be washed in.

"That I don't have to touch your pants" she added with a smug sneer. I chuckled politely. What does one answer to something like that? I was shown to my room. It was bare with white walls, a flimsy desk, some drawers and two stripped beds. The windows were covered with a fly net and wooden blinds, which were drawn. I felt like Oscar Wilde settling down to his first day at Reading Gaol.

"What time does the maid come?" I asked as a joke, forgetting that humour, like water, was in short supply here. I sat on my bed and began to unpack. The Volunteers' Matron took me on a short tour. I thought the title of Matron was deliciously camp but I was worried I may end up getting a large, soapy enema and sent straight to bed. Fortunately I didn't. We started our tour at the huge dining room where people were eating either a late breakfast or an early lunch. Our next stop was a small shop where Matron and the women behind the counter made a great show of not greeting each other. It was here that I could spend my allowance on chocolate, stamps and other such luxuries. Heavens, I would be positively spoiled.

I drank in the landscape. An old water tower dominated the centre of the Kibbutz, and beyond were citrus trees and then scorched fields. It was so Israeli, so familiar. So fucking hot! On the way back to my room I bumped into an English boy going into the room next door. When I say boy I really mean young man. Obviously he was not a real boy. We soon got chatting and he introduced his roommate who was also English. Then we called on two young English women next door and we all went for a jolly lunch. I was glad I had made friends so soon. In the canteen I piled my tray with cucumber salad, pickles, vegetables and some cream cheese. As usual, when food is free I pigged out. I felt happy and reckless. I was here. I belched. I felt sick. After lunch we took a very, very hot walk along a dirt path, behind the modern factory and over a dry stream. This was filled with rubbish, and a swarm of flies buzzed around the damp soil. Huge plastic tubs were stacked by a wall, bearing the names of Israeli ports. After a short while we emerged into a pleasant park area and I saw the pool, turquoise and tantalising. I eased myself into the icy water. "Gawrrrrrr," I gasped trying to get my breath. Meanwhile the sun was dazzling me. I swam, splashed and chatted. Then we sat on deck chairs and I turned lobster-coloured. This was fun!

The days followed a pleasant routine, beginning with an early and massive breakfast. I tried to make myself eat olives because I had once read that was what the early Zionist pioneers ate, along with cucumber in soured cream. I don't actually like olives so I left most of them, trying again the following day. I also consumed vast quantities of delicious Feta cheese and freshly baked pitta, washed down with *Botz*, which was Turkish coffee prepared by pouring boiling water over the grains. It means mud in Hebrew. Only the Israelis could call a hot beverage mud. Would one order it at Costa Coffee I wondered?

Customer: "Hi, can I have a tall, decaf, skinny cup of mud to go please."

Barrister: "Do you want chocolate on your mud?"

After breakfast we went to work. Initially I was given a job with the Kibbutz gardener. He was really hunky in a middle-aged, come-to-daddy kind of a way and I was keen to make a good impression and work hard.

"Look Mr Gardener, I have made this grass bed look real nice. Now can I take care of *anything else*?" This resulted in Matron telling the gardener off for exploiting me (If only) and I was sent somewhere else. I was then given the task of painting metal chairs in a shed so hot I felt I was in the punishment block from *Bridge Over The River Kwai*. I enjoyed the solitude in there. I savoured the smells and the thousands of details that made me realise I was in Israel. The sound of crickets, the Hebrew writing on the paint tin, the exotic weeds, the Middle Eastern songs on the radio or the sound of Hebrew news bulletins. At noon we had a big lunch in the canteen and then it was time for our afternoon break. As I grew used to the rhythm of Kibbutz life, I looked forward to my break. I went to my room to read, make myself a cup of tea and savour my daily chocolate bar. I then went to the shower block for a cold, refreshing shower and got ready for my *Ulpan*, or Hebrew class. I was often struck by the juxtaposition of some really nice facilities such as an air-conditioned classroom or a pool, with something utterly vile or filthy like the volunteers' loo.

Our teacher was a young *Mizrachit*, a Jew of Middle Eastern rather than European origin. This was highly unusual, as most Kibbutzim are composed of *Ashkenazim* or European Jews. It was nice to sit in the cool classroom and study. It was often the best part of the day. My

Hebrew was good enough to communicate in and I was soon writing little pieces of prose.

On the days when there was no class, I took the free minibus into Kfar Saba and engaged in a secret vice, a sin so disgraceful I never breathed a word of it to anyone on the Kibbutz. I treated myself to a cup of decent, decadent, capitalist coffee and sometimes even a cake at the posh Café Mozart. Here a waitress in a black apron brought *me* the coffee. There was air conditioning, classical music and above all *class*. It was delicious not to see anyone in a scruffy, blue, prison uniform or to eat anything from a Formica table. After relishing my treat I walked round the modern streets of the town, popping into the local Super Sol supermarket. I loved looking at the packaging of everyday products in Hebrew; I loved the strange smells and slightly retro feel of the products. I think it was the fusion of modern with exotic and biblical which had first attracted me to Israel. Cornflakes in the language of the bible; supermarkets in places where ancient prophets had preached. It was weird.

In the evenings there was no meal in the canteen, a result of the Gulf War when families had started taking meals in their homes. This was in case a Scud Missile should decide to plonk itself down on the Kibbutz, and wipe out the entire community. After the war people decided they actually preferred eating with their own families, rather than the several hundred other miserable people, with whom they were confined. For the volunteers there was a tiny kitchen and a large fridge stocked with cucumbers, cottage cheese, *Teisha* (9%) cheese and pitta bread. After a light supper we sat on the steps with a beer and chatted, admiring the purple hues of the sunset and the relative cool of the evening. We became close, exchanging our hopes and dreams and life stories. I also befriended a group of young Dutch women, and some South Africans.

One scourge of the Kibbutz was the abundant and varied population of creepy crawlies. Worst of all were the slipper-sized cockroaches or *jukkim*, which flew into the kitchen, making the Dutch girls scream *"Yeyzjus"* at the top of their lungs. This usually attracted a grumpy Kibbutznik with a rolled up newspaper and a dustpan. Otherwise one of us Englishmen, made of stern stuff, would be sent to dispatch the unfortunate creatures. Flies were also a menace. After a tasty slap up meal of fertiliser and cow shit, these invariably came over to our kitchen for a nice bit of neon light and a refreshing drink of blood.

The highlight of the weekend was *Erev Shabbat* on Friday night. Work stopped at lunchtime and the Kibbutz began to wind down. Clouds of fragrant steam came from the shower block as everyone rushed to get ready, and for once people wore clothes that bore no resemblance to the ladies from *Prisoner Cellblock H*. It was also the one evening of the week when we had dinner in the canteen. My favourite dish was the *Tivoli* vegetarian cutlets with roast potatoes and sweet corn. It was like eating children's food again. As there was never any rush after this meal, we lingered over our empty plates, enjoying the small candles. Outside the trees faded into darkness and the crickets chirruped merrily. The orange groves breathed their sweet perfume. It was *Shabbat Shalom,* the peace of the Sabbath.

I enjoyed chatting to an older German volunteer who was also planning to convert to Judaism. After years of feeling like I was the only person in the world on this path I had finally met fellow travellers. After dinner we were allowed to go to a special lounge with posh furniture and standard lamps. This was the Sabbath Room. Here coffee, pastries and stale biscuits were served. I am sure that these biscuits were the same, week in week out. I am not entirely convinced they weren't like those pieces of plastic food you get in the windows of Japanese restaurants, but made to look like cheap lemon puffs. The older Kibbutznikim sat with clasped hands and looks of constipated rapture listening to zit-speckled youths playing the cello. It was very refined. The room also served as a library and a little museum. Around eleven o'clock the *Mo'adon*, or Club, opened. This was located near the *Refet* (cowsheds). I loved the club and enjoyed drinking beer so cold it froze my tonsils. I nibbled chickpeas or *Bamba*, a fluffy crisp-like snack, which tasted vaguely of peanut butter. The club was lit by tea lights and played loud popular music, as well as Israeli music. Sometimes we danced or else chatted outside in the fresh air.

On the Sabbath we didn't work but spent the morning by the pool applying for skin cancer. Later, in the afternoon, we made the mile-long walk across the fields to the Israeli Arab village of Tira where the shops were open. There we sat in an open-air café nursing beers and chickpeas. For lunch we snacked on hummus and pitta. Half-pissed, red and delirious, we went for deliciously sweet ice creams at a small ice cream parlour run by a *Hijab*-wearing woman who seemed to eat more ice-cream than she sold. Tira was a strange place. My first impression was that it was half-derelict. Years later I discovered that Moslems are not allowed to borrow money with interest, and therefore prefer to build their homes in stages, resulting in a lot of half finished homes.

Soon after arriving, we were all gathered together and told we were to go to the medical block. I knew what was coming; we were going to be tested for HIV. I hated the way this was done, and felt violated. I know cats and dogs which have been spayed with more sensitivity. About a week later we were given the results on slips of paper, returned with our clean laundry in our pigeonholes. There was no counselling and I dread to think about the effect on anyone who tested positive. Would the Matron leave a little note I wonder.

"Here's your pants and socks. By the way you have AIDS and two days to clear off. Have a nice day."

"Give me scraps for the monkeys now!"

Two weeks after arriving I was transferred to kitchen duty which I found about as enjoyable as handwashing a bag-lady's soiled underwear. I spent the morning slicing loaves in a huge cutting machine before then putting the bread into plastic bags. It wasn't challenging. Around eleven o'clock each morning an unpleasant boy with wiry ginger hair came to ask for the scraps.

"Give me scraps for the monkeys now" he barked, arrogantly and without any concept of how rude he sounded. At first I thought he was a bit simple and just gave him the bread, adding an ironic 'you're welcome' which was lost on him. One day I told the Dutch girl about it, expecting a jolly good side-splitting-pants-wetting belly laugh. She informed me that the monkeys lived in a small zoo on the edge of the Kibbutz. The next day I went to visit them, where I also saw two young goats having full-on-eyes-popping-out-the-head sex. Sure enough, my new found simian friends were busy munching on crusts of bread.

One morning I was informed I was to get a new roommate. My mind began to picture a succession of hunks that would bunk down with me. "Do you mind if I walk around naked?" they would ask. In my dreams. Instead I really drew the short straw and it was clear that my camp new roommate and I were not going to see eye to eye. Hackles were raised, claws were out. Our first clash came over the tidiness of the room. My roommate decided I was messy. I said *potato;* he said *get your pants off the floor.* He said *tomato*; I said *get out of my face bitch!* Despite our differences we had long gay-related chats and he introduced me to Ethnix, an Israeli pop group whose music I grew to love. He regaled me with his trips to Tel Aviv and the carryings-on in Gan Atzmaut, Independence Park, whilst I sat open mouthed in outraged relish. After a few weeks he bizarrely began to see himself as some kind of manager. One morning, when we were sat peeling cucumbers for the lunch time salads, I noted with a mixture of puzzlement and distaste how a long-standing female Kibbutznik asked him if she could leave a few minutes early. After a moment to consider he graciously assented. Hang on a cotton-pickin' minute I thought. This woman grew up on the Kibbutz. She's Israeli. My roommate was a guest and yet he was managing her work place. Then I wondered why she had given him this power on a plate. I guess some men exude a kind of control, thinking the world owes them something. Whatever the reason I personally found him unpleasant and this was spoiling my stay on the Kibbutz.

While I was on the Kibbutz I celebrated my birthday. The day started pleasantly with a card and a cake baked in the Kibbutz kitchen by the beaming Dutch girls. They had ordered the ingredients especially and had gone to work early to do it. I was touched. Unfortunately the cake tasted like cardboard. I gagged and tried to smile rather than spit, something I am sure my roommate was doing there and then behind a bush in Independence Park. Birthday festivities on hold for the day, I went to work as usual and, as it was a Friday, I went to the club in the evening. There was something magical about being awake at two in the morning and being so close to the Israeli countryside. There was that orange blossom smell, the smell of hay in the cowsheds and a delicious coolness that was a rare treat. I'd had a bit to drink and the Oriental Remix music of Ethnix floated out of the club with me as I walked back to my room. As I staggered into my room, singing a song about strawberries in Hebrew, a bag of flour fell down, narrowly missing my head and I kicked over a bucket of water. I cursed as I pulled back my sheets to discover more flour in my bed so I shook it over the balcony onto the roof of Matron's office where, in the absence of any rain, it remained for the rest of my stay. In the morning I swept up the mess as best I could, feeling as cross as a bag of weasles. What a stupid thing to do. Was I supposed to laugh? None of the perpetrators offered to help clean up. It was typical stag night behaviour.

During our stay we were offered several free tours. We left early on a strange bus, mounted onto the frame of a truck. Everyone was cranky from lack of sleep but we were all excited. We bypassed Kfar Saba and joined the coastal road known as the Via Maris, heading north to the Galilee. As the driver was in the cab of the truck, we had no way of communicating our urgent desire to piss. The gentlemen could have improvised but there were ladies present. The slightest bump sent shock waves through my painfully engorged football-sized bladder. Our first stop was at Rosh HaNikra on the border with Lebanon, where we stayed at the Youth Hostel. As soon as the bus doors opened we charged like startled sheep into the toilets. Seconds later Rosh HaNikra reverberated to a giant collective sigh of *arrrrgggghh*! The hostel was spartan but clean and functional, and the *Kibbutznikim* in charge began unloading large bin liners of food for us. It was at this point that I noticed they were armed with revolvers. I certainly didn't remember my school teacher bringing a round of ammunition and a gun on our school trips.

In the lobby were dozens of snoozing soldiers, dusty and exhausted from a tour of duty in Southern Lebanon. They looked so young, like schoolboys in khaki. Machine guns and kit bags lay piled up on the floor. It seemed an odd place to billet soldiers. Some of them looked like they needed a cuddle. I didn't try. Exhausted teenage straight men; too much testosterone; loaded weapons. No. Bad idea. I was awoken from my musing by a bowel-chilling-goose-bump-inducing scream and saw blood seeping from the piece of kitchen roll which was wrapped around our group leader's hand. On the floor was a jaggedly open can of pickles. I winced and turned away. I hate to see good food wasted. Every Israeli al fresco meal seemed to consist of exactly the same food; Pitta bread, bitter humus, shredded red cabbage and some dips, usually made from char-grilled aubergine. Unfortunately I never really acquired a taste for it and would have preferred a nice Cheddar cheese sandwich with some pickle. Brought to me in my room by one of the soldiers. After lunch and a walk on the beach we were taken to the caves at Rosh HaNikra. These could only be reached by cable car, and stretched underground into Lebanon. It was sad to see the bricked up railway tunnel, part of a British Mandate plan to run a railway from Cairo to Beirut.

Israeli excursions have the hallmarks of route marches. There is an underlying militarism to them, a spirituality-through-blisters-and-low-blood-sugar-levels kind of ideology. By the time we'd climbed some more pretty hills, I was ready to wilt. It was early summer in Israel and temperatures rarely fall below thirty degrees. Nevertheless the view from the summit was gorgeous. Wild flowers were growing everywhere and I noted exotic plants which I had only ever encountered in bars of expensive soap. There was Aloe Vera, hundreds of red poppies, wild sage and mustard.

Our evening meal was communal and eaten at the hostel. Predictably it involved chips, pitta and hummus. I was fast asleep by 9. The soldiers had gone.

The next day was Shabbat and we drove back to the Kibbutz through the Galilee, passing some Druze villages along the way. Our guide was keen to point out how loyal the Druze were to Israel and cited their commendable war record in crack Israeli units. Many of the older men in the villages wore huge baggy trousers which some of the less enlightened volunteers thought was funny. We arrived home at dusk, a time when the Kibbutz always looked its best. The cypress trees were silhouetted against a pink sky, and the water tower loomed over the settlement, reminiscent of the old pioneering days. However my bladder was the size of a generously stuffed haggis, and such poetical musings would need to wait.

A month after arriving I was transferred to night shift at the rubber factory, a job which I hated. I hated the smell, the boredom and the stress of opening the machines and removing bits of hot, melting rubber when they got stuck. I sat listening to the religious right-wing channel on the radio because they had good music and it was in English. A soothing American voice informed listeners that all the Biblical lands of Israel should be returned to the Jews but since we were reasonable people the Arabs could keep Jordan and Syria. A nice catchy tune would be sandwiched between these bouts of lunacy and it was disturbingly easy to get caught up in the romance of the ideology. As the Extreme Right bedtime story continued I felt myself dozing off, dreaming of soft, pink Judean hills, patriarchs and a world of deliciously uncomplicated moral absolutes. Every so often a loud beeping noise informed me that a machine was sticking and I needed to don huge gloves and open up the doors in order to clear it and oil it. I have met fighter pilots with less stressful job descriptions and I was beginning to feel like a Victorian orphan in a Lancashire mill. It was my job to sweep up the rubber leftovers from my machine. The rest of the time I sat on a stool and read. I was never quite sure what I was making. It might well have been an exciting new range of women's sex aides, destined for Anne Summers shops all over the world.

Customer: "Hi, has the new *Orgasmatatron Alpayim* arrived yet? It's supposed to be really good."

Sales Assistant: "I'm sorry madam. It seems there has been a hitch. The factory in Israel burned down last week. Some problem with the machinery. Can I interest you in some Japanese love eggs instead?"

Around three in the morning I went to a little kitchen to make myself cheese on toast and a cup of milky *Nes*, Israeli instant coffee. I had discovered that the fridge in the factory had real cheese and I was determined to eat as much of it as I could. Grilled, uncooked, on bread, on crackers, I just didn't care. Cheese I wanted and cheese I would have. One problem with working nights is disturbed sleep and I arrived back to my room, awash with caffeine and dairy products, just as my roommate was getting ready for work. We had a huge bitch-slapping, hair-pulling row about this which was audible outside. Was I starting to get bitter and twisted, I wondered, scraping my roommate's toothbrush around the rim of the toilet and shredding his credit cards? I noticed a cooling in the attitude of the Dutch girls towards me.

One night, around twenty minutes after I was due to finish, my relief arrived late. By the time he sauntered in, a small pile of rubber had built up but I simply walked away, furious at being cheated out of fifteen minutes of sleep. He called me back with that endearing Israeli greeting of "hey you, you." I turned round. He was pointing at the rubber on the floor. I refused to sweep up. I was feeling humiliated and the last thing I felt like was someone watching me sweep the floor. I told him, jolly reasonably I felt, to perform an unnatural act on his own person. This soon got back to Matron and I was fired from the factory, to my great relief, and to the relief of the sexually frustrated all over the world.

My next job was working in the dining room. This involved getting up early, and to more lost sleep. By now the temperature was getting very high. My dear, dear, anything-to-please roommate wanted to sleep with the blinds closed whereas I wanted the windows open and the fan on. If you've ever tried to settle down to forty winks in the laundry room of a Thai prison wearing nylon panties and a thermal vest, you may get an idea of how hot it was. One night I couldn't stand him or the heat anymore, and so I took my mattress and sheets and went onto the flat roof to sleep. Just as I was dozing off an almighty racket started from the area of the swimming pool. The Kibbutz earned extra income by doubling up as a wedding venue. I certainly don't remember reading about this happening in the days of the Zionist pioneers, reclaiming the malarial swamps and building a Jewish Homeland in Palestine in those tough-but-oh-so-good days of the 1900s.

Pioneer 1: "Here Golda, grab this plough. We need to sow the grain and make the desert bloom."

Pioneer 2: "Oh, I'm sorry David. We have the Goldfarb wedding booked in at 15.00. Now, did you remember to book the D.J. and confirm the caterers?"

I wanted to weep with frustration. However being English, and possessing a resolute nature and good sense of humour, I chuckled the next morning when I heard Matron telling off a group of volunteers. Someone had it seemed been using the pool during the wedding reception. They were not to do it again she admonished, *especially not naked*. I could visualise it. The bride, beautiful, radiant and virginal; the groom in his suit, probably for the first time in his life. Then there would be the proud parents, the bride's mother stifling a sob. The orchestra would be playing a lively *Hora* or perhaps *Hava Nagila*. The fathers biting their nails, watching an overweight guest asset-stripping a groaning buffet table, the bill spiralling out of all control; the lobster-red arse of a sunburnt English volunteer swimming in the moonlight; the delighted shrieks of young Brummies rubbing their tits and necking bottles of Vodka.

I hated my job in the dining room. I hadn't come to Israel in order to become an Edwardian scullery maid. Our first task was to fill the breakfast buffet and napkin holders. Each table was then to be given a metal container, like something a dog would eat from, known as a *Kol Bo*. This was where the diners left their dirty napkins, eggshells, bogies etc. We then cleaned the tables using a week-old, brown rag. The breakfast serving seemed to last for ever, as many Kibbutznikim started work so early they had breakfast a couple of hours or more into their shifts. We had a short break from around 10.00 until 11.00 when it was time to start the lunch service. It was interesting to see such a huge catering operation in motion. There was a conveyor belt to take dirty plates to an army of washer-uppers, all of whom were volunteers. Huge ovens heated up tray upon tray of schnitzels or burgers, whilst others fed vegetables into gigantic pots of boiling water. I hated the job of getting hot trays of food out of the oven for the simple reason I wasn't given any oven gloves and had to make do with a dish cloth. I am a man, for crying out loud, not a TEFLON-coated ape. The pressure was unpleasant and the clients rude and ungrateful. The amount of waste generated was staggering. Before the last meals had been served, some other volunteers and I began clearing the tables. We started mopping floors and trying to close sections of the dining room. Invariably a few Kibbutznikim insisted on sitting in the cleaned sections, as it was their habit to sit in certain places and they believed this right was more important than the time and effort of those cleaning the room. This was classic behaviour from people who have been institutionalised for too long. Big, dribbling, drooling men, boorishly sitting at a table just to spite a couple of foreign volunteers who were working for next to nothing.

Another glimpse into the portals of hell came in the form of the school buses. If you have ever seen the *Bells of St Trinians* you might have a rough, very rough, idea of what it was like. Children from neighbouring kibbutzim would be bussed to our Kibbutz on a rotation basis for lunch, as volunteers crossed themselves and dived for cover. There was a cacophony of screaming, shouting and whingeing as the darlings vied for supremacy in the queue. Israeli children are often spoiled and undisciplined. Charitably I put this down to the Zionist ideals about letting children grow free and uninhibited, close to nature, and not constrained or pallid like Ghetto children. There is also a desire to spoil children before they serve two or three years in the army and childhood comes to an abrupt end. Often the children deliberately made a mess of the tables to wind the volunteers up. They looked remarkably similar to Damien from the *Omen* as they slowly mixed ever growing puddles of ketchup and Coke on the Formica topped tables, grinning with something so Satanic and Evil that Father Merrin from *The Exorcist* would have turned heel saying "sorry love, you'll need to get an expert in to deal with this one." When I remonstrated with their teachers, they didn't want to know and asked us to clean up later rather than confront the problem. One of them, a desiccated pseudo-intellectual with glasses on a chain, even told me to grow up.

I had two main coping mechanisms on the Kibbutz. One was the free minibus service into Kfar Saba and the other was my night-time walk. I relished walking through the tree-lined paths that wound round the Kibbutz houses. These were lovely and individual. Some were almost suburban. I often peeked, discreetly, through windows at book-lined rooms, lit by candles or soft lighting. Many had works of homemade conceptual art in the small gardens. I think granny had been using a chisel and some stone this time. Someone really should have taken the local artist to one side and had a quiet word. If I walked further I came to the *Pardes* or the orange groves. I thrilled at seeing oranges growing on trees, and the darkness and sweetness enveloped me. It was intoxicating and soothing. Beyond the groves was a slope with fields, and beyond this twinkled the lights of Kalkillia, a Palestinian town on the West Bank. I returned refreshed to my room where I often read or chatted with my friends. The evenings were a time to wind down and I often enjoyed long, hot showers. One reason for this was a little crush I was indulging. One of the washers-up was a French volunteer who was converting to Judaism in order to marry an Israeli woman. Let's just say she was a very lucky young lady and leave it at that. A hearty *Mazel Tov* to the young couple is what I say!

"Zis is crazy! Zis whole country is fuckink crazy"

One night there was an edge in the air, though I was unsure why. Radios seemed louder than usual. People stood and talked meaningfully. Then one of the Dutch women reported hearing a rumbling. It might have been that extra helping of hummus and pickle at lunch, I thought momentarily but apparently it sounded like, *gulp,* artillery. High above us two fighter planes screeched northwards leaving vapour trails. We went to the grapefruit groves on the other side of the main road to listen. Sure enough there was a faint booming sound. According to a permanently stoned South African volunteer it was coming from the border but he had just come back from a *camping trip* to Dahab in Egypt so no-one could be sure. We discussed the political situation and had a beer in the kitchen before going to bed. Outside I heard the German volunteer angrily demanding that she be given an explanation about what was going on.

"I demand ein explanation wot is goink on! Ve are foreigners here unt our safety is paramount." I heard a mumbled reply. "Zis is crazy! Zis whole country is fuckink crazy" she complained. I dozed off and had a strange dream about kittens, pristine toilets and a room of my own.

One weekend the English volunteers decided to spend the Sabbath in Jerusalem so on Friday morning we took the free minibus to Ra'anana Junction where we caught the red and white *Egged* coach to Jerusalem. I loved the name *Ra'anana*. I practised saying it. It is derived from the word for freshness in Hebrew although you'd need a fairly fertile imagination to capture that feeling now, stood in the heat and the exhaust fumes of the bus stop. Actually Freshness Junction would sound strange in

English, a bit like a revolutionary American innovation in feminine hygiene. It was my first visit to Jerusalem since I'd arrived on the Kibbutz and I was excited about returning. I was also looking forward to playing guide. Soon the bus was climbing the mountainous road, passing the dozens of red-painted convoy trucks that lay as monument to Israel's War of Independence in 1948. We stayed the night at an Arab youth hostel in the Old City, opting to sleep on the roof, which was cheaper and cooler. We spent the following day in the Old City exploring. By the afternoon however the day was dragging and it was also getting chilly. Jerusalem can be much cooler than the coastal plain and we had not brought enough clothing. We killed time wandering around the main park until the buses started running again at the end of the Sabbath, getting fractious and on each other's nerves.

The volunteers were divided into three main types. Non-Jews looking for fun, Jews on extended tasters of Israel and non-Jewish 'seekers'. By this I mean non-Jews who had become caught up in the drama and excitement of Israel and who wished to join it for a variety of reasons. Personally I had initially come to experience Kibbutz life, but I was developing a stronger feeling of identification with Israel. I had developed a deep and long-seated attachment to the ideals of Israel through years of reading and yearning. When I heard Hebrew songs they struck a chord as I had been listening to some of them since my mid-teens. I felt I had lived this life before through reading, photographs and music. It was like coming home. But it wasn't home. In fact at times it was downright hello-have-I-just-fallen-asleep-and-woken-up-in-a-parallel-universe alien. For many of the non-Jews there was a genuine thrill in seeing men and women of their own age, or younger in uniform, and having an adventure in this bewitching land. There was also an incredibly strong community atmosphere. It was tragic, romantic and exotic. One parallel might be the sense of carefree romance and feelings of worth experienced by young people during the Second World War. Some of the non-Jews actively sought out Israeli partners, subconsciously looking for a way to trap themselves in Israel.

Contact between volunteers and the locals was usually limited. We simply weren't worth getting to know as we came and went too often. The Jewish volunteers fared better, as the Israelis wanted them to stay and become part of the nation. The behaviour of the volunteers rarely endeared us to the locals. Drinking games were common, as was promiscuity and soft-drug taking. This got so bad that Matron took to opening our mail and looking through any photographs developed locally to see if we had been to Egypt. She also insisted on looking after our passports. The volunteers on the other hand saw the Kibbutznikim as humourless and morose, or even completely nuts. Or all three! A few of our hosts were certainly odd in the extreme, with some broken and damaged individuals exhibiting extreme bitterness. The claustrophobia of a tight community often led to petty feuds and fallings out. I was finding that out myself. Certainly, sticking pins in effigies is not something I did *before* going to Israel. Some of the older members were Holocaust survivors and often survivor's guilt and anxiety was passed to the second or even third generation, adding another ingredient to this crazy human goulash.

One day my two English friends told me they had been given a strange task. Matron had asked them to clean the air raid shelter. The German woman went into orbit when she heard this.

"Vhy are ze cleaning ze shelters? Zer will be var, und zey are keepink it from us!"

The air raid shelters were located down concrete steps on the lawn directly in front of my room and, as long I as didn't need to share with my roommate, I was not bothered. In fact an air raid might have livened things up a bit. It would be like the Blitz and we could all sing some jolly songs and give our saucepans to that nice Mr Churchill.

"And make sure you dust the corners" Matron added. Why I asked myself? Would it matter?

Kibbutznik 1: "Scuds are bad tonight aren't they Shulamit?"

Kibbutznik 2: "Dreadful Shoshana. Worse than 1991. And have you seen the muck in here? *Someone* hasn't flicked a duster around for a few weeks that's for sure; not that I'm one to name names or point fingers."

Kibbutznik 1: "You're not dear. You're not. And look at that box of Nuclear, Biological and Chemical Warfare suits. Ooooo, you could write your name in that dust you could."

Kibbutznik 2: "If there's one thing I can't abide it's a mucky air raid shelter."

This prompted me to chat to a Kibbutznik about the Gulf War. He recalled the dreadful racket of a Scud flying directly over the Kibbutz on its way to Ramat Gan. He told me about the kits given out with antidotes to chemical weapons and about the nightly drama of the raids. Little did I know that one day I would live two streets away from the place where they had landed.

Occasionally I travelled to Tel Aviv on my afternoons off. I sometimes hitchhiked into Kfar Saba and the drivers who picked me up were often Arabs. This was because the road in front of the Kibbutz only went as far as Tira. The fact I had accepted lifts from Arabs scandalised some of the Kibbutznikim. There was a great deal of suspicion and fear, and sadly it was true that there had been several cases of Israeli soldiers being abducted whilst hitchhiking. I guess hitchhiking is never a great idea but I certainly never had any problems and only met with courtesy and a desire to help. Many Arabs worked casually on the Kibbutz and I remember breaks where strong Arab coffee was served and Jews and Arabs sat together under the trees to drink together.

Tel Aviv took some getting used to. The heat was oppressive and seemed to be absorbed and retained by the concrete and tarmac. The high rise hotels along the front prevented a breeze and the pace was frantic. I envied the rich, privileged guests who could afford to stay there, sipping enormous pink cocktails by the ice-cold pool and enjoying big, fluffy towels. I walked barefoot along the beach or around the lush, shimmering Independence Park, hoping for a little holiday romance. Tel Aviv always accentuated any feelings of homesickness I had. The expanse of sea was a constant reminder of being far from home and I felt trapped. To cheer myself up I occasionally treated myself to a glass of fresh strawberry juice at Café Nordau, the only gay café in the city at that time.

In June 1992 two friends from Edinburgh came to Israel and I went to meet them in Tel Aviv. We all shared a room at the Youth Hostel near the pleasant Yarkon River, located in the residential north of the city. It was good to be with familiar friends again. We drank Gin straight from the bottle and I felt I was on holiday too as we laughed and carried on. One evening we decided to try out a gay club in Jaffa, a short taxi ride from Tel Aviv. It was magical to be in Jaffa late at night. I soaked in the atmosphere of the old Ottoman streets, relishing the cool breeze. As I heard my footsteps echo I imagined the people who had lived here before. I could feel their ghosts. The stones felt clammy to touch from the humidity and salt air. I went over to the ramparts in order to take in my favourite view of an illuminated Tel Aviv, the high rise hotels glimmering in the moonlight. A strong smell of jasmine and bougainvillea hung in the air and I could hear the lapping of the waves. It was so utterly romantic. We paid and entered *Caliph*, the latest gay club. Here we danced and drank and it was like old times. It was then I noticed a reasonably handsome, shorter man looking at me. When I returned his gaze he gave me a coy, slightly mocking look. Intrigued, I told my friends. Once more I noticed him looking at me. I went out for a breather and soon enough we were engrossed in a tonsil-licking-tongue-devouring snog in an ancient Ottoman doorway that smelt of piss and jasmine and the sea. I hadn't kissed a man for months and I was starving. His name was Avi and this was a night which would change my life forever.

After making arrangements to meet Avi again, I returned to the hostel with my friends, thrilled at this unexpected romance after a long drought in the *luuurve* department. Avi was on an extended holiday to see his parents in Israel but in fact he lived in Italy and had just broken up with his ex-partner. *Shame.* Unfortunately I had to go back to the Kibbutz.

Israel was gripped by pre-election fever in June 1992 and every surface was covered by posters and stickers. It was interesting to be here at this time and it promised to be a very historically important election. I personally decided to root for the left-wing *Meretz* party because of its liberal views on gay rights and on its two-state policy to solve the Palestine-Israel conflict once and for all. It also promised an end to draft exemptions for the Ultra-Orthodox. All its policies seemed eminently reasonable. When I broached this with Avi he became oddly flushed and explained in a choked voice that no, he would not be voting for *Meretz*. He seemed to be labouring under some strong emotion and if he had been a Victorian lady I would have reached for the smelling salts or dabbed cologne on his temples. This would be the first of many strangulated how-dare-you-not-agree-with-me conversations which would provide hours of entertainment over the years to come. The

Kibbutz was split between support for *Meretz* and Labour, and left-wing slogans were attached to prominent places such as the water tower. The day of the election dawned bright and sunny and there was an air of tense expectation as the Kibbutznikim went to vote in the canteen. During the night the exit polls began to show a narrow Labour lead and I awoke the next morning to the highly unusual sight of people smiling and wishing each other a good day. Matron told me, her voice full of girlish glee, that Labour had won enough seats to secure a coalition and that there would be wine and cake in the canteen. One hiccup in the election was that the coalition was so tight it might need to depend on the votes of the Arab parties, a fact which caused some revulsion amongst people I spoke to. In the end it was decided that a coalition with the fundamentalist *Shas* party would be preferable to *cough, choke, God-forbid* allowing Arabs into the government.

One recent development on the Kibbutz was the departure of a volunteer, leaving a spare bed in the room next to mine. Within a nanosecond of hearing the news I was packed and holding a machete to Matron's throat for the key. My roommate looked smug but in his eyes was fear. Who would he get instead? Well that question was very quickly answered with the arrival of a squat, muscled South African chap, fresh out of some commando unit or other. I couldn't wait for their first row.

A few days later I came down with the most awful diarrhoea and sickness. This was made doubly unpleasant due to the fact that the suddenness of my ailment made it necessary to use the volunteer's toilet rather than the nice clean one in the cafeteria. I sat miserably on the cracked seat, looking at spiders' webs and about seven inches of sunlight coming from under the thin wooden door. How I dreamt of the cool plastic seat and fresh Toilet-Duck-mixed-with-spring-meadows smell of the cafeteria toilet. There was a world of gleaming basins and freshly scrubbed tiles, and here I was in something worse than the famous toilet scene from Trainspotting where Ewan McGregor dives into the *Dirtiest Toilet in Scotland*. Unfortunately I wasn't ripped to the tits on jellies. If I had been, the whole experience may have been fractionally more pleasant. I soon became weak as both *ends* competed with each other for the fastest evacuation. I felt like a tube of toothpaste with a foot on it. As I was damned if I was going to work, Matron demanded I go to see Nurse. I really did feel I had stepped into a farcical 1970s Carry On film. I half wondered if I should say something along the lines of "Cor, them's a nice pair of melons nurse" upon which she'd giggle suggestively and say "'ere saucy, don't touch what'cha can't afford." Back in Reality the po-faced-wouldn't-recognise-a-joke-if-it-headbutted-her nurse could do little but let things run their course. A few packets of industrial strength Imodium wouldn't have hurt, but never mind.

One day I got a letter from my friend Andrew from Edinburgh, announcing he was coming to Israel on a visit. I felt instantly happier and immediately booked a room for us at the Youth Hostel in Tel Aviv. I took some time off and on the appointed day I took the bus to Ben Gurion airport. I waited by the gate, along with several dozen Israelis, waiting for relatives to return from abroad. Every now and then the relatives screamed and surged as passengers emerged from the gate, wearing gondola hats, and carrying enormous sacks of Duty Free. Cries of *Abba, Abba* made me suddenly alert. Was it possible that Bjorn, Benny, Agnetha and Frieda were really here in Israel? I quickly delved into my pocket, looking for a pen and my autograph book before remembering that *aba* is Hebrew for dad. Soon enough Andrew and his sister emerged. It was at this precise moment that a group of Arab women began making an undulating, guttural sound with their tongues, although this was in fact directed at the elderly man behind my friends. Once again, within just a couple of weeks I was back at the hostel with old friends.

We travelled to Jerusalem the next day, staying at a cheap and dated hotel in the Armenian Quarter. This ancient hotel had not seen a lick of paint since before our own gracious Queen was crowned. Indeed I half imagined Noel Coward to pop out from one of the enormous leather armchairs in the lounge. My room had a ghastly First World War Hospital feeling to it, with a huge iron bed and a black, dusty ceiling fan. Everything felt dark and gloomy. The bathroom croaked and groaned to the extent that I actually believed it was a living entity. I stood in the rusty, chipped bath holding a weak shower in order to wash. Unfortunately my stomach and I were still in some disagreement about the precise length of time it should be holding onto food.

We spent the day sightseeing and wandering the alleys of the Old City, focusing on the Christian sights, mainly for Andrew's benefit.

We walked the Stations of the Cross, stopping for some mint tea and almond biscuits along the way, which I suspect defeated the object somewhat. I don't remember a cheery tea break scene during *The Passion of The* Christ but then I did watch most of it whith my eyes closed. We spent a great deal of our time fighting off young boys trying to sell us things, or entice us into the shops.

"American? French? Swiss? I have crosses, statues of Our Lady fifteen Shekels, good price!" shouted shopkeepers. On the Temple Mount we visited a small museum with various artefacts from the two world famous mosques and also a selection of blood soaked shirts, a relic of some clash during the Intifada. I loved the Al-Aqsa mosque, with the huge expanse of space covered with nothing more than a thick luxurious carpet. The gold of the Dome glimmered in the sun and was in sharp contrast to the deep, shiny blue of the tiled walls. Inside the Dome of the Rock a few worshippers were praying on their knees as we walked around as unobtrusively as possible. The following day we took a shared Arab taxi from the Jaffa Gate to Bethlehem. Whilst this was less than a twenty minute drive, it was in the Occupied Territories. We therefore took our passports and hoped for the best. I was so nervous as we pulled off that I bit my nails down to bloody stumps. Was this such a good idea I thought, as we sped past Rachel's tomb? Would I be returning home via Cargo El Al with a sticker attached to my coffin? Would I emerge from captivity years later with a beard as long as roll of kitchen paper and speaking gibberish? Before I had time to indulge in further catastrophisation we had pulled up in Manger Square. Like all first timers in Bethlehem I was disappointed. I was adult enough to realise that I would not be walking into the nativity scene from Barney's New York but I had expected it to be *quainter*. The enormous British Mandate police station dominating the square bristled with barbed wire, antenna and a freshly ironed Israeli flag. Where was the snow? It was flesh-cookingly hot and the smell of charred meat floated from the cafés that surrounded the square. We entered the enormous Church of the Holy Nativity through the narrow door, built to discourage horse-riding in times of yore. It was cool, calm and smelled strongly of incense and candle wax. We descended some steps to the chapel below, where a metal plate indicated the exact spot of the Nativity. How would anyone *know* that, I wondered? Nevertheless the place felt special and holy and did it really matter exactly where it happened? Hundreds of candles flickered in the darkness and I watched as Andrew and his sister added two more.

On our last night in Jerusalem we had dinner in a smart café on Ben Yehuda Street, demolishing a cheesy, gooey flan each, along with chips and glasses of crisp white wine. I loved this long, bustling street with its numerous restaurants and bars, and its vibrant, fun-loving atmosphere. We were up early the next morning to take our last breakfast in the Ottoman Hotel from Hell. This consisted of stale pitta bread, thick, rubbery jam and slightly sour-tasting butter which smelt of sick. The waiter had dirty looking hands. I felt trouser-soilingly ill. We caught the bus to the Ben Gurion Airport where Andrew and sister caught their flight and I caught a bus to Tel Aviv and thence back to the Kibbutz.

Soon afterwards I made arrangements to go to the Dead Sea with Avi. I was a bit worried I might be too ill, or worse, think I was better, and then have an *accident* in Avi's hire car. I had certainly lost a considerable amount of weight on my fantastic new weight loss programme. In fact I was considering marketing it. I looked fantastic in swimwear and had the waist of a fourteen-year old girl.

"So, tell us about the new 30-day Kibbutz weight loss programme Andrew" the Stepford Wife-like American presenter would ask, looking blonde, fresh and fabulous.

"Hi, and let me just say what a great pleasure it is to tell you about this revolutionary product. I have a half hour bout of dysentery in the morning, a shake at lunch time and a sensible meal in the evening!"

"There you go ladies. Just give the toll free number below a call and you too could be pooping your way to a great figure!"

Despite my concerns, the day arrived and Avi drove up to the Kibbutz in his smart hired car, earning me looks of envy from the other less romantically involved volunteers. I wiggled my now svelte hips over to the car and hopped in, casting an insouciante glance back to see who was taking it all in. It was exciting to be in a car, rather than on public transport and I enjoyed the budding romance. Coquettish jokes were shared and heavily edited life stories exchanged. Soon we were headed inland and the landscape became more rugged. Beyond Jerusalem the landscape changed radically. The hills turned bare, harsh and arid. Only the occasional olive tree broke through the rock and dust, and from time to time we saw herds of filthy looking goats by the side of the road. On some hilltops were the stark white outlines of Jewish settlements. These looked more like housing estates than ideological statements, with high rise blocks and smaller houses with red roofs and solar panels. The black road shimmered in the heat ahead. I felt sweat trickle down my back and legs despite the air-conditioning. I also noticed some ugly, tarpaulin settlements with jerry cans and walls made from old pallets, around which were some rather unhealthy looking sheep. Avi explained these were unrecognised Bedouin settlements. A large green sign pointed to Biblical-sounding places such as Jericho, Sodom and the Dead Sea. Then we were at the top of a ridge and the road seemed to fall away beneath us. In the far distance was a small, black lake, which was the Dead Sea, and all around was the harsh, eerie desert of rocks. We stopped for a photo and then made the descent. The heat and the brightness were breathtaking.

After a long drive we were finally on level ground and the hills rose beside us. On our left was the Dead Sea, its surface so bright it was hard to take in. The shore looked tatty and the water level had receded, leaving an ugly waste of salt and rock.

Soon we arrived at a road sign announcing Sodom, where we turned into a secondary road. I was expecting to see the ruins of a town, and perhaps the odd Salt Person, but all there was were some rocks and small caves. Nevertheless we got out and walked around. Its bleakness was unnerving and I was glad to be back in the car once more and headed for a place I had always wanted to see, Ein Gedi. Ein Gedi was an oasis and *wadi,* deep in the rocks. I had heard songs about this place. I had collected stamps with its picture, and now finally I was here. One of the great things about travelling in Israel is that every destination has a wow factor for the first time traveller. Wow, this is where Jesus lived. Wow this is where David is buried. Wow, this is where Jacob stubbed his toe and so forth. We followed a trail, which soon became a tunnel through thick, tall reeds. A cool trickle flowed on one side, but above us were the same infernal, lunar-like rocks. The path climbed, allowing us a glimpse above the reeds and soon we were rewarded with the sight of exotic animals such as hyenas and desert dogs. Above were a couple of vultures, circling slowly. After our visit to Ein Gedi we continued to the ancient fortress of Masada. Although I had been here before on holiday it was nice to be back and we took the cable car up to the summit, enjoying the desert views below. The views stretched for miles, over flat, relentless desert with hills in the background and the shimmering Sea of Salt in the foreground. I tried to imagine the feelings of the first century Zealots, torn between surrender and slavery, or suicide. We wandered around the summit and then returned to the cable car. We stopped at the Masada Tea Rooms for a welcome lip-smackingly yummy slice of fruit tart and some lukewarm Lipton Tea which looked, smelt and tasted like a urine sample.

I was coming to the end of my stay on the Kibbutz. I no longer had any interest in my work or in meeting new people. I simply looked forward to the weekend and to my next outing with Avi in the car. This took place a week later, but this time we went north to Galilee, taking the main coastal road and then branching off towards Tiberias where Avi's sister had a holiday home. I enjoyed the drive, the music and the chat and it was not long before we were driving through fairly hilly terrain. The villages along the road were Arab, and the houses took on a completely different appearance. In Jewish towns and settlements the emphasis was on square lines and symmetry whereas in the Arab villages the modern houses had a more exuberant feel, with archways and pathways of marble, and walls of textured concrete. Each village had a mosque with slender minarets and loud speakers attached. As in Tira many houses remained unfinished due to Islamic attitudes on mortgages. It was dusk when we arrived in Tiberias. We began climbing a steep hill whilst Avi pondered the right route to take. I felt a surge of annoyance, then shock as the window caved in over me, showering my bare legs with fragments of glass. The car spun around 180% in a second. I barely heard the crash but the impact left me feeling generally sore all over. I remembered feeling the same way after a head collision in a dodgem car. Avi stared ahead in horror and shock, and then looked over at me, gaping like a mildly surprised gold fish. I had to shove the door hard to get it open. Outside, the balmy heat struck me and I crunched glass underfoot. Another car stood smashed and dripping a few feet away. It wasn't long before a lively chorus of "*Ata meshuga, ben zona cus ima shelach*" could be heard, both drivers coming out of shock. There were more references to the genitals of both parties' mothers as

I began getting our luggage out of the car. Meanwhile other drivers rallied round, helpfully blowing their horns and telling us to 'get off the fucking road.' I never could see the point in this Israeli habit of honking broken down cars. Do they think it will help or do they believe the unfortunate driver has somehow done it out of spite?

Car Crash vicitim 1: "Hey Dudu. There's quite a lot of honking. Do you think we should perhaps cut ourselves free from the wreckage of this smashed and burning car."

Car Crash vicitim 2: "*Dai* Rivkele! Relax, what's the hurry? Have some more coffee from the flask."

Car Crash vicitim 1: "But I can't drink upside down Dudu."

After an initial feeling of relief that neither of us was hurt, it suddenly dawned on me that we were stranded. It was getting dark and the car was a write-off. After half an hour or so we eventually pushed the car to the kerb and began walking down the hill towards Tiberias with our luggage. We eventually entered the lobby of a four-star hotel where I instantly felt envious of the tourists who were sat enjoying drinks and getting ready for a side-splitting-button-popping buffet dinner. Dozens of Sabbath candles were burning in sandboxes, a reminder that offices such as hire car companies etc. were going to be closed till Sunday. Whilst Avi asked if he could use a phone, at reception, I stood under the uncomfortable gaze of a doorman, looking and feeling incredibly scruffy in my Kibbutz boots, shorts and T-shirt. A surly reception clerk with a badge that read *I'm Zvi, I'm here to help,* gave a curt nod by way of a greeting. He clicked his teeth and pushed over the phone, oozing contempt from every pore. He then turned his back to do other things, which I hoped included tucking in his shirt and brushing his hair but I somehow doubted it. Just because I looked an absolute fright wasn't reason for him to let standards slip. We eventually located a garage which would sweep up the remains of the car and try to find an alternative for us. In the meantime there was nothing for it but to take a taxi for the last couple of miles to the holiday flat. Zvi, the happy-go-lucky receptionist, obligingly took his finger out of his nostril long enough to dial us a cab.

It was dark when we arrived but in the distance I could see the silvery surface of the Sea of Galilee reflected in the moonlight. "Thank you" I said to the cab driver, picking up my luggage and wiping the spit from my face. "And take a Shekel for yourself." As Avi opened the door I was struck by the cool, slightly musty, interior of the flat. Avi switched on the lights to reveal an open plan living room with kitchen and breakfast bar, and beyond, a veranda overlooking the sea in the valley below. There was a small bedroom off the living room with a large double bed. The flat had a kitsch feel to it, not helped by the presence of two life-size ceramic tigers, nor by the enormous chandeliers, items which would have raised an eyebrow at the Court of Louis XVI, never mind in a tiny Israeli holiday flat. We both felt lost and disappointed and were unsure what to do, so after a wash in the luxurious, marble bathroom (a rare treat after two long months on the Kibbutz) we walked back into Tiberias. This took us along a busy main road which felt dangerous and unpleasant. Cars shot passed at the speed of light, honking and kicking up grit. Eventually we reached the outskirts of Tiberias and headed for the shore. This was quaint and buzzing, with old Arab buildings now turned into cafés and restaurants, and gentrified pedestrian streets with crowds of holiday makers. Coloured light bulbs hung gaily across the streets, giving the town a festive air. We found a restaurant by the water's edge and sat back enjoying the Oriental music and relative cool of the evening.

We ate a *mezze* of hummus, pitta, olives and white cheese, deciding to forgo the ubiquitous St Peter's fish. As we ate we talked about our plans. Avi was going to return to Italy where he was running a small hotel. However at the end of the summer he wanted to come back to Israel and open his own business. He told me about his service in the army, where he had served in the Tank Corps whilst I simpered and cooed in admiration. The beer, the music and the pleasant evening air were all beginning to cast a spell on me. In the background a familiar Hebrew melody added to the magic.

The following morning I awoke with bright, strong sunlight on my face. It was still early and Avi was fussing in the kitchen, preparing a hasty picnic.

"We were going to make a nice breakfast" he said, with a face like a disappointed child. He seemed strangely vulnerable. After a long walk, lots of phone calls and some shouting in Hebrew, we somehow managed to get another car, and, much later than scheduled, we were driving along the circular road which skirts the Sea of Galilee. We turned off and began the steep ascent to the Golan Heights. The very name Golan Heights thrilled me and finally I was going to see them. We passed some ruined tanks and I noticed an increase in army vehicles. Jeeps, trucks and personnel carriers were driving in both directions, and at one point we needed to make a very scary, knee-gouging-buttock-clenching manoeuvre to pass a long truck with tanks on it. I did not envy the driver of that. Can you imagine trying to parallel park it? We continued to climb, passing a crusader castle and more recent fortifications. By the roadside were wild flowers, gorse bushes and rusting barbed wire. The views were incredible and the air was becoming noticeably cooler. Although I was enjoying the ride, I noticed the road was becoming increasingly congested and the drops by the side, steeper. Coupled with this was Avi's, how shall I put this, pro-active-go-getting-who's-ya-daddy style of driving. I gasped with terror as we overtook a convey of tank carriers, narrowly swerving back into lane in the face of an oncoming petrol tanker. We were so close I could smell the driver's breath.

"Are you enjoying the drive?" asked Avi, fiddling with the radio and picking up in rapid succession Radio Damascus, The Voice of Christ, and Hizbollah FM.

"Yes" I croaked in a voice thick with fear, my sphincter so tightly clenched you could sharpen pencils in it. We eventually ground to a halt in the parking lot at the foot of the chair lift, next to an Israeli army bulldozer so big it would reach the top of a double-decker bus. We took the chair lift up the side of Mount Hermon, reputedly the site of Jesus' Transfiguration according to some traditions. Suddenly the ground disappeared from under my feet with a jerk. We were alone, with mist floating beneath us, and the majesty of Mount Hermon rising in front of our eyes. At the summit we savoured the peace and the cool and Avi took a picture of me smiling, holding an Israeli flag. We were at the highest point in Israel and beyond lay Syria. Avi explained that the chairlift was for the benefit of skiers and was the one place in Israel where skiing is occasionally possible. After visiting the Golan and the new town of Katsrin we rejoined the circular road, around the Sea of Galilee, passing a McDonald's Drive-In. We found a quiet spot and I stripped down to my bare essentials for a quick dip in the cold water. I imagined how nice it would have been to be a Christian at this point. I felt like a gay man watching two women strip down to bra and panties to have a cat fight, i.e. conscious that I should really be getting something from it but totally missing the point. Our next stop, and one which I had specifically asked Avi to make, was the springs at Banyas. Like Ein Gedi I had collected stamps with it and heard songs about it. It was a magical place with a waterfall, mossy rocks and pools. The name is derived from the Greek God Pan. Nearby was a bird sanctuary and some swampy land. Until the creation of the modern State of Israel the entire area had been a malarial marsh. In its zeal for modernisation the government drained it, decimating a lot of local wildlife in the process. In later years, in an attempt to undo some of the damage much of it was reflooded, no doubt to the delight of local birds.

I was tired and crabby when I got back to the Kibbutz. It was already dark and I went to my room, turned on a soft light and listened to my music in order to relax. By now I was in such a don't-give-a-shit-about-your-crappy- failed-little -experiment-with-Communism kind of mood that I was reluctant to do any work that involved being humiliated, bitten or burnt. I was developing what our American cousins refer to as an *attitude,* and after weeks of nagging, I was finally transferred to an agricultural job. This is what I envisioned Kibbutz life to be about. I would manfully sow fields, my jaw set and determined. I would push a plough with my bare hands, singing rousing songs about Eucalyptus trees, perhaps pausing to single-handedly disarm a Syrian tank or two. At an unholy hour of the morning we piled into a van and drove to some potato fields. Here we climbed the steps onto the platform of a giant harvester. This was great fun, and soon the beast rumbled off and potatoes began flying up onto a tray. Our job was to sort them, throwing the bad ones away and putting the good ones into sacks. Within minutes the potatoes were arriving at such a rate that we couldn't keep up. Laughing hysterically, and going slightly mad from the sun, we fought a valiant but losing battle as more and more potatoes piled up. "*Allo,'allo.* You, hey you!" shrieked the driver, indicating that a slightly more task-focused attitude was expected.

The next day was orange picking. We began the day with a flask of Turkish coffee so thick you could use it to bury Mafia informants in, and some pastries which we ate sitting on a tarpaulin in the orange groves. Dawn was just breaking and the ground was damp and dewy. We then stood on a platform to pick the riper oranges and throw rotting ones to the ground. One of my last jobs on the Kibbutz was helping with the rubbish tractor. This involved piling stinking garbage onto a trailer, pulled by a rusting old tractor and then hopping on for the ride. The tractor driver was another volunteer, but a more trusted long-term one, and soon we were driving down a long dusty track to a massive rubbish tip near the perimeter fence. I found this area sinister as it was almost on the border of the West Bank and was completely deserted. The mountains of rubbish seemed alive and I could visualise them closing in on me.

My last excursion with Avi was an afternoon-only one and for this we drove the short distance to Caesarea on the coast. We wandered around the Roman ruins, many of them half submerged by the sea, and then sat for a while on the steps of the amphitheatre. I absorbed the history. It was here that Pontius Pilate had had his palace. And it was here that Avi asked if I'd like to come to Italy with him. The whole scene began to sound like a gay version of the 1945 classic film *Brief Encounter*. I took on the role of Celia Johnson, saying things in a very fast, clipped Received Pronunciation accent. "Oh, darling, no! Neither of us is free to love each other. It's *medniss*." At first I said no, at which Avi did his punctured-balloon disappointed face and said he thought I was a different kind of person but 'never mind.' He then talked about the wonders of his hotel and the idyllic scrumptiousness of it all. Absolutely no commitment would be involved; just a nice rounding off of our relationship before going our separate ways. He even offered to pay for my flight. It must have been the heat but for some what-the-hell-was-I-thinking-you-mad-fool reason I agreed. The next day we both turned up at the 1970s concrete El Al tower in Ben Yehuda Street in Tel Aviv, where Avi generously paid for my single ticket to Munich. My departure date was set for a few days hence. This definitely didn't happen in *Brief Encounter*. Back on the Kibbutz I put my affairs in order i.e. I packed my rucksack and got my passport out the safe as Matron danced a *Can Can* around the office.

I spent my last day alone in Tel Aviv, doing some last minute shopping and, as it grew dark, I walked to the beach. In my haste to get away I had seriously overestimated the amount of time I needed to kill, as my flight wasn't until around four the following morning. I walked around the point where Ben Yehuda Street and Dizengoff Street intersect in the North of the city, looking for somewhere to have dinner. Finally I found a Hungarian restaurant which was quiet and where I wouldn't be surrounded by tables of happy couples feeding each other and laughing at me, a poor pathetic wretch eating alone. I had some Hungarian soup and a salad before returning to the beach. I then wolfed down a falafel in Dizengoff Square as I was still hungry. I phoned my mother from a call box, explaining in a very edited way what I was planning to do and then had a frozen yoghurt to calm myself down. I walked for miles up and down the *Tayelet*, the buzzing promenade, listening to the sea and to the music which escaped from clubs and bars. I walked to the more secluded beach near the port, normally reserved for Orthodox Jewish men during the day and sat on the cool sand. I began making a sand city, finding peace in the creativity. As I worked I noticed a group of teenagers sat around a small fire, drinking beer and laughing softly. For some reason about ten of the boys got up, took off their trunks and ran screaming and naked into the sea, their cherubic bottoms reflecting the moonlight. It was a long night. I was weary and bored as I waited for the 222 bus outside the concrete 1970s tower block which housed the Tel Aviv Hilton. It was still the middle of the night, and everything felt damp and dewy. As the bus sped down the Ayalon Motorway towards the airport I grew excited and felt happy to be leaving. I was also looking forward to seeing Avi again. I drew little hearts on the window with my finger.

My changed journey plans did not go down well with El Al security.

"Who paid for this ticket? Why? Where are you going in Germany?" The woman with the clip board was looking at me as if I were wearing army fatigues, a balaclava, and carrying a bomb with a fizzing fuse. I explained that this was a romantic arrangement, which helped, but not a lot, and I was soon inside a curtained cubicle with my trousers round my ankles and a stomach-contractingly gorgeous young man called Shmuel running his metal detector over my crotch. Meanwhile a plain young lady in jeans was squeezing all the toothpaste out of its tube, whilst a third was holding my passport and talking on the phone.

"Oy vey" I sighed. This was going to be a long day.

"Show me your papers!"

The El Al flight to Munich was fully booked, but as it was early in the morning I was spared the usual gangs of caffeine hyped teenagers chatting in the aisles. Instead I had to listen to 280 people snoring. As we began to make our decent into Munich I caught my first glimpse of fresh, green countryside and I realised how much I had missed Western Europe.

As the plane taxied into its bay I noticed a German army tank approach and park next to us in a please-do-not-be-alarmed-ve-are-just-followink-instructionz kind of way. As I disembarked the air felt delicious and cool on my face and I gulped it down. Europe! I was almost home. But not quite. We were led into a completely separate terminal, built solely for flights to and from Israel and I nervously eyed the machine gun nest trained on us as we walked by, feeling like an extra in *Raid on Entebbe*. Personally I think it should perhaps have been pointing the other way, but that's just a suggestion and I am sure Bavarian *Landes Polizei* knew what they were doing.

Avi was waiting for me at the gate and we hugged. It felt really good to be back together and away from Israel. As we got into his rusty old car, I had a moment of unease thinking 'where is this relationship going?' but I dismissed it and enjoyed the happiness of the moment. Soon we were speeding down the Autobahn and headed towards the Austrian border, and the city of Innsbruck. The scenery became dramatic and mountainous but the sky was grey and cool and I was savouring it. We stopped for petrol at a service station and enjoyed a cup of strong German coffee and a delicious, buttery cheese roll. One food I had really missed in Israel was decent cheese and I finished every crumb before gorging myself on decadently rich and bitter chocolate. The buxom Wagnerian wench behind the counter nodded approvingly at me as I licked my plate clean. "Vos good, Ja?" she asked, her bosom wobbling alarmingly. I nodded, grinning from ear to ear.

At the Austrian border we were stopped by some rather Aryan-looking border guards with a huge, panting wouldn't-mind-a-bite-out-of-your-arse-mate Alsatian. I noticed the way in which they scrutinized Avi's blue Israeli passport and then looked at the tatty old car. For an awful moment I expected them to start barking *raus, raus* and asking to see my 'papers.' Soon however we were on our way, and we stopped briefly in Innsbruck for more caffeine and carbohydrate. From here the motorway climbed and weaved through and around Alpine peaks. After a long stretch of driving we reached the Italian border where a quick flash of Avi's *permesso di segiorno* was all that was required to satisfy the half-conscious, half shaven, half cut border guard. We were in Italy at last. The architecture changed, becoming softer and tattier. When we reached the city of Trento we left the motorway and joined a smaller road. We began to climb steeply into the Alto Adige region of mountains. I was reminded of *Heidi,* with meadows of lush, green grass and little brooks and waterfalls. I was cold and for the first time in months reached for a sweatshirt. Oh, what a delicious feeling that was. We stopped at a small town near Avi's hotel and went into a supermarket. Here Avi told me to choose something for lunch and I looked in wonder at the gorgeous range of food on offer. I chose peach nectar to drink and more cheese, a fragrant and pungent *Parmigiano* to eat on crispy rolls. We ate this in the car park before covering the last stretch to his village. I was nervous as we finally pulled up outside the small, modern hotel in the main square of the peachy Alpine village. Outside the hotel was a small covered terrace for patrons to drink on, and beyond that a cosy foyer. I noted Avi's touches behind the reception, including souvenirs from his many travels. After a milky caffeinated treat we went upstairs to his en-suite room at the top of the hotel. How wonderful it must be to run a hotel, I thought, feeling like Meg Mortimer from *Crossroads.* I put down my things and looked out of the window. From the front I could see the spire of the small parish church and the village square. From the bathroom I could see nothing but a mountain slope, covered in a verdant forest of pine trees. Even though it was summer a thin mist and drizzle hung over the trees, making it seem mysterious. What wolves and goblins lurked in there at night I wondered?

It was soon dusk and time for dinner, a huge portion of mouth-melting pasta arrabiata, with hot chilli, followed by a finger of syrupy, thick espresso. After dinner we sat on the deserted terrace and enjoyed the cool air and the silence of the village square. As I hadn't slept for nearly 40 hours, I was soon stretched out on the firm bed with cool freshly laundered sheets, away from the flies and the noise of the Kibbutz. I was asleep in seconds.

The next morning I had my first Italian breakfast. Avi served me cappuccino, peach nectar from a bottle and a sugary brioche.

"Do you want Italian cappuccino or Israeli cappuccino?" asked Avi.

"What the hell is Israeli cappuccino?" I replied, perhaps a tad abruptly. I was still trying to prise open my eyes.

"Is coffee with whipped cream from container." I really did need to do something about Avi's English I thought, uncharitably.

"I'll have a normal one please." Who on earth invented Israeli cappuccino? I suspected it was Avi. As Avi had to get the hotel ready for the season I decided to explore the village. I looked around me from the square. I was struck by the heart-stopping beauty of the pine forests which covered the mountains on all sides of the valley. At a certain point the trees stopped to reveal the stark, brooding rocks of the Dolomites. The village itself felt more Austrian than Italian. This was not surprising, as it had belonged to Austria until 1918. There was a small bakery selling baguettes, pastries and some weirdly shaped loaves that looked more like origami shapes than food. This was presided over by the sourest, most acidic looking woman ever to stalk the face of the planet. She was so sour it set my teeth on edge just to glance in the general direction of her shop. There was also a small newsagent, and a shop where tourists could stock up on such essentials as trolls, postcards and knobbly walking sticks. I wouldn't have been at all surprised if it also did a roaring trade in Swastikas, jackboots and busts of *Il Duce*. I walked into the little parish church and enjoyed the calm and spiritual atmosphere. Dozens of votive candles in blue plastic holders burned beneath a serene blue and white Madonna. By the altar was a very Aryan figure of Jesus, pulling aside his robes to reveal a purple heart. I forged on up a steep hill, following a path that gradually got narrower and darker as it entered the forest. Soon the only sounds were the singing of birds, the babbling of a stream and my out of condition, dog-like panting. I relished the green beauty and quietness of my new surroundings and made a promise to myself not to return to the scorched, concrete craziness of Israel for a long, long time. This was a trifle premature as we shall see.

We developed a routine. Avi worked for long parts of the day and I walked around the forest and the village. In the evening we would eat together in the kitchen. I was developing a real taste for Italian food along with a small, but growing spare tyre. One night Avi served me a huge plate of Gorgonzola cheese with potatoes. It was hardly Gordon Ramsay at the Dorchester but never mind.

"I'll be so fat, I won't be able to get onto the plane" I joked. At this Avi became truculent and sullen. "It seems you want to remind me of this." It was a subject which had been preoccupying me as well. Before I knew what was happening we were involved in a furious argument. I was really confused. What was I doing here? Where would this end? I began to cry, the Gorgonzola lying untouched on my plate. It was another Brief Encounter *This is medniss* moment.

"*Dai, dai,* Pucci!" said Avi, hugging me. "We'll find a solution, don't you worry." Would we? I thought glumly. I wasn't so sure it would be a solution that would be terribly convenient for me. One problem for me in the village was boredom. There was a limit to how often I could wander around the village gasping in girlish delight at the scrumptiousness of it all, or walk into the forest communing with nature. Fortunately, I could speak some Italian being a cultured and rounded individual with a flair for language. I therefore spent large amounts of time watching both *la signora in giallo* (Murder She Wrote) and *Il barce del amore* (The Love Boat) in Italian. The dubbing was truly awful, but it was pleasant sitting in the guests' lounge, drinking incredibly strong coffee, eating biscotti and watching Jessica Fletcher solve her 453rd murder.

"*Ah signora Fletcher. Cosa c'e successo?*"

"*Non sono sicuro Seth ma penso c'e un assassino qui a Cabot Cove!*"

I watched copious amounts of Italian television and, no offence if you are Italian, but it is dreadful. I mean truly dreadful. So dreadful it is entertaining. All the shows were presented by chemically enhanced geriatrics, with laughable hairpieces, fawned over by nubile, half-dressed women with lips so shiny you could shave in the reflection. The woman stared up at the men with doughy eyes as if they were attractive young studs, their completely-natural-not-a-hint-of-silicone breasts straining to pop out of the eye patch-sized bikini tops. Meanwhile, an audience of cheering Italians simpered and laughed sycophantically at the poor quality jokes, clapping enthusiastically at the right places. Back on planet Earth, I was still troubled about Where Our Relationship Was Going, but tried not to think too much about it. Rather I tried to just enjoy the chance of a holiday romance and a nice, long holiday in Italy.

Occasionally Avi's friends would make the hour-long drive up from Trento. I always found this tedious, a bit like having to listen to one's mother and her friends at an endless coffee morning. Sometimes it was fun though, and there was always plenty to eat and drink. One of Avi's friends was very camp without realising it, which I found funny. One evening we drove up to Madonna di Campilio, an exclusive skiing resort, which, even in the early summer, felt nippy. The views and atmosphere were amazing and so was the bill after we drank cocktails in the bar of an exclusive hotel. Well, they drank cocktails. I had an orange juice to punish everyone for not giving me enough attention. I wasn't paying for anything any more as I had no income. Avi had made it clear he would treat me to everything I needed, which on the one hand was nice but it was also very disempowering. It was embarrassing as Italians go through a ritual fight every time a bill arrives. They play-snatch it out of each other's hands with loud exclamations of protest, pouting and saying *non, non, o Madonna. Ah non. Dio, que genorosita!* And so on and so forth, until one of them, invariably the one who paid last time, (not that anyone is counting) graciously backs down. It reminded me of a scene from *Father Ted* where Mrs Doyle and her friend end up in Police custody, following a full-blown fight over who got to treat the other. I never had this problem. I just sat there and let Avi do it.

Sometimes Avi and I went for outings in the car, often to deserted lakes in the forest or to Trento. I liked Trento, which did not feel like an Italian city at all, but was more Germanic. Here we often went for filter coffee and strudel at street cafes, or met Avi's friends for pizza. My favourite pizza was served in the village however, at a place called *Pizzeria del Diavolo* or the Devil's Pizzeria, located inside the forest on the fringe of the village. Most of the tables were outside and were shaded by tall, brooding pines. As it grew dark the forest closed in and it felt like as if I were in a fairy tale. Except they don't usually eat pizza in fairy tales of course. The pizzas were cooked in a glowing furnace outside and were as big as bike wheels and covered in thick but simple cheese toppings, the best of which was Gorgonzola and Parmagianno.

One evening we made a longer excursion to Lago di Magiore where we strolled by the lake, before eating our own body weight in creamy pasta at an outside restaurant. We then drove back through the night, the lights of the car illuminating the steep mountain road ahead. Despite the trips and fun, it was getting to crunch time. I didn't know what to do, and unfortunately I wasn't in a very supportive atmosphere from which to make a balanced decision. Whom could I talk to? I did make a rather expensive phone call to my friend Bruce but despite his sound advice of a cooling period or a trial long-distance relationship for a while, I felt stuck.

One afternoon I had a blazing row with Avi and, filled with rage, I packed my things into my rucksack and began marching down the hill towards the main road, with the intention of hitchhiking to Trento and from there catching a train north to Germany and thence home. I felt like an Allied airman in Occupied Europe. Avi soon caught up with me in the car and persuaded me to come back, as net curtains all over the village twitched to fever pitch. I don't think anything that exciting had happened since 1954 when a farmer returned early from milking one day to discover the farmer's wife helping the postman empty his sack. Back at the hotel we talked seriously. Avi could not come to England as he was not from an EU member state and gay and lesbian relationships did not count. He did not want to continue with the hotel, although he would bitterly regret this decision later. He talked about wanting to return to Israel and the fact that I wanted to convert to Judaism interested him. He knew the right things to say. He said we would open a café of our own, his parents would finance it, and I could become a Jew and lead a Jewish life. I could become Israeli. I ruled it out. I wanted to go home. I wanted to join the police. My reaction produced anger and disappointment in Avi and we had more blazing rows, a fact which I am sure did not go unnoticed amongst the hotel guests, most of whom were elderly, and who had come to get a couple of weeks of mountain air, not an earful of two queens having a catfight in English. I began thinking seriously about this. What was more important in life, love or work, I pondered? Should I follow my old teenage dream of becoming Israeli? In Avi's room I sat and looked at his blue Israeli passport, listening to Hebrew music. One of my favourite songs at that time was called *Telavi Oti*, which means *Accompany Me*, in Hebrew. Time was running out. Conflicting feelings surged through me, love for Avi and homesickness, longing for Brighton and a career in the police and the need not to be alone anymore. It had got to the point where I could not simply say goodbye to Avi now. It was too late. It was far too late.

I had to make several deeply unpleasant phone calls home. I also put off writing a letter of resignation to the police for as long as possible. But the time came when I had to, following a conversation with my freaked out mother who had just received joining instructions for me from the police. This caused me huge amounts of anguish. I understood that I would not be able to bear to return to Brighton for many years, as the pain would be too great. I spent my days trying to get my head round the new direction my life was to take. I began reading the bible on the terrace overlooking the village square. I took notes, trying to absorb as much information as I could. In order to relax I also read and reread the English books I had received from my parents through the very efficient and dependable Italian postal service. I had a small collection of Jeeves and Wooster stories which comforted me, but I could not bear to read any of the Miss Read books, with her reassuring tales of English village life. When would I see my green and pleasant land again, I wondered with pain? I was really missing it now. I missed bookshops and pubs and the sound of English voices. I missed the soft countryside and red brick houses. I missed the attitudes of the people and the relative informality of their interaction. Italians, it seemed, dressed up for absolutely everything.

Italian Husband: "You look smart darling!"

Italian Wife: "Ah *si, mio caro*. I am popping down to the corner shop for some milk. Have you seen my pearls?"

I was desperate for a conversation that did not involve pouting and saying "*Oooooh Madonna!*" or "*Vero, vero*" at the end of every sentence. I was tired of the inbred, ex-Gestapo woman from the bakery looking me up and down every time I went into the square. Above all I was tired of the extended holiday that was now in its second month. Despite this

I tried to get some enjoyment from life. I still looked forward to our meals and excursions, and it was interesting to observe the comings and goings of the long-term hotel residents and of the villagers. There were the two elderly sisters from Milan who had been coming to the hotel every year for the last two decades and who were staying for the entire month of August. Apart from Avi, these two old dears were the sum total of my lively *Sex and The City* lifestyle. In the early mornings some of the villagers came into the bar of the hotel for their cappuccinos and brioches but never lingered. One of the most interesting characters was the hotel cleaner, a rather earthy and somewhat simple woman who relished gossip. One day she made me cringe when she looked viciously at one of the guests and her teenage daughter.

"*Non e normale questa raggazza. E mongolina*" she hissed. She was referring to the young woman's Down Syndrome and had no sense of respect or tact. She seemed to feel that talking in a deafening whisper about the situation to me was more appropriate than just treating the guests with some basic respect.

The area was not entirely devoid of gay life and Avi pointed out small lay-bys in the forest where truck drivers stopped to read dirty magazines. A generous scattering of condom wrappers indicated that reading magazines was not all that went on there. There was also a small lake which Avi assured me was Alto Adige's answer to Sodom and Gomorra but apart from me, Avi and an elderly Dutch couple with a camper van there was not much going on. Gay life was discreet but there were lots of Joe Ortonesque encounters to be had for those willing to seek them out. In Trento the scene centred on a rather tired looking park, with lots of elaborate toing and froing and dropping of hankies etc. It all seemed a bit Jane Austen for me.

Closeted gay married man 1: "Ah *signore*. You 'ave a dropped a your 'ankie."

Closeted gay married man 2: "Ah silly me. *Grazie signore*."

Closeted gay married man 1: "Is a ma pleasure. 'Ave seen you 'ere before, yes?"

Closeted gay married man 2: "Indeed. *Ascolta*, ma wife's at a da bingo. You fancy a wank? *Si?*"

The park was where two of Avi's closest, campest and most closeted friends had met. Another member of the 'gang' was a straight cousin.

This lady was an absolute hoot, partial to a *grappa* or three, and completely unaware that not only all our party, but also her elderly uncle were gay. We all had to pretend we were straight, easy for me because I had nothing to say anyway, but a real challenge for the rest of them. This was all delightfully dysfunctional but I couldn't really see the point. Why not just tell the woman we were gay and have done with it? It was obvious to everyone else, and I am sure the lady was no fool. Unfortunately there was a misogynistic undercurrent amongst some of the group. When I challenged this, one man became quite flushed and rounded on me for being so naïve. Concepts such as ecology, animal rights, coming out and feminism seemed utterly alien in Italy if the present company and the TV were anything to go by.

The elderly grandmother of one of Avi's friends fascinated me. This tiny woman was well into her 90s, and lived alone in a huge dated apartment near the station. Her kitchen reminded me of Ann Frank's secret annex, with a huge gas stove and a deep Butler-style sink. The shelves were lined with shiny paper and stacked with jars of dried pulses and pasta. She prepared coffee from a massive, espresso maker which was placed directly over the flames of the cooker. This was blackened from years of use; indeed I imagined she had been making coffee for the local *fascisti* with it back in the thirties, perhaps rustling up a couple of crunchy biscotti from the other ingredients on her shelves. The lady had no teeth, giving her a skeletal appearance, and she had more facial hair than I did. She spoke in a guttural, rasping dialect. If I had been a child I would have wet my pants and needed the urgent services of a really, really good child psychologist.

Time was ticking on, the season was coming to a close and we started to make plans about moving to Israel. Before going home, Avi wanted one last holiday in Europe, and I naturally wanted to see my family. So early one September morning we packed up the old Golden car and set off north.

"It's very small" said Avi

We drove for hours, crossing into Switzerland and pausing for a light picnic by a glacier. We passed fleetingly through charming Swiss villages, yet without really stopping to get a true feeling for them. The scenery was spectacular. We passed Swiss cows wearing huge bells, and then wooden chalets and of course, massive snow-capped mountains. Our first proper stop was the city of Zurich, where we drove around for nearly an hour, before finding an affordable hotel. Once we had showered and unpacked we explored the town on foot. We passed a shop which sold shoes to Swiss drag queens, a poster in the window advertising *Einen Grossen Tranny Schuen Angebot*. Now that's what I call a niche market. Dinner was fast food, and then we went to a gay bar, which was half empty. We should have known. It was ten o'clock and this was Switzerland. We left Zurich the next morning after a breakfast of crispy rolls and plum jam. We then joined the motorway, heading north. The travelling was making me constipated and I longed to get out and actually *do* something more than sit and listen to Avi's tapes. We were visiting some of the most beautiful places in Europe and not seeing them. It was frustrating. We stopped for the night at a gay hotel Avi had found in the *Spartacus Gay Guide*. This was located in an odd and depressing one street village close to the university town of Heidelberg. I couldn't quite see why we had made the detour to stay in a gay hotel when we had the world-famous city of Heidelberg on our doorstep. We left early the next morning, 'did' Heidelberg, then it was back in the car for another gruelling, bowel-sealing leg up the *Autobahn*. It was getting dark and I was tired, crabby and in need of fresh air. We had been driving for hours and were approaching the industrial conurbation of Essen. We had already missed our turning for Maastricht in the Netherlands, where we had planned to spend the night, and I was worried where we would finally end up. As we passed the lights of distant cities I imagined the lives of the people there. Would they be settling down to dinner? Had they been at work? I envied them their homes and settled lives as we forged ahead towards the end of this fairly rootless and disorientating day.

"Turn left!" I shouted suddenly, spotting our exit and we found ourselves heading towards the Dutch border at last. After another long drive we arrived at the outskirts of Arnhem. I experienced a strange sensation of familiarity at the rows of semidetached houses, built in the 1930s Amsterdam-School style of architecture. At a distance, the streets looked almost English. I needed to be home. In the centre of Arnhem we soon discovered that every hotel for miles around was fully booked because of the anniversary of the famous Second World War battle. All I wanted now was a bed and something to eat. Above all I wanted silence and I wanted to get out of that bloody car. I would happily have stormed into a hotel, grabbed an ageing war hero by his medals and thrown him into the street if I had thought I could have his bed. I finally gave up as the hundredth Dutch landlord shook his head regretfully, wiping a beer glass on a tea towel. All around were smiling, cheerful guests getting ready for a good night's sleep in their sensibly pre-booked bedrooms. I shook my head as I got back into the car, Bonnie Tyler screeching her way through the same songs that I had heard three times that day. I felt like the Holy Family arriving in Bethlehem on the eve of a particulary important cup final. We resigned ourselves to driving onwards to the next big town, Utrecht. It was now well-past dinner time. We discovered a similar problem. Everything was full, or else way too expensive for us. Eventually we saw a large B&B by a canal and drew up. There was a room for us and mercifully we could get out of the car. I felt as though the seat had actually become part of my body, and that my DNA had somehow merged with it. As we went upstairs Avi seemed angry.

"What's up?" I asked.

"That fucking man!" he cursed. The reason for his ire, it transpired, was that the owner was a fellow Israeli and had not given Avi the customary discount due to Israeli travellers. The following day it was hellish trying to drive into Amsterdam and find a hotel and a parking space. After an hour and a half of trying, we found a dreary B&B overlooking the Amstel and Avi parked, probably illegally, on a bridge. It was great to be back in Amsterdam, my favourite city, but this was not how I wanted it to be. There was no time to unwind, to revisit my special places. I wasn't happy or particularly relaxed.

I was sad to be leaving Amsterdam so soon the next day but we needed to get away before the traffic wardens gave us a ticket, and we had a ferry to catch that evening from Rotterdam. At dusk we set sail; tomorrow I would be home. Early the next morning whilst we were still at sea we had breakfast, fuelling up for the day ahead. Avi gorged on a full English breakfast, consisting of grease with bits of rubbery meat in it. I had a slice of bread and marmalade, feeling sick. Avi was also quietly making a stack of sandwiches. A rather brusque member of crew told us it was not allowed. "I am going to eat them now!" Avi protested, pretending to raise one of the two dozen cheese sandwiches to his lips.

The dawn was grey and misty as the Humber Estuary began to narrow. I had not seen this view for over fifteen years. I was in England. I felt emotional, a feeling compounded by the fact we were arriving not at Heathrow or Gatwick, but in Yorkshire, my birthplace. I felt like saying "'ee ba gum" and pulling on my braces. An unpleasant altercation ensued when we turned up a couple of nanoseconds late on the car deck. The Dutch drivers, never internationally renowned for their tact and patience, were tooting, and making obscene gestures. One of them seemed to be suggesting that we avail ourselves of his middle finger for purposes best left to the imagination. Avi replied there was an irregularity in the Dutchman's family tree. Views and feelings exchanged and vented, we drove off the ferry and onto the quay side. We stopped at passport control. A sour pinstriped suited immigration officer took one withering look at our tatty golden car with Italian number plates and at Avi's Israeli passport, and then ordered us to pull over, adding a frosty 'sir' in the condescending way that the English have perfected. This delighted the Dutch occupants of the car behind us who honked their horns in undisguised glee. I sat miserably in the cold car as the immigration officers interrogated Avi for nearly half an hour. I began to fear they may not let him in at all. We drove out of the port into Hull, feeling upset. Soon we were making for my birthplace of Beverley. This was a very strange feeling as I had not been here since I was a little boy. Nevertheless I recognised it, squealing at my first sight of the Race Course, the Westwood Hospital and the Minster. It was still early in the morning and we decided to walk around the market place and then go for coffee at an old fashioned tea shop.

"Is this coffee or tea?" asked Avi sipping a hot, milky beverage. I tasted it.

"I am not sure" I replied; It was good to be home.

We drove up to my old home, a 1930s semidetached suburban house which was smaller than I remembered it. I remembered the window, through which my mother had accidentally shoved her hand. I remembered the tree whose berries I had proudly eaten before an unedifying rush to the hospital. Then we drove to my school, and suddenly I was six years old again. Here we learned about the baby Jesus and I had bought my mum bubble bath as a Christmas present at the fete. I remembered crying with frustration because I couldn't tie my shoelaces. Mum was always there to meet me, at the same gates where I was standing now. How odd life can be. One day you are a little boy of six, playing in the garden and then twenty years later you return, on your way to Israel. Who could have imagined life turning out this way? Sighing, I got back into the car and we drove out of Beverley. We made our way through more familiar Yorkshire countryside, passing fields of haystacks and thick hedgerows. We paused for a photo at the border between England and Scotland before forging ahead to Edinburgh. Avi did not feel comfortable at the prospect of staying at my parents' home so we agreed to find a B&B. I had misgivings about this, and felt suddenly sad. I just wanted to be home.

It was interesting watching Avi's interaction with Scottish landladies, and to see the result of cultural differences. Scottish landladies believe that their B&B is their fiefdom and that guests are there under sufferance. Israelis believe that hotel owners are out to cheat them and that it is their duty not to be a *sucker,* the worst insult to any Israeli. We drew up outside a row of gruesome-looking B&Bs, boasting fine Scots names like *Ben Grabbit, Dunsmiling* and *Borstal View*. I felt as if I had just entered one of those hostels for released prisoners, the kind that are featured on *Taggart* just after a decapitated corpse has been found in the Willow Tearooms and the first sick joke has been made. Avi lost no time. "We need double room, three nights."

The venomous, blue-rinsed woman's nostrils flared. "I'll see what I have" she said, her voice cold enough to freeze sperm. When she had retrieved the key, Avi demanded to see the room, before agreeing to it. Mrs Mc Frosty did not like this one little bit but silently led us up a cheaply carpeted staircase to a depressing double room.

"My terms are £35 a night, bed and breakfast." She folded her arms and eyeballed us defiantly. And there was me thinking holidays were supposed to be fun.

"It's very small" said Avi, obviously expecting the woman to crumble and reduce her price, giving him *ha nacha*, the expected discount.

"Well you can take it or leave it" the now fizzing landlady snapped, turning heel. "Let me know what you want to do."

"Let's just go" I hissed. We stalked out as quietly as we could, the net curtain twitching frenziedly behind us. I think the poor woman needed a wee lie doon and a bit shortbread to recover. We decided to stay at the gay hotel in the New Town, paying the usual supplement for the privilege of being greeted by a gay receptionist, and having exactly the same facilities as any other hotel.

It was finally time to see my parents. I found it difficult to be at home again, yet not be staying. I looked round at the familiar large drawing room, at its wooden floors, the rugs and the view out over the Forth Estuary. Here was my mum's couch, my grandmother's Chinese vases, a copy of the Radio Times, listing programmes I wouldn't be staying long enough to watch. It was sad and strained for the whole family. Nevertheless we had a delicious home-cooked meal and I was given the birthday presents that I had missed whilst on the Kibbutz. While my father was talking to Avi, my mother tried to thrust some letters and joining instructions from Sussex Police into my hand. The general drift seemed to be "'ello, 'ello, 'ello. Wot's happened to you then Sir?" I could not bear to look at them. When it was time to return to the hotel I had to disguise how upset I felt.

Avi and I had different priorities for the few days we were in Edinburgh. I wanted to see family and friends. Avi however wasn't happy.

"I want to see real Scottish cows!" he announced. I was about to suggest a visit to the Jenners' Sale when I grasped his meaning.

"You mean you want to go to the Highlands!"

"I want to see real Scottish scenery, with cows with horns and mountains and lakes."

"But that's miles away!" My father later suggested a compromise. The following day we drove to the Trossachs and Loch Katrine, wild enough to satisfy Avi and yet close enough to avoid me getting deep vein thrombosis. We then returned to my parent's home for dinner, and the same sadness returned. The following day we needed to leave for Ireland. My father had planned a route for us, and although it looked straightforward, a traffic jam on the outskirts of Edinburgh held us up. We were getting seriously late for our ferry. By the time we reached Dumfries the road was wide and clear so we drove as fast as we could, throwing up a vapour trail for miles behind. The old car rattled and hissed at the punishment it was receiving but Avi drove it mercilessly. We screeched to a halt at the queue for the Larne ferry with just seconds to spare, steam coming off the tyres and smoke bellowing from the bonnet. We disembarked at Larne where we came face to face with a row of RUC police officers in dark green uniforms and peaked caps. The officers were armed to the teeth but looked jolly polite and well turned out, and I am sure they would mind their Ps and Qs if they decided to shoot you. A couple of them were women and it was odd to note the combination of sensible shoes, tights, knee-length skirt and thick body armour. One of the women looked mumsy and middle aged and strangely vulnerable. She smiled at me as she waved us past.

Belfast looked like Newcastle with terrorism. It was Victorian, red-brick and of course drenched in a thin, constant rain. Many buildings were derelict and there was a distinct edge in the air. Occasionally we passed army vehicles but mostly it was the RUC who were on patrol, armed and very, very alert. We didn't linger in Belfast, beguiling though it was, and made our way south, passing the outskirts of Londonderry. It felt strange to be driving through Northern Ireland, and seeing signposts to places I had been hearing about for decades on the news. As the border drew closer I noticed an army roadblock ahead and wasn't sure if Avi had seen it, as he was fiddling with his cassettes.

"*Dai*. Is not for us!" he announced calmly, keeping his foot firmly on the accelerator.

"Erm, I think it might be" I replied, staring ahead in horror as a paratrooper stepped out into the middle of the road. Meanwhile Dolly Parton was giving it all she had with *Stand By Your Man*. Avi decided to stop and the soldier rapped on my window.

"Alright there lads" he said in a thick Lancashire accent. "Thought you weren't stopping there, for a minute." His face was painted black and his helmet was decorated with twigs and leaves. In his arms was a self-loading rifle. Meanwhile two other soldiers were walking around the car, stooping to check underneath. After a quick chat about our travel plans he waved us into Ireland.

"What a big mess you have in your country" pronounced Avi.

"That's a bit like the pot calling the kettle black isn't it?" I bridled. This ignited a circular and irritating row all the way to Dublin, the seedy, depressing and highly overrated capital of Ireland. As usual on this car journey from hell we arrived without reservations, and late. Dublin oozed unwelcoming vibes as we drove around looking for hotels. I was given the task of jumping out the car and asking if there were rooms free and eventually I struck lucky, finding a clean and reasonably comfortable place near the centre.

"Hello there. Do you have a double room by any chance?" I asked.

"That oy do" replied the rotund and jocular owner cheerfully. This was all going swimmingly. I went outside briefly to get Avi, who then arrived carrying our luggage.

"Ah, now would that be two gentlemen?" asked the owner still smiling, but not, any longer, with his beady eyes. I looked at Avi, and replied that yes, it would be for two gentlemen.

"Ah now well, you see that moight be a problem" he continued the key now firmly back on the rack. "Oyve only a double bed but that wouldn't do at all now, would it?" He continued to smile in that sickly sweet way of Christian bigots, with their sending-you-to-hell-with-a-cheery-wave-and-a-packed-lunch attitude. Personally I am a great believer in twin beds, not particularly enjoying a sweaty grunting, farting body with morning breath anywhere near me when I am sleeping. However on this occasion I would gladly have accepted a bed with the owner and his wife, watched over by a life-sized picture of the Holy Father himself.

"No, no, that wouldn't do at all" beamed the bigot. "You might want to try in town. There moight be some places that cater for that sort of thing there. Good noight." We had no choice but to look for somewhere else that might be more amenable to 'that sort of thing.' We ended up finding a lovely, and very pricey modern hotel and booked in for two nights. I stretched out luxuriously on the wide, double, faggot friendly bed and soon fell asleep.

We had a huge Irish breakfast the next morning, which was basically a full English breakfast but served in Ireland with 'Irish' tea and a slice of black pudding for Avi. We called in at the tourist office. Avi had got it into his head that we might spend the day driving (Oh please God no!) to the West Coast of Ireland but thankfully the unsmiling cuss behind the counter almost laughed in his face at the very idea. (Thank you God!) Instead we explored Dublin Castle, the courtyard of Trinity College and the city centre shops, before going for a walk along the river and over the famous arched pedestrian bridge. In the afternoon we drove (Why God? Why?) the short distance to Malahide. I loved this beautiful old home which smelt of damp and history. I found something incredibly peaceful in the atmosphere of the bedrooms and imagined ghosts and troubled spirits stalking the chilly corridors, rattling chains.

"Come on, *dai*, let's go" said an impatient Avi, chomping at the bit for some CD shopping. I did however insist on being taken for a traditional Irish Cream Tea. Despite the outrageous price tag, it wasn't the freshest scone to ever pop out of the microwave. I swept up my broken teeth and went to pay. After Dublin, our next overnight stop was at the border town of Dundalk, which sounded nice in the book but which was sinister and vaguely threatening. We checked into the Best Western and then walked around the drizzle soaked streets looking for something to do that didn't involve knee-capping or drug-taking. Avi had promised me a slap up Irish meal to celebrate our last night on the Emerald Isle and against all the odds we found a posh restaurant with table cloths and candlelight. Here we stuffed ourselves on salmon steaks, followed by trifle, then coffee and After Eight mints. One of the pitfalls of eating in the United Kingdom or Ireland with Israelis is their confusion about restaurant etiquette. An Australian friend once told me about how her Israeli partner had read the entire description of the dishes he was ordering.

"Hey you! You! 'Allo! Miss" snarled my friend's partner.

"Yes?" replied the English waitress, by now very put out and selectively deaf.

"Gimme the Delicious Selection of Marinated Vegetables, the Succulent Salmon cooked in a Fragrant Blend of Summer Spices and Served in Cranberry Jus."

"Anything else?"

"Yes, gimme a slice of Oak Roasted Smoked Trout on a Bed of Crisp Seasonal Lettuce."

"'s that all?"

"No, I want a glass of The Mellow, Fruity, *Chateau Foofo de Put*, Redolent of Apricots and Strawberries. And hurry!"

Avi wanted to sample Guinness in a traditional Irish pub. This did sound rather nice, and I pictured myself writing our initials with my finger in a thick, creamy froth, perhaps adding a little heart shape. There would be a roaring fire and a small local band would be playing traditional Irish ditties on delightful and quaint instruments. All the time friendly locals would be raising their glasses, winking and wishing us top o' the mornin'. We ventured out into the steady rain which had replaced the drizzle. After a long search we located a pub that didn't have bricked up windows or pints of rhesus AB negative evaporating in the doorway. There were a few locals who barely glanced at us. A couple of toothless and loutish looking men were playing darts. We bought two pints of Guinness from an emaciated woman with a dog's-arse mouth and a voracious heroin habit, then sat down in a discreet corner of the ghastly little venue. I took one sip of the foul drink and gagged.

"I don't like" said Avi pushing it away.

We went back to the hotel. Early the following morning we set off like bats out of hell and soon reached the border, passing the massive army post at Warren Point. We made straight for Belfast, where we promptly got lost. The Victorian streets began to look the same, and I was alarmed by the huge murals, painted onto the ends of each terrace. These featured surprisingly well painted depictions of men in balaclavas, holding aloft Kalashnikovs. Invariably they boasted some slogan such as *You Are Entering Free West Belfast* or *Hip Hip Hooray For The Shankhill Butchers*. The streets looked mean. Seriously stop-here-and-you'll-get-shot-quicker-than-you-can-say-what-ho mean. Some of the terraced houses where boarded up with pieces of plywood, whilst others were derelict and burnt out. I noticed Irish tricolours fluttering from windows and TV aerials. I am sure this was all perfectly quaint, and under different circumstances I would have been overjoyed to don a green, white and orange top hat and do some River Dancing, perhaps touching my forelock and winking. Today however, I thought it best to keep my 'white English ass' in the car.

"Look, we're lost!" said Avi, swerving to avoid a barrage of petrol bombs and a volley of machine gun fire. "Ask someone the way." I am generally a communicative happy-to-mingle-with-the-locals kind of a guy. Indeed part of the fun of travelling is the chance to stop, chat and exchange small gifts with ones' hosts. There was however no way I was going to open my plummy English mouth anywhere near the Falls Road. I could sense snipers fixing me with their sights, drooling with blood lust. Even the army was nowhere to be seen. Fortunately for us, we eventually found a main road and arrived at the port of Larne in time to catch our ferry to Stranraer. At Stranraer we began our long and exhausting drive through the Pennines, and the Yorkshire Dales. By the time we got to Yorkshire it was dark, and the bleak, desolate hills were shrouded in a thick fog. It was a scary, arse-clenching-bile-swallowing drive, with about three feet of visibility ahead of us, and on several occasions we hit the verge. This induced fits of merry, girlish laughter and we both saw the funny side, with Avi threatening to extract my testicles from my scrotum and put my eyes out with them should I not rethink my approach to backseat driving. Meanwhile I suggested that if he couldn't drive then perhaps he had better not try. We crashed through the grass verge of a Little Chef somewhere near a hamlet called Inbreeding-On-The-Mire. Here we opted for a dinner of beans on toast. This took some ordering as Avi insisted on mispronouncing the word as beams. Meanwhile Avi, and for that matter I, had difficulty understanding the half pig half gnome who was serving.

"D'jur wan brown tuuurst?"

"Sorry?" asked Avi.

"Tuurst? What tuurst d'jur want?"

"I want beams."

"Yurwot?"

"Beams."

"Beams? Wots them?"

And so on and so forth. Oh, how we all laughed. I was glad when we reached the outskirts of York and found a B&B. After a rest, we walked around the old Shambles and medieval streets, before finding a pub. The following morning we visited the Minster and Castle area. It was strange being here again, as York was a place mum had always taken me to when I was a child. In the afternoon we drove to Hull, and caught the ferry to Zeebrugge. From Zeebrugge we drove through Belgium and into Germany, forging ahead for hours down the Autobahn. The plan had been to stop in Stuttgart, but after more than an hour of looking for a hotel we decided to leave and try elsewhere. We eventually found a cheerful hotel in the countryside with a balcony overlooking a forest. I wanted to just stay here, relax and actually enjoy our holiday. I was exhausted. What's more, my dear old friend Mr Constipation had returned as a result of hours in the car. The travelling was a *strain* in more ways than one.

We arrived in Trento late the next evening in a thunderstorm. We stayed at a pass-me-the-razor-and-let's-be-done-with-it awful pensione on the outskirts, which appeared to be run by the village idiot. Our requests for simple indulgences such as water, light and a door which locked were met with insensible laughs and shrugs. The next day we returned to the village in the mountains where the afternoon was spent packing up the hotel. We then returned to Trento, this time staying as guests at Avi's friend's home. After selling the car for scrap to an Albanian refugee, we returned to a slap up meal of creamy pasta, slices of tuna steak and fruit salad.

"I need to go for a walk" I said. Everyone looked at me as though I had just announced I was carrying Satan's child. Was I being frightfully rude I wondered? Had I committed a social boo boo? Despite the surprised looks I needed to escape. I had been in the car for days. I wanted fresh air, exercise and some silence. I wanted to feel the blood carousing through my flabby buttocks. That night I lay awake on my mattress on the floor, listening to the pounding rain and thunder. When I woke up it would be time to go back to Israel. I didn't want to go. I just didn't want to go. The alarm clocks rang at four the next morning, and by half past four I was sat with all Avi's friends in the hired minibus, with luggage piled up beside me. We arrived at Verona airport in plenty of time to catch our flight to Rome, where we changed terminals. Above us, on a gallery, was a machine gun nest. Dozens of soldiers and armed police hovered nervously around us. I went through the check in without thinking or feeling. I just wanted to get the whole thing over with. I felt trapped. This was a nightmare.

"Ma hu oseh po?"

We arrived in Israel in very different frames of mind. Avi's friends were in a buoyant holiday mood, perhaps tinged with sadness that they would be saying goodbye to a friend. Avi was gearing himself up for a return to Israeli life. I was completely freaked out and powerless. It felt horribly familiar as I stepped out onto the tarmac. The same balmy heat, the smell of orange blossom and the same view of concrete and palm trees. We hired a mini-bus and after an initial grinding of gears and mounting of kerbs, we were soon speeding down the Ayalon on our way north, bypassing Tel Aviv. It was around dusk, the sky was turning purple and the palm trees were silhouetted against the sky. A warm, blossom-laden breeze was blowing through my hair. The radio news came on with the by-now familiar *"Kol Israel mi Yerushalayim. Shalom rav."* I had first heard those words as a teenager, in my bedroom in Luxembourg. I had finally found the frequency, after weeks of searching. I remember jumping out of my skin, feeling as though I had just cracked the Enigma Code. Back in the present I couldn't quite make out the gist of the broadcast but the words El Al and Amsterdam came up several times. My heart sank. An El Al 747 had crashed in Amsterdam. Avi immediately turned up the volume. It was a cargo plane and it had hit a housing estate.

We arrived at the holiday house in Tiberias late at night, feeling tired and cranky after the long journey. All I wanted was to be alone and yet I was surrounded by a bunch of half strangers, speaking Italian and trying to unfold camp beds. The next day was the eve of Yom Kippur and I had decided to fast. We all went to a small Orthodox synagogue in the village for the Kol Nidre service, and I immediately experienced an unpleasant feeling of alienation. A hard-core of worshippers prayed, moving their lips rapidly but looking around the room and staring at newcomers. This was not the Judaism I was used to. This felt harsh, fundamentalist and conservative. I missed the soft organ music of West London Synagogue, and the delightful, polite, and gentle rhythm of the service. I missed the inclusive, respectful liberalism of British Reform Judaism. I remembered the terribly English Kiddush after the service, where women dressed for the Ascot Races and the men wore suits so sharp you could slice bread with them. We would nibble *petit fours* and have cups of splendidly weak tea. Well, obviously not on Yom Kippur, but at least the service would have been meaningful. In the morning Avi made a big show of asking everyone to eat and drink outside, and not in the house. Inevitably the day dragged and tempers frayed. Claustrophobia was rising in the one bed roomed flat with its six occupants. We were also all pretending to be straight again. Yawn! I went through the motions of this, hating myself for doing it and doing it as badly as I could.

I felt I should say something like "Yeah, yeah, I'm a tit man myself. By the way, has anyone seen my knitting? I left it on top of the complete works of Oscar Wilde." At dusk, we broke the fast with an al-fresco meal in the garden. There was a selection of salads and dips, and the mood improved, but I noticed more and more that I didn't really fit into the group. I was beginning to resent Avi's attention being so thin on the ground. Whilst I appreciated the situation was stressful for him, it was also hard for me, and I wasn't surrounded by comfortable friends. I recalled one of the first questions my friend Jane had asked me during the short visit to Edinburgh with Avi.

"Andrew, what are you doing for money?" she asked anxiously in a teashop in Crammond when Avi was in the toilet. I had shrugged. I was now in a situation where I was totally financially dependent on someone else. Not only that, but I was depending on someone who no longer had an income, and yet was spending his savings alarmingly quickly.

We spent a day in the Galilee before driving south along the Jordan valley the following day. The scenery became brutal and arid, the road shimmering into the horizon. The sun was merciless. Above, a couple of vultures circled and by the roadside we passed a Judas tree. Meanwhile I was sulking, or *taking some time out* as I preferred to call it, because my position in the front passenger seat had been usurped by one of Avi's friends. The journey was tiring, but we forged on along the desert highway, passing Jericho, a dusty and shabby collection of breezeblock houses, and then onwards, past the Dead Sea. It was dark by the time we eventually reached Eilat where we had to endure the tedium and stress of trying to find a hotel with four vacant rooms at a price that suited. This involved walking into reception after reception, and trying to haggle with teenage staff. Meanwhile hotel guests lay by moonlit pools, sipping huge cocktails with little umbrellas in them. After about an hour and a half of this, we found rooms at a modern three star hotel. Avi reached into his pocket for an inch thick wad of crisp Shekels. It was a relief to stand under the pounding hot shower, washing the sweat and dust of the journey off my body. Feeling more fragrant but very hungry we all walked the short distance to the seafront. We went to a fishy alfresco restaurant, where group dynamics resulted in a very expensive bottle of wine being ordered. The owner's eyes reflected Shekel signs, as he uncorked the bottle with a flourish, mentally planning his next holiday and nipping off to make a down payment on a Saab. I winced, thinking of the bill and wondering if it would hurt when I finally had to sell one of my kidneys to get by.

"*Chin chin*" said Avi and his friends, clicking glasses. I wanted to weep.

The following morning I woke up to my first true Israeli hotel breakfast. I had heard legends about these buffets, but had always believed them to be an urban myth, exaggerated beyond all proportion and added to over the years. I was soon to discover for myself that the legend was in fact true. In the dining room were three banqueting tables, with silver platters of food laid out on crisp white table cloths, decorated with bunches of fresh flowers or heaps of tropical fruit. Avi, a seasoned veteran of such affairs, was silent but determined, and I, a mere novice, entered the fray with caution. I selected a vast array of cheeses, Feta cheese, blue cheese, Israeli white hard cheese and some cottage cheese, for health reasons. After all, just because a girl's on holiday doesn't mean she can let herself go. To go with the cheese was the entire contents of a bakery, fresh and fragrant rolls, brown bread with seeds and bagels to name but a few. There was also sweet, succulent watermelon, which was the ideal accompaniment to the salty cheese. I went in for the kill, with a staggering mound of scrambled egg and smoked fish, some blinnis and a little cherry tomato on the top, which is supposed to be good for *men's health* as my mother always says, making me simultaneously cringe and confused. At our table conversation was fitful and muted as we got down to the serious business of clawing back some of our hotel bill in the form of free food. To round off, I selected hot pancakes with maple syrup and some fruit salad. Surfeit, and bored by the Italian conversation that seemed to revolve around Avi and his wonderful driving-stroke-organisational skills, I observed the scene around me. I watched Israelis in their natural habitat, hunting and gathering. Men with hairy backs and sunglasses hanging around their necks hovered close to each other, jealously competing to see who could load the largest amount onto their plates. I began to wonder if it was a virility thing.

Male Hotel Guest: "Look at that prick and his six omelettes. I'll show him who can eat the most omelettes around here. Here mate, seven fucking boiled eggs, you wanker. Yeah, seven, oh no. Look, eight, yes, eight fucking eggs I can eat, I'm that hard."

Meanwhile the women-folk were also hard at work, although this time it was more a show of look-at-me-eating-all-this-and-still-staying-slim-enough-to-fit-into-my-wedding-dress. Their body language seemed to say "Cor, look at this huge, enormous, greasy piece of potato latke I'm eating. My, however do I do it, eat like this and still stay sooooo slim? Look at you, stuck with that plate of melon and a figure like a horse" Staggering out of the restaurant, we passed a queue of guests waiting to join battle. I was reminded of those old photos of soldiers returning from the Trenches passing those on the way to replace them.

"It's fucking hard in there mate. Good luck to ya. They've got bloody waffles and cream, the bastards." We spent the day on the beach, which was boring, and I began thinking unkind thoughts about Avi's friends. Every now and then the sounds of the beach were drowned out by the roar of planes, coming in to land at the airport, located in the town centre. It was strange to see a street with shops, pedestrians and hotels and then, incongruously the entrance to an airport. Once again dinner was lavish, and once more we had the don't-do-this-in-front-of-my-friends-you-bitch versus the are-you-nuts-spending-all-the-money-on-holidays argument. The following day, flatulent and bloated from breakfast, we loaded ourselves into the van and drove north, through the desert. At the Dead Sea we stopped at one of the large hotels by the edge of the sea, where we would spend the night. We spent the afternoon in the brine, enjoying the novelty of reading and floating. Then we, erm, floated in the sea some more before wishing we had perhaps just stopped here for an hour or so. The issue of money reared its ugly head again the next day. We stopped at a service station and, as we queued for our meals, Avi discreetly indicated that we could not afford to eat a big lunch. Meanwhile his friends were being served steaming platefuls of fish and boiled potatoes, and chocolate mousse to follow.

"You know what, after that big breakfast I couldn't eat another thing" said Avi, poking me discreetly, cracking one of my ribs and winding me.

"Oh yes, mmmm, me too. A bit of bread's all I fancy" I said flatly, sounding like a dissident at a Soviet show trial reading a prepared statement. I sat and watched as they tucked into their meals and, as it was hours since breakfast, I realised how hungry I was. I felt like a pet cat at a seafood party. As we piled out of the restaurant I seized the chance to take a couple of boiled potatoes off a plate and eat them quickly. A couple of hours later, we arrived in Jerusalem and drove round the city walls. We then made our way to the Holocaust Memorial at Yad VaShem. It was at an exhibition dedicated to illegal immigration that I began to crack with impatience.

"Look, all these people died because the British didn't let them in" tutted Avi.

"Oh my, these damned British" tweeted his best friend. I had grown used to being invisible but this was too much.

"I don't think you lot were that innocent either" I muttered. The friend looked taken aback, rather like an elderly Victorian woman being confronted with an extraordinarily rude child.

"You elected Mussolini for goodness sake, so don't you lecture me about my country's history." I can be a tiger when roused.

"Mussolini was not anti-Semitic" retorted one of them.

"That's right. And he made the trains run on time" added another. "It was the Germans who forced him to pass all those anti-Semitic laws."

"Oh that makes it all right then. No need to take any responsibility. And look at the way your country behaved in Ethiopia. You used gas and aeroplanes to reduce an independent nation to slavery." I hadn't realised my Italian was this good.

"But they weren't Jews!" protested the first friend, looking for, and getting, nods of support. My word, what did Ethiopia have to do with anything? Avi was puce with anger that I had chosen to mar his day out with his friends, and I sullenly followed the group around the rest of the museum as they engaged in that incredibly annoying habit of audibly continuing a discussion without including you. I began to find Yad VaShem exclusive due to its focus solely on the Jewish experience. In the years to follow I learned that some Israelis reacted very badly to claims by other groups that they also suffered genocide. "It was different!" they retorted angrily, when it was pointed out that gypsies suffered more, proportionate to their numbers. It is certainly true that there is a difference in systematic genocide and war casualties, but there have been many examples of genocide in history. What made the Jewish experience unique was the recent nature of the Holocaust, the fact that it happened in a modern, liberal and Western society and that the numbers killed were so high.

By now I was tired of being with Avi's friends. It was time for Avi and I to start our new life together rather than be on holiday, frittering away what money was left. Back in Tel Aviv Avi's friends stayed at a hotel, and Avi and I stayed with his parents. I was nervous at this prospect but saw little alternative for the time being. Avi's Iraqi-born parents lived in a ground floor flat in Givatayim, a leafy town neighbouring Tel Aviv and Ramat Gan. Avi's mother and father rushed down the path to hug him, shouting untranslatable words like *"nu"* and *"halan."* Meanwhile I stood around awkwardly, feeling like the turd that wouldn't flush. Finally, with the prodigal son suitably welcomed, his parents turned their gaze to me.

"Hello" I nodded. "What ho!" Avi's mother smiled gently, sizing me up in a not-quite-sure-about-you-yet kind of way. His father literally looked me up and down.

"Oh my" I said to myself. "This is going to be fun, fun, fun."

"By the way" said Avi's mother, looking backwards "the water has been cut off, while the plumbers redo the bathroom." I sat on a plush My-Little-Pony-Made-Horribly-Real style sofa, drinking coffee so thick I needed to chew it whilst Avi retold the sagas of our trip, rehashing them to suit his audience. One of the least enjoyable aspects about staying with your in-laws in a two-bedroom flat is not having any privacy whatsoever. An additional snagette was that Avi's parents didn't realise I was, in fact, their son in law in all but name.

"Hi mom!" I wanted to wave, before plopping myself down on pop's knee. I had actually been billed as a visiting 'friend' who was working for a tour company. I am never clear why people need to embellish their little cover stories with such nonsense. Personally I hate lying about my sexuality, and vowed never to get into such a situation again, unless I was pinned against a wall by a group of Nazi skinheads, in which case I'd be the first to shout "crack open the beers and show me to the totty."

"*Ma hu oseh po?*" asked his father in Arabic-accented Hebrew, meaning "I say old boy, what is your charming friend planning on doing career-wise in the foreseeable future?" He was now staring straight at me, looking like a rather cross rattle snake.

"*Yesh lo cesef?*" (Does the gentleman concerned have recourse to any financial funds?")

"*Hu yehudi?*" (Is the gentleman of the Hebraic persuasion?). When given the answer that I was not, in fact, technically a Jew in the fullest sense of the word, but that I was interested in signing up to the covenant of Abraham, his father tutted and pronounced "*Tehiyu bayot, tamin li*" (I can see a few difficulties along the way there old chap.) I was beginning to find his father's habit of talking about me in the third person less than endearing. Frankly, I felt like a child. This was confirmed when I needed to make *pi pi*. As you may recall, the water had been cut off in the bathroom and, short of having a big steaming and enormously satisfying piss in Mrs Avi's prize azaleas, or better still in her gleaming kitchen sink, I had to resort to making this need widely known.

"Take him to the park" said his mother. I couldn't help but wonder what she did herself when nature called, but politeness forbade me from enquiring further. It would raise an eyebrow, even in Israel, to see an elderly, smartly dressed Iraqi woman, squatting down behind an Aloe Vera and relieving herself.

Resident: "*Shalom geveret.* The plumbers still there are they?"

Avi's Mum: "Yes Mrs Levi. Terrible! I say, you wouldn't happen to have any tissue paper would you?"

Resident: "Yes of course. Oh, do mind your shoes, you're splashing!"

As I emerged from behind a tree suitably refreshed, I decided to broach the subject of number twos, or *kakis,* in the local vernacular.

"Wait till we go out tonight and you can do it then" Avi graciously offered. That evening we drove back to the hotel where Avi's friends were staying.

"Go to the toilet in the hotel" urged Avi helpfully, but unfortunately I had *changed my mind.* We spent the evening in Old Jaffa spending fistfuls of Shekels on drinks and food. Every now and then one of Avi's friends would attempt some more conversation in Italian with me but by now we were running out of things to say that didn't involve *Mentioning The War.* I felt like screaming "I don't want your pity-talk. I want my own friends. I wish I wasn't here. I wish I was in Police College and getting ready to start work in Brighton."

I spent the night sleeping chastely on the sofa in my pants, praying I wouldn't need to go for a poo poo and that no-one would find the two-litre bottle of "iced tea" that I was keeping by the side of the sofa. In the morning we sat in the immaculate kitchen in uncomfortable silence, drinking Arabic coffee from small glasses. Breakfast consisted of flat bread and a selection of cheeses. I was merrily munching my way through a tub of some delicious white cheese when Avi told me, discreetly, that it was rather expensive. Avi's mother asked Avi what my parents thought about me coming to Israel, once again bypassing me. I would not have been surprised if people had started spelling words to each other.

"Don't tell the boy, but we'll hide the C.H.E.E.S.E in the F.R.I.D.G.E" they would end up saying, as I sat drooling and licking my upper lip in the corner of the room.

On the last day of his friends' visit, Avi had to hand back the minibus and say farewell to his friends. I sat in the hotel lobby, counting the minutes before I could be free of them. Now, finally, we might start getting somewhere with our lives, rather than having a holiday.

Renting a flat in Israel is horrendous. The whole ghastly process begins in one of dozens of shabby little offices along Ben Yehuda Street. These premises are presided over by cheaply dressed lieges, ensconced in elephant-size swivel chairs, behind desks that are bigger than most church altars. Their bodies are shrink-wrapped inside polycotton shirts, their limbs lubricated with copious pools of malodorous days-old sweat. We entered such an agency and were greeted by the agent with a friendly what-can-I-screw-you-gents-for grin and several tablespoons of sweat so potent it would shy a police horse.

"Shalom, shalom, gentlemen" he splashed. We explained what we were looking for, basically something cheap, nasty and central.

"Hello, we'd like something cheap, nasty and central please. Preferably with a chipped enamel bath and someone else's dumped clothes thrown in."

"I have just the thing" nodded Nylon-man sagely. "Nice flat. Good. Yes. You are my friends"

We walked to a 1930s two-story block in a very hot, tree-lined street in the north of Tel Aviv, near Independence Park. The road was narrow and residential and the trees exuded a strong, pungent smell. I was eager to see inside the flat and waited impatiently whilst Nylon-man fumbled in his pocket for the keys. At least I hope it was the keys he was fumbling for. Inside, the flat was dark. All the blinds were closed, allowing just tiny slits of light through. Specs of dust hovered in the air, and I adjusted my sight to take in the new surroundings. The flat was dated, with a 1930s-meets-1970s feel. The bathroom contained a derelict museum-piece washing machine and a green art deco bathroom suite that was both stained and chipped. The kitchen had an old-fashioned gas cooker, tiled floor and small wooden units. The wide living room was separated from the bedroom by a partition. Despite its short-comings, we decided to take the flat .We therefore handed over obscene amounts of American Dollars, the local Shekel not being trusted. Neither were we and had to provide the names of guarantors. Initially, I believed these were simply referees and was shocked to discover that guarantors were in fact making themselves legally liable for any damage or breach of contract. We returned to Avi's parents' flat in Givatayim. Later we went for a walk in order to have some privacy. As we walked, a sense of rising panic overtook us both. Avi began to mourn Italy and I just wanted to press a button and make the whole meeting-Avi-and-moving-to-Israel thing go away. Nevertheless, we had fixed a date to move in the following week and there was little we could do about it now.

The first thing we did upon getting the keys was to open the blinds and cast our eyes over the shabby, filthy flat. We set to cleaning with vigour, and filled bin-liner after bin-liner with pairs of old shoes left by the previous occupant. I soon built up an intimate profile of this woman. I imagined her to be Russian, from the piles of Cyrillic magazines. She seemed to have been a bit of a lady about town from the discarded lipsticks and tatty high heels. I am assuming it was a woman, though it might well have been a six-foot Israeli drag queen called Shlomo. Inside the fridge was an ancient lettuce, festering in a pool of brown water, along with some nail varnish and a pair of soaking wet tights. I was given the task of scrubbing the inside and outside of an enormous fitted wardrobe. Then we both scrubbed floors, dusted dead flies off the tops of doors and threw away an old gas mask. We sluiced bucket after bucket of black water down the toilet and made numerous trips to the bins around the back of the flat. "You filthy, filthy mare" I muttered, as I fished a pair of panties from behind the fridge. Tights in the fridge, panties behind it? What had the woman been doing? After hours of backbreaking work, Avi produced some pitta and red cabbage, with *tachini*, a grimace-inducingly bitter paste made from sesame. As a special treat, we each had a can of *Prigat* Nectarine Nectar and some Elite chocolate. This was obviously the *value* brand, and tasted like Wartime rations, the kind of chocolate even POWs in Colditz would gag on.

Very soon after moving in, I decided to go for a walk because the air was oppressively hot. I walked through the small port of Tel Aviv, just north of the park, my t-shirt sticking to my back. I was engulfed in a haze of fumes from rotting fish, diesel, and tar. I walked further and further along the quay, pausing to look at derelict warehouses. Here were enormous barrels of oil, rolls of plastic rope, and broken fishing nets. My thoughts were interrupted by a loud peel of thunder, and then the sky turned black. The brewing storm was Biblical. The temperature dropped and the sea looked angry. Thick, heavy rain started to pound the quayside. It was ferocious and I struggled to stand upright in the lashing wind and rain, vainly looking for shelter. I started to run, my clothes now as wet as if I had been swimming in them. Lightning flashed, and seconds later there was more eardrum popping thunder. I got home ten minutes later, dripping pools of water all over the tiled floor. I stripped off my clothes and made myself a cup of milky coffee as the storm raged outside.

Shortly after moving in, the political situation began to deteriorate in the north of the country. The border town of Kiryat Shemona came under regular rocket fire with families living in their shelters for days on end. In Tel Aviv however life continued unaffected and it was time for us to open our business venture.

Avi's family had offered to help set Avi up in business as a way of enticing him back to Israel, though it now seemed that this was not perhaps going to be the generous EU-style handout Avi had expected. When his father had promised cash, it transpired it was going to be a *wedding present*. Avi had some savings, and we spent days meeting with various real estate agents in unpleasant offices, discussing possible premises. Many of the contracts offered were for a minimum period of a year, and there were large initial deposits to be paid and guarantors to be secured. We went to view a small café in Ben Yehuda Street which had previously been a fast food outlet selling Middle Eastern snacks. It had space for around eight tables and had a small area outside. Tired and exhausted, we decided to take it.

"Hebbi Grismus!"

We took the keys and arrived to take charge of the abandoned café. Our first task was to open the fridge and I was almost sick. The stench of rotting food was overwhelming and we filled bin liners with old hummus covered in thick mould, along with cartons of solid, sour milk. We spent hours scrubbing the grimy surfaces and sweeping away grease so thick you could fry chips in it. The kitchen was tiny with little natural light, making the task claustrophobic. There was a single toilet under a staircase at the back of the café, which was only accessible by going outside and down stairs. I needed to clean that too. I almost wept as I imagined at what stage of my police training I should have been at now. I could have bought myself a little flat in Brighton. I could have been developing friendships and learning an exciting career. Why had I been so stupid? I wanted to weep as I scrubbed around the festering shit-caked toilet. We embarked on a spending spree for new equipment the following morning. We visited dozens of wholesalers in the area surrounding the Old Bus Station, searching for a cheap espresso machine. I thought anxiously of all the money we were spending and wanted to get open for business as soon as we could. We launched the café two days later. It was getting colder and colder in Israel as winter set in. The days were mostly dark and gloomy. As we were getting ready for work I asked Avi, once again, about Christmas. We had agreed that I would travel home, and I was clinging on to it. My parents had organised a holiday cottage for the family and they wanted to know what dates I would be home. Avi wouldn't commit and I reminded him that he had promised to get his mother to cover.

We opened the doors and got ready for our first customer. We waited. And waited. It was so silent even Trappist monks would have freaked out. Avi sat despondently at the counter and I brushed the floor again. Hours passed and not a soul came in. Eventually Avi sent me to the printers to copy some fliers. I then went into the street to try and entice customers. It was dark by the time we got our first customer, though this was merely Avi's brother in law. Soon the rest of the family arrived and Avi tried to make six different kinds of pasta, all at once. It was like *Ready, Steady, Cook* but with everyone ripped to the tits on a suitcase of undiluted Colombian cocaine. The kitchen was too small for me to do anything except wash up. Avi became more and more flustered as the pasta turned soggy and the other dishes grew cold. I was greeted by angry comments, with customers asking where the food was. Israelis are not at their most effervescent when hungry and getting poor service. Seeing customers in the café was an incentive for more to come in, and soon we were full, each table waiting for longer and longer periods, getting crosser by the minute. It was chaos. Some groups left. Others got half their order whilst their partners went without. Whenever someone decided to order fresh carrot juice I wanted to scream as this produced a huge amount of washing up. The kitchen was becoming filthy as we both tried to work around each other. Avi's brother-in-law was furious and later took his family away for slices of take-away pizza.

We eventually got home at around midnight, exhausted and stressed out. However, we were back early the next morning and Avi tried getting the new espresso machine to work. A young Italian-Israeli woman arrived and I rushed to serve her, longing to feel useful, and weeping tears of gratitude.

"I'll have a cappuccino" she said, which was the one thing we could not do, the machine not having warmed up yet. She very kindly agreed to have a cup of instant coffee instead. We never saw her again. Avi became more and more withdrawn, sitting alone, listening to maudlin Italian songs about the 'Sadness of Venice' or the 'Death of a Dream'. Meanwhile, I sat learning Hebrew and brooding about Brighton. I imagined walking on the pier, strolling through the Lanes and decorating a little flat in Kemptown. What had I done?

Compounding the gloom was the grizzly kidnapping and murder of a border policeman, and ongoing rocket attacks on the north of Israel from Lebanon. Life was grey. Avi then sprung it on me that I wouldn't be able to go home for Christmas. I was gutted and furious. We had a huge row and I stormed out of the café, sobbing silently all the way back to the flat. I sat in the gloomy, cold living room crying and ignoring the phone. The fights became more and more frequent.

We were unsure about my legal standing in Israel. I could only stay if I were a Jew, or legally married to an Israeli citizen. The awful prospect that we might not be allowed to live in the same country dawned on me. After all we had been through, giving up my career and following Avi to Italy, the refusal by any state to recognise our relationship seemed cruel. If we had been a straight couple we would have at least had the option of marriage. Who is a Jew is a highly contentious issue in Israel. It was with great reluctance that I followed Avi to the Orthodox Beth Din in Tel Aviv to see a rabbi and hopefully start the conversion process. I hated the whole sorry episode. I did not want to be an Orthodox Jew. Indeed I couldn't. I was a gay man with a sex life. We entered a dingy room, filled with tatty books, and with little natural daylight. Behind a desk was a very devout and very bearded rabbi, and whilst he was obviously kind, he was dismissive of my request.

"He must come back in a year" he told Avi, ignoring me as if I were a small child. I couldn't help but stare at the man's filthy clothes. His trousers seemed to shine with dirt and there were patches of dried food on his black jacket. Somehow God and God's love for humanity seemed absent from the whole meeting. As was detergent and deodorant. Did this man care for my soul I asked myself?

Shortly afterwards I wrote a letter to the rabbi at the Progressive synagogue, Beit Daniel. Needless to say he did not reply. Rabbis are nearly always dismissive of enquiries about conversion, certainly in the initial stages. I therefore decided to go to a service one Friday night. I liked the synagogue with its plain, modern interior and relatively easy-going atmosphere. However, it just wasn't the same as a British Progressive synagogue. I missed the people and sounds of England. The services were enjoyable, and were followed by a *Kiddush* of wine and bits of pastry. There were no English families, but there was a tall elderly Dutch woman who fascinated me, with her crisp manners, no-nonsense shoes and teeth you could shuck oysters with. I couldn't understand why anyone wanted to leave lovely fun-loving freedom-embracing Amsterdam in order to live in Israel, but each to their own.

The rabbi was young and left-wing, with outspoken radical views. One cold evening he decried from the pulpit the illegal deportation of some 450 Hamas activists, to a hill top in Lebanon. This had become an ongoing saga in the news and followed months of terrorist activity. As soon as he had spoken the congregation erupted into a very unsabbath-like commotion.

"I didn't come here to listen to your damned political opinions," yelled one congregant, puce with anger.

"Shame on you!" spat another venomously. It was not what I was accustomed to at the decorous West London Synagogue, with its top-hatted wardens and waist coated beadles. There, the only commotion would be the odd tut when the choir fluffed an *amen*. Sectarian conflict was rife in Israel, and was a source of much bitterness, usually unedifying. I heard stories about Ultra-Orthodox Jews bursting into Progressive synagogues and attacking the congregation. This was often because of women dancing with the scrolls, an act which had the effect of driving the Fundamentalist assailants to extremes of violence. Bus shelters with 'indecent' adverts were torched, cars were stoned if their drivers were violating the Sabbath, and there were times when Israeli soldiers killed in action were denied a Jewish burial because of status issues. Even secular Israelis were wary of Progressive Jews, adhering to the old adage "I want the synagogue I don't go to, to be Orthodox." In politics I was disgusted to see the secular left-wing Meretz party working in coalition with the Ultra-Orthodox Shas party, ditching values left, right and centre.

I often detected conflict within my new synagogue as well. Some of the old guard liked things done in a particular way whereas the rabbi was an innovator. On his birthday some ladies presented him with a new prayer shawl. He thanked them with thin lips and never wore it. After the service there was usually a chance to socialise, and I spoke to a tall bespeckled French man called François. We instantly hit it off and began walking together. He was also interested in converting to Judaism and, after a few walks, he told me he was gay. We had a great deal in common and for the first time in my life I could discuss my commitment to Judaism and to Israel, as well as the complex and thorny issue of religion and gay sexuality. Eventually I was able to arrange a meeting with the rabbi to discuss my conversion and in mid December 1992 a Beth Din was convened at the Progressive synagogue. Three rabbis sat around a plastic table in the synagogue hall and the atmosphere was cordial. I was asked about why I wanted to convert and about my attitude to Israel. I described my first feelings when I was 15 and living in Luxembourg. I talked about my sudden and profound interest in all things Israeli and Jewish; about how I gave up eating meat and started keeping the Sabbath. I talked about my first visit to a synagogue, my days at West London Synagogue and then at the gay-friendly synagogue in Notting Hill. I described the dark, lonely days of living in Edinburgh and finally the Kibbutz. When the meeting concluded I was told that I was now an official candidate for conversion. I was to follow a course of instruction for the next year. This was good news, but I was left with the prospect of a year of being unable to live or work in Israel legally. Moreover, a complex loophole in the law meant I would need to return home to England to complete the conversion process in order for it to be recognised by the State of Israel. Only Progressive conversions carried out *abroad* were recognised.

That Christmas was the worst I have ever spent. I was so homesick I was distraught. I felt a tremendous sense of guilt at the idea of my family sitting in a huge holiday house without me. Had I ruined their Christmas too? I blamed Avi for it, and the fact that we were so quiet compounded my anger. In the morning I walked to the beach and sat on some rocks, looking out across the sea, wishing I were home. It was strange being in Tel Aviv on Christmas Day as the entire city was functioning normally with no indication whatsoever that it was Christmas apart from the glimpse of a Christmas tree in the lobby of the British Embassy. At work I did my tasks sullenly. On several occasions customers would wish me a *Habbi Grismus*. I was not sure what to make of this. Was it a put-down, implying I didn't belong? Was it something for them to say to show off? How could I possibly be having a happy Christmas? Did I look like I was having a happy Christmas, I thought. I wasn't exactly skipping around the miserable little café singing *Frosty The Snowman* as I wiped the skidmarks off the toilet. I was relieved when the day was over but I had similar feelings when New Year's Eve 1992/1993 came around. I am not a great one for singing

For Auld Lang Syne, showing strangers my arse or puking up behind a bus shelter in Trafalgar Square, but I had memories of much happier New Years than this. I also felt that the New Year had little to promise and was actually dreading it. Around midnight we had a small flurry of customers, consisting of some drunk prostitutes and their customers, who had come in for a snack. Of course they could have been middle-aged women out with their dads but if they were then their relationship would be what Americans refer to as 'inappropriate.' It came as a shock when I discovered there were prostitutes in the Holy Land. I felt like a little boy being told that Santa wasn't real, or discovering the truth about where meat comes from.

"*Zonot!*" hissed Avi's mother discreetly in my ear, perforating my left ear drum, and using the Hebrew term for women-following-a-different-but-no-less-valid-career-path-in-the-sex-industry. The main red light district was located on Allenby Street in the older part of the city. There were some adult cinemas near the old Central Bus Station and the notorious Gan HaChashmal Park, where gay rent boys hung out. "Don't ever go there. Is big danger!" Avi warned me, ungrammatically, on several occasions. I couldn't see why. Did he think I was going there to make money, in which case it was very flattering but times weren't that hard. Yet. Or was he intimating I needed to pay for it? At night the unfortunate women began to appear on street corners, wearing fur coats (in the Middle East!) and high heels. Others wore tight, short skirts and PVC jackets. There was a clear distinction between the Israeli-born prostitutes and the new arrivals from Russia and Eastern Europe. The Israeli women nearly always refused to have sex with either Arabs or Orthodox Jews, and this is where the Russian women exploited a gap in the market so to speak. The police kept a discreet eye on them, cruising slowly up and down the main roads, the blue lights flashing constantly. We were walking home one wet and miserable evening when a police car drew up quickly. One officer got out quickly whilst the other eyed me up and down from inside.

"*Ma yesha lecha ba tik?*" he barked, motioning to my bag. I immediately opened it for him to check.

"*Mi eyfo ata?*" he asked.

"*Mi Anglia*" I answered. Meanwhile the policeman ignored Avi completely. He then thanked me brusquely, and got back into the car.

"You dealt with that very well" said Avi, nodding sagely. I am not sure what else I could possibly have done in the situation. I supposed I could have yelled "You'll never take me alive copper!" before running down the street, screaming 'God is great' in Arabic. What was interesting was that they identified me as suspicious and foreign so quickly. What did one need to do to fit in around here? This was a question I tried hard to answer for many years before giving up, and deciding I couldn't be bothered.

Occasionally we went round to Avi's parents' house in the evenings. I found this fractionally more pleasant than sitting in our own flat but one problem was that their house was so cold and no one but me seemed to notice. Israeli homes are built to be cool in the summer with large, wide balconies or *mirpesset* becoming extensions of the living room. They always have tiled or parquet floors rather than carpets, and of course they are not centrally heated. This can be unpleasant in a cold winter when the homes feel draughty and cold. Being the lowest of the low on the pecking order there was little I could about this, except stare wistfully at the single bar on the electric fire and shiver ostentatiously. We usually sat starchily watching TV, and it felt humiliating to have no input as his father flicked restlessly from channel to channel. I watched in frustration as I caught a glimmer of some favourite programme flash by, such as *Holiday* on BBC World TV. Instead we watched news programmes followed by hour-long commentaries on the news. During these endless talking shops Avi's father would tut and mutter imprecations, fulminating against Arabs, the Israeli left, the Israeli centre, Ashkenazi Jews, women politicians, the government and Europeans. "If it winds you up that much, why not just turn the bloody news off?" I felt like screaming. Meanwhile his mother went to the kitchen, returning with welcome date pastry and cups of hot coffee, which I drank shivering, much like Scot of the Antarctic stumbling across a Starbucks and being handed a piping hot Gingerbread Latte.

As a treat we occasionally went to the cinema. One of the first films we saw in Israel was Gianni Amelio's *Ladro di Bambini,* a tear-jerking, wrist-slashing Italian film about a policeman who needs to drive two orphans across Italy. Avi sank deeper into homesickness and I wanted to cut my own throat. However the must-see film that year was *Schindler's*

List. Few films had ever had such an effect on me. It was a long film, nearly three hours, and one so shocking and brutal that I left the cinema in a state of profound sadness and anger. For many Israelis it was vindication of the existence of the State of Israel. For older Jews, and those with European roots the film was recognition of their experience and going to see it was a form of pilgrimage.

On a few occasions Avi's parents came to visit us, or rather him. I was told to stay in my corner behind the wardrobe and act straight, which I found tiresome. And not particularly easy, being a fairly *exuberant* chappy. I was sat on my sofa, reading *Treasure Island,* as Avi showed his parents around the flat.

"Why has he got a cross on the wall?" asked his mother, looking at my St George's Cross flag. "I thought he wanted to be a Jew."

"Er HELLO!" I wanted to say, crossing my arms and squaring up. "I HAVE a NAME!"

The more I read about religion in Israel, the more disgusted with the religious fundamentalism of the Ultra Orthodox I became. I was shocked by their poisonous attitude to gays and their determined campaign against progressive Judaism. My attitude was further cemented at the end of January 1993, when the Lubavitcher Rebbe in New York was declared the Messiah. It all seemed so *silly*.

François, my new French friend, was staying with a Belgian family of new immigrants. This family had recently arrived in Israel and were living in a squalid ground floor flat near the centre of Tel Aviv. The woman was Jewish, her husband wasn't and the children were adapting, in that amazing way only children can, to adversity. The youngest child, barely a toddler, was already gabbling away in Hebrew. The others were also proficient, tutting scornfully at their parents. It was the husband I felt sorry for. He had left his job and his friends and was now unemployed and unemployable, living in a hovel in a Middle Eastern cauldron of political and religious strife. A scarf of his football team of Anderlecht was all that was on display from his own life. He sat chain smoking and watching the TV screen, with its unintelligible stream of news and adverts. His main task was going into the yard to pick up hypodermic syringes thrown over by junkies as the children had taken to playing with them.

"Look *Maman*. I am a nurse and I am going to make FooFoo all 'ealthy ba givin' her a little injection in 'er bottom."

"Ah, *non cheri*, put zat down zis instant!"

"*Oui papa*."

Occasionally the unfortunate man passively aggressively suggested to his children that if they were at home in Belgium they would be able to see their grandparents. This had the desired effect of getting them to wail with grief. I felt sorry for him and I projected my own feelings of alienation and frustration onto him. "Why did you come here?" I wanted to scream. "Why don't you go home? Look at what you've become!" Obviously I didn't actually say anything. It would have been a tad rude as I was enjoying a cup of his coffee and a cheery slice of apple cake at the time. François later told me that he upbraided the poor man for his lack of *Zionist Get Up And Go*. He deplored him for not supporting his long-suffering wife and her courageous decision to up sticks, leaving one of the wealthiest countries in Europe, in order to end up living off the social in a Levantine bed-sit. As for football, well the irritating little man had simply to go and support Maccabi Tel Aviv. Why, the man was positively mule-like in his persistence in not mastering Hebrew and reading the works of Bialik in the original. The woman on the other hand was displaying the characteristic hysterically-positive traits of someone who realises they have just made the most God-awful-life-wrecking-irreversible-going-to-regret-this-till-the-day-I-die-and-beyond kind of mistake.

"And of course zis is a wonderful place vor ze whole family. Zer woz nothing for us in Belgium anymore. It was so pampered and I am sure we would 'ave been killed. Mimi put zat packet of grade one undiluted 'eroin down zis minute!"

François was about as fanatical as a Progressive Liberal Jew can be. He was zealous in his Zionism, slating French Jews for not giving up their pampered lives and hopping on the next El Al flight out of Charles De Gaule airport. One of his favourite topics was the threat of *Something Round The Corner*, by which he meant *Holocaust; The Sequel*. This always seemed a bit far fetched to me. Whilst I can certainly see that Anti-Semitism is growing in Europe, I fail to see that the only thing to do is get a plane to Israel before it's too late. I do feel there may be a few warning signs first. François thrived on Holocaust survival stories and was never happier than when recounting the tale of some unfortunate neighbour's grandmother who had not made it to the travel agent on time. He was impatient of all who did not share his fusion of left-of-centre Zionism and touchy-feely Progressive Judaism. He told me his father had all but disowned him for wanting to convert, and he horrified me with stories of French Anti-Semitism. He had decided to convert after visiting the Holocaust shrine at Yad VaShem in Jerusalem. Although I didn't care to mention it at the time it did seem a fairly *negative* reason.

"What first attracted you to Judaism daddy, was it the Sabbath, the Jewish sense of family, the traditions?"

"Why, no you silly billy. It was the gas chambers...Now did I ever tell you the story about the family from Dieppe who didn't get through to El Al Telesales before it closed?"

François had an abiding dislike of all things German. "If I ever go to Germany, it will be with a Kippa on my head and sandals on my feet!" he announced bombastically, his blue eyes flashing with anger. I am always a bit wary of what I call the Martyr Displacement Complex amongst converts. It's as if they feel that once they are a Jew they can deflect any dislike others feel towards them and blame it on Anti-Semitism.

Convert: "You hate me because I'm a Jew don't you? You vile Anti-Semite."

Non-Jewish Person: "Actually no Mr O'Connor. I am just a bit miffed that you're shacked up with my boyfriend." There are some converts who do get a serious kick out of their first experience of Anti-Semitism. It gives them a sense of identity.

Convert 1: "Oh look! My first brick through the window. I shall treasure it always."

Convert 2: "Yes well, it's not as exciting as the time I was turned down for that rowing club."

Convert 1: "But you can't swim."

Convert 2: "Oh, that wasn't the reason and you know it!"

When Avi was at work, François and I went for walks to Independence Park or along the *Tayelet*, a promenade walk by the beach. We talked for hours, sometimes until I was slightly hoarse. Often however, I was alone. To relieve my boredom I sometimes spent afternoons watching old Israeli films, enjoying the weird sense of nostalgia for an Israel I felt I knew from my adolescence, but which in fact I knew only through reading and music. I love Israeli cinema. It is human and emotional and honest. I enjoyed seeing the old cars and the architecture of the 1960s and 1970s. One of my favourite films was *Zohar*. This Israeli classic depicted the tragic life of Zohar Argov, a singer of melancholic *Mizrachi* music. Argov's music is still widely popular in Israel and one of his hits, *Perach Be Gani,* or 'You are The Flower In My Garden' had been re-released when I was on the Kibbutz, haunting me with its melody and lyrics. The film shows Argov's rise to fame and then fall, into a hell of drug addiction and rejection in love. In the end he hangs himself in a police cell. Another film I watched at this time was *HaKaitz Shel Avaya*, which was a very touching but disturbing story of a young girl growing up in the 1950s. Her mother was a Holocaust survivor and the film reflects the confused and traumatised state of mind of her generation. In one harrowing scene the mother shaves the girl's head when she discovers nits. Later she pays children to come to her daughter's birthday party but they leave, presumably wary of the mother from hell and her trusty, rusty clippers. Sometimes I watched a very dated version of Candid Camera. I enjoyed this because my Hebrew was just about up to it and it was accompanied by hits from the 1970s. It was also surprisingly funny, especially when a man pretended to be blind and asked a passerby to help him into his car. And who says the Israelis don't have a sense of humour?

Nothing depressed me more than a visit to the Ministry of Interior in the huge 1970s tower block, in the south of Tel Aviv. This involved getting up at around 5 in the morning and catching a *Sherut* along Ben Yehuda Street. The south of Tel Aviv was depressing. It was shabby, pissy and dated. At its heart was the iconic Migdal Shalom, once the tallest building in the Middle East. Groggy eyed and stressed, I opened my bag to be searched and then took the lift to the Ministry of Interior office, a Kafkaesque nightmare of bureaucracy. Poor and badly dressed immigrants lined the walls and watched, eagle eyed, for a chance to jump the queue. Others clutched little tickets with their number.

"Serving number 456" announced the clerk, with the distain of someone whose job is cleaning a piece of particularly foul smelling shit off a shoe. Outside the sun was getting hotter and the sky turned to a brilliant and unnatural blue that taunted me, reminding me how far I was from home. After a couple of hours waiting, I was at last seen by a large-framed wild boar of a woman. She had the face of the woman who had been round the block a few times and had discovered early on that life was really, really tough. Her body language was large and like many Israelis with a rubber stamp, she had a tinsy winsy attitude problem.

Without bothering to waste time on frivolities such as *hello, thank you* or *please* she extended her calloused and grasping trotter to snatch my documents. She did this with a practised flourish that obviated the need for even eye contact.

"Why you want extension?" she asked finally, as my whole being screamed "I don't! I don't want to be here! I want to go home! I want to turn back the clock and I wish I'd never come!" Nevertheless I had to play the game and talked about wanting more time to explore this beautiful country etc. Obviously not believing a word of it, she made the formal pretence of believing me. She stamped my passport with an extension, and I paid her some Shekels. Relieved, I left the building.

I walked through the older streets of the Florentine area of Tel Aviv, which had a lot of character but which, in the wrong frame of mind, was depressing. A few blocks away was the Yemenite Quarter, with its low rise hastily built houses and unpaved narrow streets. Nearby were some fine exuberant examples of turn of the century houses, dating back to the very beginning of Tel Aviv. These had little turrets and some had frescoes. The heavy wooden blinds reminded me of my childhood in Luxembourg. This illustrated the very European tastes of the first immigrants in the 1900s. I then cut through to the seafront and the Opera Building, an arcade with air-conditioning. I loved it here as it felt European and had posh cafes and shops. In order to get rid of the crappy post-Ministry of Interior feeling I would treat myself to coffee at Kapulskys, the chain of upmarket Israeli cafes, specialising in rich, decadent cakes and pastries. Armed with an extension of my tourist visa I returned to our own café, and to my tasks which consisted of scrubbing, cleaning, washing up, and serving customers. As the café was usually deserted, I seized the chance to learn some Hebrew, or to read about Judaism for my conversion course.

The days remained gloomy and rainy. Sometimes this was cosy, and we drank cappuccinos, chatted and listened to music, whilst Avi's remaining savings merrily floated out the window. To pass the time we made up stories about people in the street, especially the rather severe looking owner of a rival café. Occasionally she stopped to stare at us, leaning on her broom and sending telepathic hate vibes. Next door was a cigarette wholesalers. Here lived three of the largest, most vicious testicle-chomping-face-removing looking dogs I had ever seen. They would have dwarfed the average pony and were also quite *virile*, seeking to impregnate any living female of any species that walked past. Often I heard screams of "*'allo! 'allo!*" as potential customers ran away to the sound of blood chilling barks, doggy language I think for "Oy, I ain't finished you tease!" Fortunately for Avi and I the dogs were all *batting for the other team* and had no homosexual leanings what so ever.

The festival of Purim, the traditional Jewish holiday for fancy dress, was looming. About a week before the festival I decided to go to Beit Daniel, the Progressive Synagogue, for a Shabbat morning service. It was an ordinary *shacharit* service, with a moderate turn out, and nothing more exciting than a scroll reading planned. Being the largest Progressive synagogue in Israel, the congregation was well used to greeting strangers. Unfortunately, one newcomer, a seven-foot Swede who was hoping to convert to Judaism, got slightly confused with the dates *vis-à-vis* Purim. Purim was the following week. He arrived late, just as a fifteen year old girl in braces was about to read from the scrolls. He was dressed as a Viking. He had painted his face with a blue and yellow Swedish flag, and he was wearing a kind of fur robe as well as the traditional hat with horns. Oh how we did all have a jolly chuckle about it! The man never returned. I think he subsequently embraced Islam.

During Purim Avi decided it would be an absolute scream for us to dress up and go to a gay club. I loathe fancy dress but despite my misgivings I allowed myself to be cajoled into donning a silk dressing gown, a 'Chinaman hat' and high heels. Avi gave me a thick application of make up. I felt ridiculous. Avi was dolled up like a hirsute version of the Chinese character from Rupert the Bear. We took a taxi to the south of the city, just as most English people in the world were settling down for a good night's sleep. We queued for a large gay club, which was packed out and horror of horrors, not everyone was wearing fancy dress. I hate clubs. I hate crowds. I hate late nights. I hate loud music. This was not my idea of fun, not by a long chalk. Now I could have coped, just about but then I was jolted by huge shove from behind me. I looked round and saw a high-cheek boned teen queen, gesturing impatiently that he couldn't see the stage because of my hat. A couple of others then joined him shouting *"Allo, allo,* roughly translated in this case as "I say would you mind awfully? You know? Thank you." I felt the very essence of my soul shrivel and die from mortification, and swiftly took off the offending hat.

"Why are you taking off the hat? I took ages making that!" Avi protested.

"I am not wearing it!" I protested. A girl knows when she's reached her limit and reached it I had. After a few seconds more of this, I petulantly decided I was going home.

"I'm going home. Are you coming?" I pouted, my lips glossy with lipstick, my eyelashes fluttering in white rage.

"Fucking hell. You spoil everything" spat Avi, venomously buttoning up his toggles and tucking away his faux-pony-tail. "Sometimes I think you do it on purpose."

"Oh piss off!" I hissed over the music, pulling up the fishnet tights which had slipped down during the course of the evening. Minutes later we were standing in a chilly Allenby Street, looking for a taxi. A bored looking prostitute eyed us up, more I suspect out of curiosity rather than as a serious business proposition.

"Taxi" I roared, waving furiously and with as much dignity as I could muster. A grinning taxi driver sailed by, laughing and waving. That night in bed I began plotting a revenge scenario that involved Avi, a length of barbed wire and a vat of lemon juice.

One day we decided to finish up earlier than usual and I went into the kitchen to make myself a cup of tea. I noticed someone looking into the café. He then entered and Avi asked if he could help. At this point the man produced identification and asked who I was and what I was doing. Quickly I replied that I was Avi's friend and was just making myself a cup of tea. He aggressively replied that that was bullshit and that we had better tell him the truth. He threatened that I would be deported and that the café would be closed down. I was terrified. He then filled out a two-page yellow form and left. Stunned we went home, but the next day I returned to work, if that is what we could call it, as business was virtually non-existent. What choice did we have? As if decreed by fate the wholesalers next door made an offer on the lease, and a relieved Avi agreed. The café closed the next day and Avi was obliged to take a temporary job in a hotel. I became unemployed. I desperately searched around for something I could do and about a week later I found a job selling places to *Moshav* volunteers. A *Moshav* is a collective farm, a bit like a Kibbutz but more commercial. The families own shares as well as their own homes. Moshav volunteers work much harder, and under tougher conditions, than Kibbutz volunteers but get paid a lot more. In order to attract workers, they paid people like me a commission for each recruit. This involved standing on street corners with leaflets and approaching backpackers. It was soul-destroying, demeaning and fruitless. I did find some potential recruits at the old bus station but it was noisy, smelly and dispiriting. I asked myself the by now familiar question "what was I doing here?" One taxi driver asked me the same thing, rolling down his window. He said "Go home! We don't want you" and then drove off, after spitting in my direction. I decided not to continue with my new career in sales.

As it was now spring, the temperature soared. With nothing better to do with my time, I often went to the beach and made sand cities. I was feeling desperately homesick and I loathed the heat and the bright blue sky. I often made little English villages in the sand, complete with parish churches and wished they were real. I tried to avoid eye contact with the patronising walkers who came over to look.

"Oh look! How pretty! What is it?" a group tanned young women in Post-It-sized bikinis would ask. "Ooooo *eze yofi* How *sweet*." Oh, the shame! I felt embarrassed and pathetic. One peril of being on an Israeli beach is an incredibly annoying game, usually played by hairy men, dressed in swimming shorts that are two sizes too small. This involves hitting a ball back and forth using bats, but the noise generated is such that it can drive a man insane in less than five minutes. For a while it was under consideration by the Chinese government as a replacement for the tried and tested dripping water torture. Plick plock, plick plock went the little ball, as the men playing shouted instructions at each other. Plick plock plick plock "LEFT, LEFT." Often a pair of calloused, hairy feet came crashing through the centre of my sand city as the ball veered off course. Without so much as a sorry the offender would scoop up the ball and resume the game. I toyed with the idea of burying broken glass in the centre of my sand city but questioned the morality of it. Once a pair of plick plock players even asked me to get out the way. I refused outright. It was strange how my highly creative sand city game was seen as childish whereas middle aged men with bats and a ball was cool. Whilst I was spending my days on the beach, Avi had found a job as a dogsbody in a cheap hotel in Bat Yam. Doing menial work was obviously hurting him, and he often came close to tears.

"I used to be the boss. I had good money. I had a car. I had holidays. People respected me" he wailed. The situation made me feel awful and I redoubled my job hunting. I went into a pub near the old port where I saw an advert for workers. Some young Israelis were busy cleaning windows with screwed up newspaper and I asked how much the salary was. A woman quoted a figure and I winced.

"And that's per hour is it?" I confirmed, disappointed.

"No, no, no. Per day." I asked for the job anyway, but when I admitted I had no work permit she refused. She kindly wished me luck anyway.

"My husband doesn't understand me"

One of the only ways I could think of making any money apart from resorting to 50-Shekels-an-hour-and-nothing-kinky prostitution, was to offer private English lessons and so I invested a little money in making some photocopied posters with my phone number on them. This generated a few replies. One of my first customers lived in nearby Ramat Gan and was a young new immigrant from a former Soviet Republic which I couldn't pronounce but which sounded something like a Greek appetiser. I was incredibly nervous before the lesson, as I had absolutely no experience. What would I say? What could I teach her? She lived in a damp smelling flat, stuffed with heavy, dated furniture. I imagined this was the in-thing in Tzatsiki-stan, and settled down to a cup of weak tea and a biscuit so stale it crumbled in direct sun-light. There were some banana-flavoured boiled sweets, which tasted as I imagine nail varnish would.

"My husband doesn't understand me" she announced, as we started the lesson and for a sinking moment I thought she might 'slip into something more comfortable' and try and sit on my lap.

"He say English lesson waste of money. But I need. I need vor my art. I am actress."

After enduring an hour of this, I left with a belly full of nail varnish and a pocketful of Shekels. Another customer was a blond haired and blue eyed Hungarian immigrant, who was filled with utter contempt for her new home.

"I only came here so I could get out of Hungary" she told me. This attitude was fairly wide-spread. I soon ended up coaching a succession of Eastern Europeans, preparing them for interviews with the Canadian and American immigration authorities. The Hungarian student's home was squalid, with huge quantities of 'ladies things' left lying around for all to see. Tights hung up to dry, a hairdryer lay on the floor, cotton wool and a range of beauty products were strewn around. On a couple of occasions I needed to use the toilet. For those of you familiar with Kim and Aggie from the British TV programme *How Clean Is Your House* I need say no more. Skid marks in the loo, hair in the sink, mildew and shrivelled sponges harbouring some of the deadliest microbes known to man, all testified to her laid back you-only-live-once-so-why-prolong-it approach to hygiene. I soon learned the art of flushing with my elbow. I decided that there was no part of my own body which was less clean than the taps and forwent cleaning my hands.

Another I'm-an-Oleh-Chadash[1]-get-me-out-of-here student came from that vibrant, buzzing, oh-so-sexy metropolis of Kursk. She was bitterly dissatisfied with the large centrally located flat which she had been allocated and which was partly funded by Israeli government money.

"I hate them" she announced. "They are like black apes. Their language is like monkeys." I bridled and asked why she stayed. She was honest and cited the generous handouts, and the fact that it was easier for Israelis to get visas than Russians. She boasted about how she wanted to go to Canada and claim political asylum. I wasn't massively keen on my new life either but I recognised that was not the fault of the people of Israel. Both the student and I had chosen to live in Israel, for whatever reason, and I thought her attitude was inappropriate. I was also angry that she was planning to use Israeli money to travel to Canada, where she intended to bring Israel into disrepute by claiming asylum. I found her racism nauseating. I presumed she considered Avi and his family to be monkeys too. Another client was also under the illusion that Israel somehow owed her a living. How wonderful everything in Russia was! Oh, the culture, the professional advancement, the weather, the forests. What a mistake it was to come here. She claimed she had been tricked into coming by the Jewish Agency. When I asked if she'd like to return to this Soviet Garden of Eden she changed the subject, and lamented

---

[1] An *Oleh Chadash* is a new immigrant to Israel. The word has very positive connotations and status and the person is entitled to special benefits and rights.

that her children were starting to talk like monkeys. Not surprisingly many Israelis began to resent this. Unfortunately, as I was often mistaken for a Russian by both Russians and Israelis, I began to get caught in the crossfire. It irritated me on both counts. The Israeli Jews of Arab origin had little time for the new arrivals. During the 1960s and 1970s the *Mizrachim* had had to contend with discrimination and racism from the European Jews. However by the 1980s the *Mizrachim* had become the majority and the Likud party had won its first ever victory on the back of their votes. "They call us *tchach-tchachim*!" roared the newly elected Likud Prime Minister Menachem Begin. He was referring to an insulting term for the *Mizrachim*, roughly translated as *riffraff*. The *Mizrachim* had had it hard, they had fought for equality and they were not about to be called 'monkeys' by new arrivals from the USSR.

My anxious parents decided they had best visit me, to see what the hell was going on. I relished the opportunity of being spoiled for a few days. They stayed at the concrete 1970s Carlton Hotel on the seafront, a short walk from our flat. As soon as they had checked in I was enjoying a hot, powerful shower, made even more delicious thanks to a bag full of expensive shower gels and other toiletries which I should have received at Christmas. Smelling delicious, we walked the short distance to a posh Indian restaurant I had chosen. Avi met us and I savoured the occasion. I was no longer used to luxury, something I realised when the waitress told me I didn't need to keep passing her my dirty plates and the dishwashers asked me to leave the drying up till later. The food and wine were delicious, and I stuffed my face on vegetable curry, chapatti, and pickles. I felt normal again. The following morning I was treated to a prodigious waist-expanding-hip-swelling breakfast at the hotel. After gorging myself on pancakes and syrup, a small mountain of buttery scrambled eggs and a bowl of healthy salad, we took a taxi to the Museum of the Jewish Diaspora in the north of the city. I loved this museum, which was full of models of famous European synagogues and photographs from a lost Jewish world. We visited the fascinating Ben Gurion House, a strangely intimate museum, in the former Prime Minister's old home. This was full of dusty books, stacked tightly on floor to ceiling bookcases. We saw his old sofa, the tiny kitchen, which looked remarkably like the one in our flat, and then the bathroom and the couple's bedroom. Glass cabinets displayed the souvenirs and knick-knacks from his travels. There were letters from other great leaders of the 40s, 50s and early 60s and a plethora of black and white photographs. I irreverently imagined the founder of the State of Israel boring visiting dignitaries with them.

Paula Ben Gurion: "David, do you really think Mr Ghandi wants to see all those pictures? More tea Mahatma?"

David Ben Gurion: "What do you talk, Paula? Look, Mahatma, this is me in prison under the Turkish occupation. And that's me with the old Dalai Lama."

Paula Ben Gurion: "David! Mr Ghandi didn't come all this way to look at these photographs. Anyway shouldn't you be getting ready to start the 1956 invasion of Egypt or something?"

In the afternoon I showed my parents our flat and then we went back to the hotel, where I watched TV with my mum, enjoying tea from room service with shortbread brought from home. Meanwhile my father went for a long walk. The following morning we boarded the coach to Masada at an underground car park under Atarim Square. The car park smelled of stale piss and exhaust, but thankfully we were soon onboard the luxurious coach and crawling out of Tel Aviv on the Ayalon freeway. I was in my element, showing Israel off to my parents and relishing the unaccustomed leisure time.

After a long drive the coach began to wind its way down towards the Dead Sea, passing modern we-live-here-now-so-piss-off Israeli settlements and then the more desolate desert landscape. We eventually drew up at the hill top fortress and queued for the cable car. On the summit the guide described the tragic siege and then suicide of the Zealots who preferred death to Roman slavery. The guide explained how the Romans had attached burning slaves to a giant catapult in order to set fire to the defences. A child in our party found this breath-stoppingly hilarious. A gentle but hot breeze caressed my face as I stared into the distance, picking out the Dead Sea and an endless landscape of rocky desert. I remembered coming here on previous occasions. Once with Avi and once years before, by myself, when I had met a handsome young Frenchman with a hired car. "Ah, Jean Paul!" I sighed. "Dear, sweet, underpant fetishist Jean Paul!" Where was he now I wondered wistfully?

Our next stop was the Dead Sea. I had also been here before, but this time I was being treated to the proper 50-Shekels-and-a-fluffy-dressing-gown experience. We were ushered through into the modern spa, smelling of sulphur and cooked food. Here I eased myself into a hot Jacuzzi of salty water, and then walked outside to the shore, yelping in pain as the hot wooden boards burnt my heels. The rest of the distance was covered by a special van as the water levels had receded so badly. I waded into the tepid water and let myself float. As much as I tried I couldn't sink. I lay back, the water up to my ears and chin, the salt stinging a small cut on my arm. Next to me a man was lying back, reading *The Jerusalem Post*. To round off a perfect day my parents bought me a slap up Desperate-Dan-Cow-Pie lunch at the very place where I had enviously watched Avi's friends eating months before. The following morning we were ready for another exciting trip, this time to Jerusalem. Our guide was nuts; a mad South African-Israeli woman with tight corduroys and a bright pashmina. As soon as we had cleared Tel Aviv she kept up a lively banter, pointing out the derelict tanks on the Jerusalem corridor, and the fauna and flora that lined the route.

Our first stop was the five-star ooh-la-la-month's-salary-for-a-bowl-of-nuts King David hotel where we picked up some more passengers. Being an experienced traveller with a bladder the size of a baked bean, I made a dash for the luxurious toilets in the basement. These were so posh even our own dear Queen, Elizabeth the Second, would have no hesitation doing a royal jobby in them. Our second stop was the Mount of Olives, where we were allowed to get off and take pictures, ignoring the boys hawking postcards and the men in Arab head-dress selling camel rides. We drove through the valley of Kidron to the Western Wall concourse. I stayed with my mother in the forecourt, as she was nervous about being left alone. We followed our guide into the Arab market, heading for the Church of the Holy Sepulchre. The shouts of the street hawkers echoed in Arabic off the ancient, gloomy walls and as the crowd got denser my mother became more distressed, looking like a flushed version of Munch's *The Scream* but less cheerful. At the junction with Via Dolorosa our tour party came face to face with another group, resulting in pedestrian gridlock. For some reason, perhaps sensing trouble, shopkeepers began pulling down the blinds of their tiny shops. Detecting the rising hysteria in my mother, I called to my father who was by now several feet away in the thick of the crowd. An elderly Indian lady pulled out a hip flask, let my mother neck most of it and then finished it off herself. I led my mother along a different route, praying I would remember the way and not stumble across an underemployed cell of the *El-Aqsa Martyrs' Brigade*. The passageways I chose were lively and filled with tourists but were not too crowded and soon we had reached the safety of the Jaffa Gate. Thank God I thought as I shooed my hyperventilating mother out into the wide open space around the huge medieval gate. We sat on a bench and waited for the rest of the party to catch us up. They arrived 40 minutes later, but I was sorry for having missed the Holy Sepulchre. Once we were all reunited and safely back on the bus, we were driven to the Knesset, Israel's parliament. After being thoroughly and rather enjoyably searched we went to the viewing area and gazed out over the chamber, by now so familiar from news broadcasts. I felt privileged that I had seen it. I even felt a little maiden speech coming on. Our final stop in Jerusalem was the Holocaust memorial at Yad Vashem. Here we were led into the dark children's hall, in memory of the million or so Jewish children who had been murdered. My father's poor eyesight wasn't up to the dark, and I had to lead him by the hand. In the darkness were illuminated black and white photographs of smiling children, long since dead. A deep, resonant voice read out names and ages in a variety of languages. "Rivka Cohen. Warsaw. 12 years old," "Malka Gold, *bat steimesre*" and so on. It was relentless. As we emerged we all felt so depressed that we laughed nervously. "Right, what's next?" asked my mother emerging from the gloom. What was next was the return trip to Tel Aviv, which we did in the rush hour and in the dark. As the coach descended slowly from the Judean Hills onto the Plain of Sharon the guide gamely tried to make us sing Israeli songs such as *Halleluia*, that all-time favourite Israeli Eurovision hit. "Nooooooo" I begged silently, not songs on a bus with my parents! Please. I searched in my pocket for something sharp. I was sad to see my parents leave, waving goodbye at the gate of the departure lounge and then returning to Tel Aviv alone on the 222 bus. I felt depressed and desperately wanted to get on the plane with them.

My life felt really bleak. I had no job, and was not allowed to work. I had no room of my own, and only had a sofa and a chest of drawers behind a wardrobe where I could be alone. Avi was miserable working in a cheap hotel, earning an eighth of what he was getting in Italy. My days had little structure so I filled them with idle pastimes, such as sitting on the beach or reading. My mother had started sending me parcels and I began to look forward to them as POWs would greet their Red Cross rations. Often I got some real Scottish Shortbread, which I would ration and allow myself just one piece with my coffee at 11. I then had another nibble at 12.00. And then another small bite at 14.00 etc.

I became very bookish. Books were an escape from the depressing routine. I trawled the cheap bookshops in Allenby Street for novels, especially English classics such as Jane Austen or Dickens. I felt I could escape back to a fantasy England, through reading. I also devoured *Rumpole of the Bailey*, chuckling at the antics of this bumbling but astute English barrister. Occasionally I treated myself to a brand new book at Steimatsky's on Dizengoff Street. I loved Steimatsky's, which had the bonus of being air conditioned. My clothes were becoming shabby and unsuitable, and I had to endure the ignominy of Avi, who was smaller than me, giving me cast off clothes, which he thought would suit me. They didn't. I looked like a shrink-wrapped clown. Not letting the matter lie, Avi then dragged me to cheap clothes shops in Allenby street where I tried on loud, poly-cotton pimp's clothes. In order to make life bearable Avi and I clung onto our small rituals. These included watching favourite TV programmes such as *I Love Lucy*, or *Archie*, and enjoying thick, sweet Turkish coffee and pastries. We also had evening walks to the park, and trips to Jaffa or the beach.

One treat of my own, which I kept for the days when Avi was on morning shift, was to visit the beach at Ga'ash, just north of Natanya. I took a *Sherut*, or shared mini-bus taxi from the Central Railway Station. I found this much more pleasant than the bus, and could ask to be dropped off anywhere along the route. Once the *Sherut* was full, and everyone had paid by passing the fares to the driver from the back, we pulled off. Soon we were speeding down the coastal highway and I sat back to enjoy the passing scenery of palm trees and modern tower blocks. Huge, plastic signs advertised yoghurts or telecom services in Hebrew and the glare of the Mediterranean was constant on our left, just beyond yellow dunes. As soon as we had passed Kibbutz Ga'ash I shouted the familiar command of "*Ta'azor bevakasha!*" and the driver pulled up by the side of the highway. I needed nerves of steel to dash across the triple lanes, resting on the central embankment. This could take up to ten minutes as psychotic, blurred drivers whizzed by at speeds that would have freaked out an experienced astronaut. Beyond the road the path led through grassy dunes, and the sun was unbearably hot. As the road and the roar of traffic receded, the path began to fall towards the sea. Sometimes I saw soldiers training here. I felt so sorry for them in their helmets, struggling beneath the weight of their full kits. The path cut through the rocks and I could see the sea and the beach. Once on the beach, I turned right and walked for about half a mile, under the scary looking cliffs. This always freaked me out, thinking that, were the sea to come right in, I would be trapped. I imagined I could see scratch marks left by some unfortunate nudist who had cut things too fine. Thousands of pieces of jetsam and old plastic bags were caught in the cliffs, adding to the general bleakness. Soon I came to some rocks, with little pools left by the outgoing tide, and I pitched my towel. This was Israel's gay beach and clothing was optional. It was remote enough for people to do anything they liked. I enjoyed the solitude. Occasionally off-duty soldiers or older men walked by, wearing nothing but flip-flops, sunglasses and a snarl. I could sit for a couple of hours and read, or snack on a picnic.

On those days when Avi was working nights I sometimes walked to Independence Park. I enjoyed walking around the park, with the strong smells of bougainvillea and honeysuckle mingled with the salty brine of the sea. The sound of the sea below the park was audible. Dozens of men walked through the park, slowly and purposefully. Often the men would chat with their friends, before moving off, and there were benches and picnic tables where groups sometimes gathered. It was in the bushes and behind trees that any action happened. The bushes were smelly with urine or worse and were littered with used condoms. Despite the "humanity" of it all, there was a sense of camaraderie in the park. It was also an eye-opener to see priapic Orthodox Jewish men in black coats lurking in the undergrowth. It was as if Teyve from *Fiddler on the Roof* had suddenly stopped singing *Tradition* and had burst into a tit-rubbing, body lotion-squirting rendition of *It's Raining Men*. Or perhaps "♪ *If I had a big one, ladida dadi dididay, all day long I show it in the park, rumpy pumpy fiddlydididay.*"♫♪ Meanwhile Golde and Tzeitel would be at home plucking chickens rather than following them into a bush. I often felt anger towards the Orthodox men, despising them a little for their hypocrisy. Perhaps I shouldn't have judged them, and cannot imagine the social pressures they lived under. I also imagine that their general appearance counted against them in the Youth orientated, body fascist atmosphere of the gay scene. Now and then I noticed Arab men there too.

I found it hard to stay in the flat, especially when it was so hot, and every night when I was alone I went for long walks with my Personal Stereo, finding the loud music and exercise soothing and motivating. I often walked down Dizengoff Street, Tel Aviv's main thoroughfare, enjoying the buzz and the elegant shop fronts in the neon glow. I was a flaneur, walking unseen but seeing through the city streets, rootless and free to roam wherever I wished. Many of the shops had a retro 1970s feel to them, and I was often reminded of my childhood fantasies of running away to Israel. Well I was here now, and it was not the strawberries-and-cream-and-a-glass-of-Pimms picnic I had imagined.

In March 1993 violence flared suddenly. One morning I was horrified by a full page colour photograph of a knife sticking in someone's back. The victim's white shirt was bright red with blood and I felt scared. Meanwhile, missile attacks resumed in the north of the country and in order to contain violence within Israel the government once again sealed the West Bank and Gaza Strip. Despite the violence life for us continued as normal.

In order to save Shekels, we often made the short bus trip to Allenby Street and the notorious *Shuk HaKarmel*. This market was crammed into a narrow pedestrian street, and reminded me of a traditional Arab or North African *Shuk*. At the entrance to market were dry goods, such as huge metal saucepans, plimsolls and crockery. Further in were stalls selling *Mizrachi*, or Arab-Jewish music. The stallholders tried to outplay each other, with a cacophony of songs, most of which seemed to be mournful wails of *chabibi*-this and *chabibi*-that, with the occasionally *oooooh-ooooh* thrown in. Shoppers pushed each other relentlessly, and the heat of the midday sun added its own irritant to the situation.

As we pushed onwards, the main road disappeared from view completely, and the narrow lane began to feel oppressive and claustrophobic. *"Alo Alo, bananot stei shekel lekilo"* yelled one stall owner, holding up some mangy-looking bananas with a show of reverence.

If you so much as looked the stallholders in the eye, they would have a kilo of rotten fruit wrapped and in your hand before you could say Yakov Robinson. We often bought our fruit here, with Avi taking on the role of alpha male hunter-gather, whilst I obediently carried thin plastic bags of oranges, mangoes and guavas. At the heart of the market were produce stalls selling meat and fish, the stench attracting flies and repelling shoppers. There were enormous plastic bins, filled to the brim with hacked off chicken legs, feathers and heads. Dead fish lay on beds of crushed ice, their mouths agape and little pieces of plastic parsley laid out to make the whole scene of carnage look appetising. Just when the shopper felt they had indeed reached the very gates of hell, the lane widened into a large car park, the sun blindingly bright. One day I was appalled to see a stallholder grab the arm of an elderly Russian man, accompanied by his equally elderly wife. They had stolen a saucepan from his stall. The stallholder grabbed back the pan and then gave the man two resounding slaps across the face. The couple walked away impassively. After finishing our shopping we had a welcome seat and can of ice-cold guava nectar, before catching our bus home. The words 'hot and bothered' didn't even begin to cover it.

Something needed to change. I thought of ways to speed up my conversion, and I was impatient at being asked to wait out the full year. I had, after all, been trying to convert for years. I could speak Hebrew reasonably well by now, and I had a depth of knowledge that few other converts had. The waiting was a formality as far as I was concerned. Unfortunately one of the rabbis at the synagogue didn't see it that way and accused me of 'holding a shotgun to his head.' It was in fact only a bar of soap, which I had fashioned to look like a gun; some people don't half exaggerate. I then took the step of contacting the Union of Liberal and Progressive Synagogues [2] in England directly, stating my case in writing, and going over the local Beth Din's head. Although it was a tad naughty of me, it worked, and the ULPS said they would agree to my conversion, provided I sat before their court and got circumcised. I would need to return home for this. A rather cross rabbi from the Israeli

---

[2] The Union of Liberal and Progressive Synagogues, now known simply as *Liberal Judaism* is one of the two progressive streams of Judaism in the UK. Both movements recognise each other's conversions.

Beth Din asked to see me and eventually we agreed to compromise. He contacted the Reform Synagogues of Great Britain Beth Din in London and a date was set for June. With this in mind I then decided to do a month long Certificate in TEFL course. My father arranged this for me at a private language school in Edinburgh. I had turned a corner and life was starting to look good again.

In April I experienced the two solemn days of *Yom HaShoah* and *Yom HaZikaron*. The first of these was the official Israeli commemoration of the Jewish Holocaust. This began on the evening of the day before, as with all Jewish Holy Days. As it got dark, all places of public entertainment closed. This included cinemas and cafes, and the TV began showing only gloomy documentaries about the death camps instead of *The Young and The Restless*. One of the great things about Israel is that it pulls together as a nation, celebrating and mourning together. One of the drawbacks is your favourite TV programmes get cancelled. Avi told me, in no uncertain terms, not to play any German music that day. I had certainly not planned to play *Ride of The Valcyrie* at full volume, perhaps donning a breastplate and a horned hat, but didn't think a little Schubert or Brahms could hurt, surely. Would Handel be allowed, I wondered, or would he too be tainted with the stigma of Nazism? The next morning I went to the Dizengoff Circle a few minutes before eleven in the morning. I stood on the elevated square, looking down on the roaring traffic below. At the stroke of eleven the traffic suddenly stopped, and the drivers got out of their vehicles. At that moment the haunting sound of the air raid sirens rang out, and continued for two minutes, sending goose bumps down my spine. I tried to say a prayer for the victims of the Holocaust, but I am not very good at saying prayers on demand so I stood in silence. As soon as the siren had stilled, the drivers got back into their cars and everyone unfroze. It was as if God had hit the pause button. About a week later a similar thing happened on *Yom HaZikaron*, the day when Israel remembered its war dead. As before, all places of entertainment closed down, but instead of documentaries about the Holocaust sad Israeli films, usually those with some military angle, were aired. This time though, there was something nice to look forward to once night came, *Yom Atzmaut* or Independence Day.

As soon as it was dark Israelis got ready to celebrate their independence and took to the streets, often with huge blow up plastic hammers. Crowds began to converge on Dizengoff Street, and in particular the elevated square, and fountain. The traffic had been diverted, so it was possible to walk under the square, as well as stand on top of it. A huge set of loud speakers had been erected in the square and was pumping out upbeat Israeli golden oldies, as well as songs by Chaim Moshe, Ilanit and old Eurovision hits such as "I want to be a polar bear" or whatever it was called; the one sung by the boys with the huge Jew-fro haircuts, in the 70s. Another favourite anthem was *Ani Noladati LaShalom*, meaning *I Was Born To Live In Peace.* Meanwhile groups of police stood by vigilantly, armed to the teeth and looking for anything suspicious as party-goers waved huge Israeli flags and did high-fives. We went home after eating some sunflower seeds and drinking cans of Maccabi beer.

Soggy Hula Hoops

The day finally came for me to return home. I paced the departure lounge excitedly, pausing to stare out of the wide windows at the shimmering runway and at the wide-bodied jets, queuing up for take off. To pass the time, I browsed the display of *tiphilin* and prayer shawls at the Lubavitch stall. The Lubavitch are a Jewish equivalent of Evangelical Christians, although unlike Christians they have absolutely no interest in converting those outside the faith. Their goal is to bring back Jews to Orthodoxy. They had no interest in a Reform convert like me. The bearded rabbi ignored me and instead encouraged more likely looking men to come and try on the items. Personally I found the idea of strapping a little leather box onto my forehead in order to pray a bit silly. Would God refuse to listen if one didn't put it on I wondered irreverently? I imagined a dying man in the desert, gasping a prayer with his last breath. "Aha!" would boom a celestial voice. "Aren't you forgetting something Mr Levinsky?"

Soon it was time to board the cramped Sardine Airlines charter flight to Gatwick. It felt good to hear English accents around me again, and to see the pleasant, if totally false, smiles of the cabin crew. Five hours later I saw the green, irregular patchwork of fields of England and my spirits rose still further. I was home. It was great to be back in England and I soaked in the sights and sounds around me. Even the tatty old trains looked wonderful as I sped towards Victoria Station. I left my bags at left luggage and went for a long walk around London, visiting my favourite places such as Covent Garden, Soho and Piccadilly. Satisfied, I picked up my luggage and took the underground to Kings Cross for my train to Edinburgh.

I thrived on my new routine of studying and returning home to my parents' house, where home cooked meals were waiting. After dinner I nearly always went back into the city to meet my friends, or I went to their homes and chatted for hours on end. I had a whole month away from the stress of Tel Aviv. I could find my centre again. I had friends around me. My surroundings were comfortable and the weather was pleasantly warm, rather than face-peelingly hot. It was great to be learning something new, and I enjoyed the lessons at the small heading-for-bankruptcy-at-the-speed-of-light language school near Edinburgh's Meadows. Every morning I walked the two and a half miles from Ravelston, climbing up the Mound and gazing up at the breath-taking views over Edinburgh. At the school I learned the basics of teaching English as a foreign language. Towards the end of the course we started doing practical work, teaching small groups of real students and being observed, which was stressful but exhilarating.

One evening, my friend Andrew took me to a church service at a notoriously high Episcopalian church. A I-wouldn't-so-much-as-dream-of-touching-the-altar-boys-your-honour congregant with a lazy eye and breath even a dog would be ashamed of, explained that the church was so high they had to 'scrape their priests off the ceiling' and 'had smoke every Sunday.' "Sorry?" I replied, confused. What was the man talking about? I had never attended a church service before so I was naturally curious. I was instantly struck at some of the similarities between Christianity and Judaism. "Oi! We say that. That's our line!" I wanted to protest when the priest said "Open our lips and our mouths shall declare your praise." One thing that was very different to West London Synagogue however, was the procession of crucifix with the intoxicating smell of frankincense and myrrh which was bellowing out of the incense burner. I had certainly never seen rabbis Tabbik and Gryn doing that at West London Synagogue. At one point the priest moved up the aisle of the church sprinkling holy water over the congregation. I shifted uncomfortably in my seat. Splush, a great wet drop of holy water hit me square in the cheek. "I hope you don't dissolve" giggled Andrew mischievously. I wiped off the holy water, worrying that I was now a card carrying Christian.

As the TEFL course neared its end, I was faced with the reality of going back to Israel. I wished I didn't have to. In fact I was dreading it. However two thoughts overrode my misgivings; my forthcoming conversion and seeing Avi again. At the end of the course in June 1993 we needed to sit a written exam and do a practical lesson, both of which I passed. All the teachers and students went to the pub together. And then it was over. I was a qualified TEFL teacher.

My brother-in-law drove me the short distance to the doctor's surgery from my hotel in Ealing, on a sunny Sunday afternoon. I felt incredibly nervous as we rang the bell to the surgery. Seconds later, the smiling, friendly doctor answered the door and led us through to his office.

"Lovely day isn't it?" he said jovially.

"Absolutely. Bit cooler than yesterday" I replied, wiping beads of sweat off my forehead.

How typical of the English to stand discussing the weather, I thought. In less than ten minutes the man was going to cut off part of my penis. In the days when we still had hanging I imagined the executioner would engage in social pleasantries as well.

Executioner: "Nice day for a hanging isn't it?"

Condemned Man: "Oh quite. Am I your last hanging of the day?"

Executioner: "No, in fact it's quite a funny story…"etc.

Back in the present, I took off my redundant sweatshirt and sat down.

"I thought it might rain, but it didn't" continued the doctor, pulling out a drawing pad and pen.

"No. I hope it rains soon" I added.

"Anyway let me just explain what I am going to be doing today" he said, getting down to brass tacks. He then drew a penis and, with a rubber, he then deleted part of it. I am sure you get the picture. I certainly did. We then moved through to the surgery itself, where the examining bed was already laid out with a sheet of blue paper, whilst all the time discussing unseasonable rainfall.

"Can you just pop your trousers and pants off for me" he asked, before enquiring about my holiday plans. He pulled on a pair of surgical gloves with a theatrical plop and washed around the area concerned with some disinfectant and cotton wool.

"We're going caravanning this year" he announced, taking an enormous *Carry-On-Matron*-sized syringe from a drawer and sticking it into a phial of anaesthetic.

"Oh lovely! Anywhere nice?" I asked, wincing at the sharp jab of the needle into my foreskin. Meanwhile my brother-in-law gave me a manful how-ya-doin'-buddy rub of my hair.

"Cornwall actually" he replied, repeating the injections at various points on my penis.

"Cornwall's lovely at this time of the year" I added conversationally looking in alarm as my cock turned swollen and blue.

"Now I am just going to say the blessings" he said, putting a small skullcap on his head. I tried to look as reverential as I could, with my pants on the floor and my cock now an alarming purple.

"Baruch ata adonai, elohenu melech ha-olam asher kidushanu be mitzvotav u tzivanu le mila" he announced as calmly as if he were lighting candles on Friday night or breaking off a particularly moist piece of *cholla*.

"Now then.." he mumbled, selecting a pair of razor sharp surgical scissors. I looked up at the cracks in the ceiling and tried hard not to listen to the snip snip snip of the scissors. I actually felt like I was at the hairdressers. I could not feel any pain.

"Would you be wanting to keep the foreskin?" asked the doctor, holding up something that looked like a slice of uncooked bacon or a soggy, bleeding Hula Hoop.

"Oh, not really thanks" I added, horrified.

"Are you sure? I can pop it into some preserving fluid for you, or I can donate it to the medical school dermatology department" he offered. Why on earth would anyone wish to keep a foreskin in a jar? Would you show it to people over tea and crumpets? Would you keep it with knick-knacks on a shelf, along with plastic gondolas from Venice and a miniature plate that says *Souvenir from Clacton*? Perhaps I could give it to someone as a gift, or find a more practical use for it such as donating it to a serial killer who needed to let out his human flesh suit.

"Now, I am just going to stitch this up and that's you all set" he beamed weaving surgical thread through what looked like a fish hook. "Oh how jolly!" I thought. Minutes later the doctor was wrapping my penis in thick rolls of bandage and recounting an hilarious episode about an overbooking at the caravan park. Obviously when I say that he was wrapping my penis, I do mean that it was still attached to my body. I gingerly pulled up my pants and trousers and asked the doctor about aftercare.

"Well I would avoid any sexual activity for a couple of weeks" he replied, slightly unnecessarily in my view. Did he imagine I would be hoofing it down to the nearest gay club for some hot guy-on-guy action, or perhaps engaging in a particularly vigorous bout of frenzied masturbation?

"Someone told me I should have a bath with Dettol in it" I suggested. The doctor winced.

"I should imagine that would be very painful" he replied. "No, best not. Just a tepid bath or shower would do."

He gave me some ointment, I gave him a hundred pounds and we were good to go. My brother-in-law drove me back to the hotel and then said goodbye. I settled down into the comfortable bed to sleep off the anaesthetic. After a couple of hours there was a knock at the door. It was Avi, just arrived from Israel. We hugged and laughed and then Avi said "let me see, let me see."

A hello-darling-you-are-the-apple-of-my-eye would have been nice but never mind. I eased off my tracksuit bottoms to reveal a mass of bandages and, oh-shitting-hell's-bells it had been bleeding! A large rusty stain of blood had dried. Avi looked greener than a Saudi flag. I resisted the urge to phone the doctor, as he had said to expect such an occurrence. I therefore left it alone, praying I wouldn't develop gangrene and spend the rest of my life as a eunuch. We spent the afternoon walking around Ealing. Well, Avi walked, I did a kind of bandy-legged waddle like a cowboy who had just done an unexpected jobby in his pants. The following day we took a train from Kings Cross to Edinburgh for the start of our holiday. I enjoyed the trip, despite Avi's paranoia that someone would steal his suitcase every time we made a station stop. I could not see why someone would wish to leap off a train at Doncaster with a case full of Avi's off-white Y-fronts. I loved pointing out the wonderful views from the train window as we passed over the bridges at Newcastle and Berwick, and then rode along the Northumbrian coast.

At my parents' home I did my best to disguise my discomfort, preferring as a general rule not to discuss my genitals with my family. My mother had prepared a meal for us and for several of my friends, and I felt very happy. The following day Avi hired a car and we drove with my mother to the Highlands of Scotland. The scenery was breathtaking as always, with a welcome sun turning the glens a bright green and blue. I felt a twinge of unease as Avi applied tried and tested Israeli driving techniques to the narrow Highland roads, pedestrians and cyclists spinning silently in the air in my rear view mirror. There was an hilarious cultural misunderstanding when we came face to face with another driver on a single track road. It is hard to decide what to do in such situations. Does one reverse several feet to the designated passing bay, perhaps with a gracious wave? Or does one face the elderly local driver with mouthed imprecations, implying that the geriatric driver is unusually close to his sister before then shaking a fist and revving the engine aggressively? It's a tricky one.

We spent the night at a small bed and breakfast, before continuing to the seaside town of Ullapool in the far north west, where we met up with my father. Here we stayed at a truly whacky hotel. My parents stayed in the hotel-proper, whilst Avi and I stayed in the bunkhouse, in a much cheaper room with two bunk beds and a functional bathroom. The hotel had a wonderful lounge on the first floor with skylights and a library. There was also a bar with an honesty box and a liver-pickling-blood-vessel-cracking range of malt whiskies. On the ground floor was a gift shop that stocked a surprisingly large collection of gay and lesbian books, as well as many delicious smelling Highland soaps and shampoos. Unfortunately they didn't stock any industrial strength pain killers, or for that matter rolls of bandage and cotton wool. This meant we had to stop at a local chemist.

"Is everything OK?" asked my mother in a voice that implied a great deal more. Yes, something was afoot. Nevertheless, I enjoyed being together as a family as we sat with our pre-dinner drinks. Avi was relaxed, charming and sparkling. It was the first time I'd really felt accepted as a couple by my family. There is a line in the New Testament where St Peter has a vision in which God tells him he is henceforth allowed unkosher food. Avi had, it seemed, also received this message loud and clear, and ordered a huge piece of crab. I stuck to a more kosher piece of grilled salmon. We had enormous portions of dessert to follow, whilst my mother got stuck into the wine. We had coffee and shortbread in the lounge, with more drinks to follow. I sampled a range of smoky, malty whiskies and by the time I got to bed I had almost forgotten I had part of my penis missing. The effects of the alcohol, rich food and full moon began to make me feel amorous. Seconds later I froze in horror as I felt the stitches grow taut. Ullapool was awoken by a blood-curdling scream. The next morning Avi tucked away huge portions of unkosher black pudding, bacon and pork sausages, whilst I nursed a caffetiere of Arabica coffee and a fistful of painkillers. Our excursion that day was a boat trip to see the seals. This took place in a smaller than imagined boat, and soon we were being tossed and pitched from side to side. The combination of painkillers and post-circumcision trauma were making me feel sick. It was with profound relief that I disembarked at Ullapool but Avi was not content.

"Go tell him we didn't see any seals" he said at last.

"Sorry?" I asked, gulping back down a mouthful of my lunch, which had tasted better the first time I'd eaten it.

"We didn't see any seals. Tell him we didn't see seals."

I knew Avi well enough by now to realise that the best thing to do was simply to give in. I went up to the skipper, a gruff Scotsman with a red beard and piercing eagle eyes, who was doing something butch and dirty with a yard of oily rope.

"Aye pal?" he enquired.

"Right, now the thing is, my dear friend,…may I call you Jock? The thing is Jock, my Israeli chum here was rather hoping we might see some seals. And we didn't."

"Aye. So?"

"Well my chum rather feels that it was part of the tour."

"Aye, well I cannae dae mitch aboot that, ken."

"No. Absolutely. Well not to worry. Another time maybe. Cheerie pip."

"Aye whitever pal."

I walked off as the man muttered something that sounded a bit like 'English banker' although I wasn't sure what he meant by that. I didn't look particularly financially career orientated.

"The man's really sorry there were no seals. He says they are all hibernating" I explained.

"Ah, OK" said Avi mollified.

The following day we drove back to Edinburgh, stopping at the town of Pitlochery, where we had lunch. Here I finally managed to persuade Avi to try haggis.

"Go on, it's nice" I urged. "It's made with offal."

"What's offal?" asked Avi dubiously.

"It's a Scottish delicacy" I replied.

Avi stayed a couple more days in Edinburgh before returning to Israel, and I prepared myself for the Beth Din, which was scheduled for later that week.

The morning of the Beth Din was sunny and warm. It was great being back in leafy, suburban North London once again. How I wished I could stay! I loved the softness of the streets, with the mock Tudor mansions and well-tended front gardens. I was incredibly excited as I went into the former manor house where the rabbinical court was being held. I waited outside the office, admiring the beautiful Georgian mansion. It was strange to think of all the previous inhabitants of the building. I wondered what they would make of all the present day goings on.

"Andrew?" A bearded rabbi was smiling, and holding open the door. I stood up, shook his hand and went into the large former drawing room. Behind a desk were two other rabbis, also bearded. There wasn't a pair of rabbinical boobies in sight. Was I in the right place, I wondered to myself? Had I got the Orthodox Beth Din by mistake? I had grown so used to women rabbis it seemed odd that there were none present. The rabbis took it in turn to ask me questions about my faith, asking me how and why and when it had all come about. They asked me about living in Israel and then asked me to read the *Shema* prayer in Hebrew. Satisfied, one of them asked me how the circumcision had gone and although what I wanted to say was "It wasn't as bad as I thought" I felt really nervous and actually said "It was an agreeable surprise." As soon as I had said it I cringed. What a stupid thing to say. "It was an agreeable surprise." It sounded like I had turned up there to get a bunion removed and the doctor had said "tell you what mate, we're doin' 'arf price snips. Can I tempt ya?" And then I would say "Cor not 'alf, me old China. *What an agreeable surprise!*" The rabbis explained that my conversion would not be recognised by Orthodox Jews, but would be recognised by the Israeli Ministry of Interior, for immigration purposes only. If I wanted to get married, or buried presumably, I would need to go to Cyprus, as Israel does not have civil marriage. This was to prevent anything unsavoury happening, such as Jews and Moslems getting married. The short thirty minute flight to Larnaca would of course deter anyone considering such a step, and thus keep the status quo safe. I could imagine such lovelorn lovers, saying their tearful farewells.

Lover 1: "I love you *habibi*."

Lover 2: "Me too, my darling. But you are a Christian Arab. And I am an Israeli Jew. If we didn't have to take an afternoon off work and catch the twice-daily ferry to Cyprus I'd marry you like a shot, you know that don't you."

Lover 1: "Alas yes. Oh, well. I suppose we'd better go and marry our own kind then. See ya."

Lover 2: "Yeah, whatever. Bye."

I explained to the rabbi that I wasn't planning on getting married in the near future, and that I didn't care if the Orthodox recognised it or not. The first was true, but the second began to fester in the years following my conversion, and I constantly felt that I was somehow not a real Jew. We came to the part where I was given a new name. As they weren't happy with my first choice of Rachel Bat Sara Lolita Lasagne, I gave them my choice of Golan Ben Avraham. They needed to confer about this. Was Golan a genuine Hebrew name? When they had decided it was, and one of the rabbis had half-jokingly asked if I was planning to annex him, I was given my *Teudat Giyur* or conversion certificate. I looked lovingly at it. It represented years of spiritual travelling. Feeling incredibly happy I went downstairs to the *Mikveh*, or ritual bath. This was it! This was finally it. I hastily pulled my clothes off, leaving them in a heap. I peeled off my underpants, glanced at the scabby but healing scar on my cock, and then eased myself into the cold water of the pool. It was deep enough to cover my head, and as I let myself sink, I read the blessings printed on a laminated card on the wall. I emerged and plunged three times and then climbed out the water. I was a Jew. At long last I was a Jew. And there was no-one here to share the moment with me, a fact I would grow used to over the following years of DIY Judaism. I wondered what would have happened if I had slipped or had some kind of fit. If I were the last conversion of the day I might well have been found early the following morning, floating face down.

Rabbi: "Oh no, not another one Mrs Pringle! We really should get some sort of CCTV system in there."

Mrs Pringle the cleaner: "I wouldn't mind rabbi, only I need to get in there and scrub the grouting this week."

Rabbi: "No, no, don't worry Mrs Pringle, we'll sort it out. Miriam, could you get someone from Maintenance to drag Mr Reid's body out of the Mikveh?" I left the *Beth Din* proudly wearing a skullcap, which I felt I was entitled to wear now. About ten days after the Beth Din I met my friend Andrew and we began a two-night break together in London. I had booked a pleasant three-star hotel for us in Kensington, and as soon as we had checked in we threw ourselves into London, first visiting Liberty's, where we had afternoon tea, and then exploring Westminster Cathedral, travelling to the top of the church spire in a lift. In the evening we had a disagreeable Chinese meal at a notoriously rude restaurant in Soho where I consumed my own body weight in MSG.

The following morning we went to the gay and lesbian friendly synagogue in Notting Hill. I greeted the rabbi, who kindly noticed how much weight I had put on since she had last seen me. When it was time to do the Torah blessing she called me up, using my new Hebrew name, and almost doing a double take when she saw what it was. I proudly and nervously read the blessings. When it was all over, we had an informal pot-luck lunch. And that was it. Again, I felt like something was missing. Friendship? Community? The support and fellowship of other Jews? My foreskin? I left Andrew sleeping, early the next morning and travelled to Gatwick airport for my charter flight back to Israel. As my parents were buying me the ticket, I felt it was only fair to get the very cheapest and this was it. I hated waiting in the queue. I wanted to turn around, run away, just never go back to Israel. But I couldn't because of Avi. I had to go back out of love. Why couldn't we get married and then we could live in England? It was the first time I had ever truly suffered because of discrimination. I cursed the Conservative government and boarded my flight.

"I am going to prescibe parafin and some laxatives"

The plane flew to Eilat first, before stopping at Tel Aviv on its way back to London. When I got my first glimpse of Israel, instead of the familiar Tel Aviv coast line, I saw red, rocky desert. The sight was dazzling. I was enjoying the descent until we lost altitude suddenly, then banked so steeply there were gasps amongst the passengers. Soon we were almost on our side, and my face was pressed against the window. I could see the Red Sea from one side of the plane and the Sun from the other. After this incredibly tight turn we flew bile-inducingly low over Eilat, so close to the blocks of flats I could see people watching TV. I could even read the subtitles. I am convinced one woman winked at me from her balcony. Another waved, wringing out her tights in the kitchen sink. Just when I had resigned myself to death there was a bump. We were on the ground.

Everyone had to clear immigration at Eilat and I emerged into the furnace. I was expecting to become a citizen immediately. Indeed I was under the impression that I could become a resident by producing my conversion certificate to the passport officer. A nonplussed clerk told me, unnecessarily curtly in my opinion, to go to the Ministry of Interior, and stamped my passport with a tourist visa. Everyone was made to clear customs, with special checks to see who had brought back any expensive electrical items, or huge amounts of foreign currency. Israelis have a delightfully disrespectful attitude to authority, and it seemed everyone's pockets and luggage was bulging with contraband, perfectly content to run the risk of a fine. One woman had two stereos and a

TV in her bra, whilst an elderly man was swallowing a condom full of diamonds. I read a wonderful joke about this.

A man arrives at Ben-Gurion Airport with two large bags. The customs officer opens the first bag and finds it full of money so he asks the passenger about how he had come by the cash. The man replies "You will not believe it, but I travelled all over Europe, went into public toilets and each time I saw a man pissing, I grabbed his dick and said, "donate money to Israel or I will cut-off your testicles."

The customs officer is stunned and mumbles: "well...it's a very interesting story... what do you have in the other bag?"

The man replies "You would not believe how many people in Europe do not support Israel"...

After the quickest of cups of coffee we were loaded back onto the stifling plane, and were soon bound for Tel Aviv. We approached Ben Gurion airport by flying in low over the scorched Judean Hills, rather than over the coast. As soon as the back wheels of the plane touched down and I had relaxed, the engines went into full throttle and we shot back up into the sky. The applause turned to screams. We circled for a while before trying to land again, this time successfully. Thankfully the silly habit of captain-clapping was suspended, though one educationally disadvantaged Israeli woman did manage a strangulated cheer. I glared at her and she stopped. Avi was there to meet me, and soon I was back in our flat in Tel Aviv. Although I didn't want to be back, I was in a much stronger position than when I had left. I had my TEFL qualification, which I hoped would enable me to get a job. As I was now a Jew, I would soon be a resident and could start to normalise my life. I lost no time in trying to get things in order. One of the first steps was to return to the Ministry of Interior, armed with food, drink, reading material and a cyanide pill in case it all got too much. I was served once again by the wild boar and this time I had some questions for her. She took my conversion certificate, the fruit of a decade of spiritual travel, glanced at it and then slouched off to photocopy it.

"I want to ask you a question" I said, gulping in fear. There was a pause as she registered her shock. A scowl and a raised eye brow indicated I should continue.

"Does this mean I need permission to leave Israel?"

"Why you should need permission? *Ani lo mevina*? This is Israel not Russia"

"Someone told me some *Olim* needed permission to leave." I felt claustrophobic, cautiously eyeing my black British Passport in her hand. I imagined her suddenly stamping it with something along the lines of "Permission To Leave Israel Denied For Ever. Must Die Here and Dogs To Shit On Grave."

"If you are *Oleh Chadash* you must pay back all the benefits you get from the government before you leave."

"What about the army?"

"Maybe you need something from them. Is not problem." Her talon tightened round a stamp.

"I think I need more information."

"You want or not?" she was getting nasty.

"Can I be a temporary resident?"

"For up to six months. Then you must decide." I agreed to this, and she stamped my passport with an A1 visa, allowing me to work.

The following day I arrived at the British Olim Society office in Ibn Gvirol Street seeking information about my position. The enthusiastic representative explained the context. Immigrants from poor countries were given much larger benefits to get them started, their property not being worth much in Israeli terms. They received tax free electrical goods as well, though many had been getting the cheaper goods, only to resell them to Israelis and then leave the country. In order to stop this practice, immigrants from certain countries needed permission to leave Israel. With regards to the army, I would be allowed to leave at any time until I got a call up date, after which time I would need written permission. I would be allowed six months as a temporary resident and after that time I would become a citizen unless I opted not to be. Even if I opted not to be, I would still be liable for military service, as a permanent resident. As long I was Israeli and living in Israel the British Embassy could not offer me any legal protection. If I travelled abroad then both countries would offer me protection if I needed it. I would be forbidden from using a British passport in order to enter or leave Israel.

I now needed to find a job. One of the first places I tried was the British Council on HaYarkon Street, overlooking the sea. I desperately wanted to work here. It looked smart, professional and reassuringly British. There was a good-size library and large classrooms with modern equipment but although I sent in my CV, there were no openings. Nevertheless, the British Council was a place of refuge for me. In the library I heard soft English voices and could read as many books in English as I wanted. One day I thrilled at hearing the librarian put an Israeli student firmly in his place.

"Hey you! I want informations about courses in England."

"Excuse me."

"I said 'Hey you! I want informations about courses in England."

"No. I heard you the first time. 'Excuse me'. It's what you say when you want someone's attention. And information doesn't have an *s* at the end of it."

"*Ma?*"

I sniggered discreetly from behind my Encyclopaedia Britannica.

Downstairs was a predictably named café called Shakespeare's, selling quiches, salads and delicious-smelling main courses, which I couldn't afford. I sat here for hours, pretending to be in England, although the blubber-melting heat, the screech of brakes and the palm tree pushing against the glass did spoil the illusion rather.

In the autumn we decided to move to a new flat in the slightly posher Usshiskin Street, facing the pleasant Yarkon river and park. We met the landlord and landlady, and discussed the contract. The toad-like couple, who lived in Jerusalem, used the property as a summer pad. Very soon after serving tea and lemon-wafer biscuits they began showing off. Seizing on a casual remark about an African mask, they launched their double act.

"Oh we've been everywhere" boasted the smug, blotchy man, his smile making me feel slightly creeped out.

"We've been to El Salvador. We've been to America" added his wife, scarcely pausing for breath.

"Four times, four times we've been to America" added Mr Toad, a piece of lemon wafer caught in the corner of his mouth.

"Japan. Australia. You been to Australia?" asked the woman, not stopping for an answer.

"Erm, how much is the council tax?" I asked.

"Alaska. Amsterdam, Ankara" reeled off the man. I had a horrible feeling he was actually going to go through the alphabet. I was thinking of a few of my own. "Arsehole, bore, cu…" before I could finish my thought we were back in the Far East.

My life flashed before my eyes when the man reached for a drawer.

"Nooooooooo not holiday snaps!" I began bargaining with God, promising anything if He would but hear my plea. Fortunately it was merely the contract, which we signed for a limited six month lease, and soon we were settled into our bijou new home. I had my own box room and I relished my new freedom, arranging my things and behaving like a young girl in her first Wendy House. From the window I could just about make out the sea and the power station, where I saw small passenger jets making their final approaches into Sde Dov airport. It was impossible not to see across into neighbouring flats, and I often sat like an English James Stuart in an Israeli version of Rear Window. Washing lines were strung between the buildings; on Saturdays these were always groaning beneath the weight of dozens of army uniforms, as mothers washed their sons' uniforms. Despite the upward move, I became homesick and the gloomy weather didn't help my moods. It was an awful winter. The sky remained a shiny brown colour, forever threatening rain. This, when it came, was torrential and brown. On the radio I listened to the equally gloomy lyrics of Aviv Gefen and his nihilistic messages. I went for long walks, usually up the river bank, looking at the fat water rats and passing a small zoo with tropical birds in cages. Other times I passed the point where the Yarkon meets the sea, and entered the old harbour.

One night at around nine o'clock, I became aware of an annoying tooting noise outside, which I ignored. A few minutes later Avi let himself in, grinning. "Come" he announced so I followed him down the communal stairs and out into the street. As it was raining and I was in my slippers I wasn't pleased.

"This better be good" I muttered.

"Look" said Avi. In front of me, parked under a tall, dripping palm tree was a purple Simcha, an incredibly dated car that must have been at least a decade older than me.

"Omigod!" I gasped. I climbed in gingerly, still in my slippers, and ran my hand over the plastic seat cover and museum piece dashboard. With a blood curdling, joint-dislocating jolt the car sprang into life and we flew round a corner in third gear. Soon I was enjoying the novel experience of being driven around in our own car. After a few minutes we were speeding along HaYarkon Street, passing Independence Park and the concrete monolith of the Hilton Hotel, heading for Jaffa. I rolled down the window to enjoy the wet, cool wind in my hair, glimpsing the cafes and bars as they flew by in a neon blur. We were soon in the creepy Ottoman backstreets of Jaffa. Avi pulled up at the famous all-night Arab bakery and returned with two piping hot filled breads, similar to Italian Calzones, but filled with a sour, white cheese and herbs. We drove to the beach and sat in the car eating them, looking out at the dark sea.

A few weeks later I began noticing an extremely unpleasant sensation down below, *at the back*. This grew steadily worse, with the result that I could no longer go to the toilet. I soon started feeling pasty and uncomfortable. There is a peachy British advert for laxatives where a woman pours plates of food into her handbag to symbolise constipation. It had got to the point now, where it wasn't so much plates of food in handbags but cement mixers and bin liners. I strained and strained but my swollen and vice-like sphincter proved too powerful. I felt ill and liverish, and when François called his first words were "You've put on weight."

This is one of my pet hates, this casual, off-the-cuff remark about other people's weight. What is one supposed to say by way of answer.

Thin Friend: "Hello. You've put on weight."

Fat Friend: "Yes I have become a bit of porker, haven't I? Look at me with my huge, flabby thighs and elephantine butt. Shit, I am FAT."

Now, if you are one of those people who has ever told another person they have put on weight, can you please answer one little question. Why?

Is it designed a) to make us feel better b) to draw attention to something that we hadn't noticed before despite the fact that we all wear clothes and have mirrors or c) to encourage us to lose weight. If it's c, then do you think people like feeling fat? Is it such a pleasant situation that we would wish to indulge in it, were it not for your selfless attention to our well being.

I suspect François was trying to become ever more authentically Israeli by saying the first crass thing that came into his mind.

"Ah *sacre bleu*! 'am not Israeli enooof. 'a know. 'al tell zat old woman she looks like un *sac de patat*."

It is true that tact is not a virtue universally held by all Israelis. Don't get me wrong. Some of them are charming, so charming in fact that your average fairytale prince would hand in the towel of defeat saying, "You damned Israelis have got me licked!" On the other hand some of them can be downright rude. This was brought home to me when I was teaching a middle-aged dentist's wife one evening. The woman lived in a shrine to kitsch. There was so much white leather and suede that Elvis himself would have flinched. It was our first lesson and I noticed her eyeing me curiously. "Why your parents not get your teeth fixed when you was child?" said the jowly, discourteous cow, before going in for the kill with "*ze lo aestitit*" which is Hebrew for "you *are* a goofy bugger aren't you?" This was a bit rich coming from a woman who was wearing so much make-up she could barely blink and whose thick, throat-coating perfume was more like a Weapon of Mass Destruction than a toiletry. I was stunned by the woman's almost childlike and naïve rudeness. I remember once chasing a dwarf down a street in Hull but then I was a child and allowed a certain amount of leeway in matters of etiquette. It seemed that this woman had little grasp of the ins and outs of what's done and what isn't, and for her own good I really do think someone should have taught her some basic manners.

Me: "No Mrs Finkelstein! It's bad to point at people in wheelchairs. Naughty! No coffee and cake at Kalpulsky's for you!"

Mrs Finkelstein: "But look! He's got a funny face with blotches!"

Me: "Stop it now you bad woman!" Looking apologetically, "I'm sorry, she's 56 you know!"

Passer-by: "Don't worry! We were all in our mid-fifties once."

But I digress. I made an appointment at the Basel Square Medical Centre, a small tower block with all manner of specialist doctors.

"I think I had better take a look" said the well-spoken doctor, pulling on a rubber glove and lubing up. I braced myself, almost crying with fear and pain. I imagined I looked like something from a Tom and Jerry cartoon as my eyes popped out of their sockets and I emitted a deafening Scooby Doo "oooooooooo" sound. Enjoying this, I was most decidedly not.

"You have an anal fissure" said the doctor pulling off his glove as I groped around trying to find my eye balls. It sounded awful. Was it life-threatening I asked?

"I am going to prescribe paraffin and some laxatives and give you some ointment. You must have hot sit baths."

What was a sit bath I wondered? Was it the opposite of a stand bath? As I was pondering this, the word 'operation' floated unwelcomely into my consciousness.

"If it doesn't improve" the doctor added.

The thought of an operation on my anus in an Israeli hospital was not filling me with unmitigated gaiety. Fortunately, the paraffin and laxatives soon did their stuff and the ointment soothed my sphincter down to the size of a small doughnut before the month was out.

As Avi and I were struggling with money we didn't go out much. When we did, it was usually to the HeShe Bar, a rambling, half empty gay bar overlooking the Karmel Market. The HeShe Bar was one of my favourite venues in Israel. There was a roof terrace where we could sit to enjoy the cool night air and sip our ice cold beer. There were few customers, but the ones that did frequent the place seemed genuine and friendly, and there was little of the attitude that unfortunately existed in some other bars. One evening we decided to drive to the bar, rather than take the *Sherut* taxi. After getting lost Avi drove straight into the now empty *Shuk*. We squeezed through the narrow street, lit only by moonlight. I relished the Gothic Levantine atmosphere. Perhaps life in Israel wasn't so bad after all.

I was allowed to work now, and I managed to find a temporary job in a town called Yahud, a 45 minute bus journey from Tel Aviv. My job was to input data onto a computer. This became forehead-thumpingly-hair-clutchingly boring after less than an hour. The bus journey also became a drag, and the early morning rush hour lengthened it considerably. Nevertheless I enjoyed the feeling of being at work in an office; it made life feel relatively normal. The office was located in a villa in a suburb, and getting there involved a long walk, passing an orange grove and a ruined mosque. I was often left alone in the office and took this as an opportunity to put my feet up and read, and before you judge me, you should, dear reader, have seen how little the sharks were paying me. Sometimes the boss was present and he used an intercom to buzz me. One day his voice buzzed loud and clear, spoiling my mid-morning break. Indeed I had just unwrapped a chocolate wafer Elite biscuit, a bit like a Kit Kat but not actually nice. The boss said "make me a coffee." Just like that. No 'if you've got a minute' or 'could you' or even a straight forward please. Just 'make me a coffee.' It wasn't even my job to make his coffee. I felt humiliated as I boiled the kettle, but then recalled how one of my friends coped at his office when dealing with people he disliked. "Fancy a coffee" he'd ask, whilst drawing up a thick, moist, juicy mouthful of phlegm. I starred at the cup. Could I? Would it be *ethical*?

One day I lost my identity card on the bus home. Avi was furious and spent the next hour on the phone to a rather unhelpful representative of the Dan Bus Company. In the end my card was found but I would need to go to an office in the town of Lod to collect it. I decided to do this on Friday morning when I was not working and caught a *Sherut* taxi from the Old Bus Station. Lod is located a short distance from Ben Gurion Airport and is one of Israel's most Arab towns. Formerly known as Lydda, the town was one of the wealthiest Palestinian towns. In 1948, during the War of Independence, a massacre reputedly took place here, when Israeli forces wanted to clear the area of its hostile population. Like all tragedies in the Palestine-Israel conflict only those who were there know the exact facts, but it is true that thousands did leave their homes. As soon as I got off the shared taxi I felt ill at ease in Lod. It was not a nice town. I eventually found the lost property office in the large bus depot and got back my identity card. Next to the bus station was the ruined Dahamash Mosque, which according to several sources was where the massacre happened. I shuddered. I then strolled around the decaying old town, where the Palestinians lived. What I really wanted to see was the Church of St George. I had expected to see an English parish church, perhaps with a fete outside and some old ladies selling homemade jam. Indeed, I was expecting nothing less than *St Bartholomew's* from the Vicar of Dibley. Perhaps a woman vicar would pop out wearing a bra over her cassock and offer me tea in the vestry. Instead I found a locked UPVC door, covered in Arabic graffiti. The writer didn't seem to like Jewish people very much if the star of David, blood-dripping dagger and Swastika were anything to go by. I caught the *Sherut* back to Tel Aviv, and found myself next to a Jewish lady with a bag full of dead chickens, their feet sticking rigidly out of the thin carrier bags.

"*Eze chaim kashim yesh lanu baeretz!*" she repeated every few minutes between moans. This is loosely translated as "ain't life in Israel hard!" We passed the airport. 'I wish I could go home' I thought as I saw an El Al jet shoot overhead with a roar.

On Sunday I was back at work, and chatted with my only colleague, a rather fiery but otherwise pleasant Israeli-Iranian woman. We occasionally had long caffeine-fuelled chats, and sometimes she asked me to help her with her English. I really enjoyed doing this. In fact I would much rather have been doing that full-time than work in the office. Which is just as well, as I got fired three weeks later. I wasn't bothered about this as I hated the job, but I suddenly realised that I was no longer paying health insurance and that worried me. Although there is a mechanism for the long term unemployed and the elderly to be covered by the Kupat Cholim Klalit Health fund, this did not apply to me. I would die a horribly slow death in a gutter, or need to resort to prostitution.

I started looking for a new job. One day Avi brought home an advert for someone who could speak English and use computers. This seemed ideal so I walked to the small office off Ibn Gvirol Street for an interview. This all went swimmingly, the huge man behind the desk enjoying showing off his command of broken, pidgin English. We discussed terms and a possible start date. As an after thought, he asked me to go and speak to a short, pony-tailed young lady in the other room with whom I would be working. After a quick chat, she asked me about my experience. I said I could use a word processor and had been entering data into a data base. She looked nonplussed for a second before horror spread over her face.

"This is a programmer's job!" she exclaimed. "They need you to run this!" She turned and pointed at a wall of computers, which were whirring and flashing like the control deck of the Starship Enterprise.

The following morning I took the bus to the South of Tel Aviv, feeling the gloom and dirt of the area seep into my mood. I was supposed to go for an interview for shift work at the post office sorting office. About half way there I got off the bus, turned around and went home. I had had enough of making myself look stupid.

A seventy year old man called Sue Ellen

Avi and I had never truly settled into our new life in Israel, and we often dreamed of returning to Europe, perhaps to Italy, where Avi still had a valid identity card. The snag was that the card was valid only for two more years, and it stipulated that Avi had to be self-employed. I would be allowed to work, as I was an EU citizen, and I was more than happy to leave Israel. Avi became misty eyed, as he described the old days of hard work in the summer, followed by long, extravagant holidays. He recalled the cool, mountain air, the delicious fresh food, the *joie de vivre* of the friendly locals and the ease with which we could visit Switzerland, Venice or Austria. I was sold on the idea. I wanted quiet, normality and beauty in my life. In the hope of finding a solution Avi booked ten days off work, and bought us open-jaw tickets with El Al, flying to Paris and then back from Milan for Avi, and returning from London for me. It was an epic journey which for Avi took on the form of a pilgrimage, a journey to his old life. For both of us it would finally lay to rest the idea of living in Italy. It began with an overnight El Al flight to Orly Airport.

We arrived at dawn the following morning and even before the plane was going slow, never mind stopped, hairy arms had begun to reach into overhead lockers and seatbelts were snapping open like pop corn. I remembered a joke about an El Al captain making an announcement. "Ladies and gentlemen. Please remain seated with your seatbelt securely fastened until the aircraft has come to a complete halt. And for those of you still sitting, Happy Christmas." Sod it, I thought and daringly stood up. Outside I greedily gulped in the cool, fresh air of Europe. It was very, very cold but it was bliss. We took the train into Paris where we found a cheap, depressing hotel in Montmatre. It was the kind of hotel where failed writers go to die alone.

Our room was taller than it was wide, making me feel as if I were sleeping in a particularly unpleasant and drafty lift shaft. The flocked wallpaper was fading and peeling and the room smelt damper than a Victorian sewer. As soon as we had checked in, Avi said he wanted to go to bed. I was shocked. How could anyone wish to sleep when they had just arrived in Paris? Nevertheless, I felt better when we woke at lunchtime. We ate at Flunch, a chain of cafeterias I had discovered as a student in Aix-en-Provence. Here we enjoyed a meal of chips, cheese salad and a small carafe of lip-suckingly-eye-clenchingly tart wine, followed by a rich chocolate mousse. "Ah," I sighed happily, loosening my belt; this was the life. We walked happily around Paris, both more relaxed than when we were in Israel. We visited the Eiffel Tour, the Sacre Coeur, and the Arc de Triomphe and in the evening Avi suggested doing our own thing, i.e. going to saunas. I readily agreed to this, seizing the chance to explore on my own. We chose a sauna each, so that there would be no embarrassing meetings by accident. It was here that I made a couple of new French friends, an attractive couple with a forthright and explicit approach to having their needs met. *Ooo la la* I thought. Feeling wonderfully sated, I walked along a drizzly Boulevard de l'Opera, where I met Avi for a quick meal at McDonalds. The following day we slept in, and I was awoken by the urgent ringing of the phone.

"Monsieur" said a shrill, hectoring voice.

"Ah, yes. I am sorry. We're coming down."

"But monsieur, this is too stupid. It is after eleven."

"Yes I known it's after eleven. *Un petit moment s'il vous plait.*"

"Ach, tell her to f…" began Avi as I put the phone down and jumped out of the lumpy bed onto the cold linoleum floor. We packed as quickly as we could and left the hotel in disgrace, the Gorgon landlady counting a wad of crisp bank notes behind us. We had no time to lose as we dashed to the station and then to Charles De Gaul Airport, where we caught an Air France flight to Verona. I was struck at how quiet the plane was. Apart from two businessmen, we were the only passengers. This did not of course improve the service we received from a pouting stewardess, who poured our tepid coffee with disdain. Indeed had she been washing a tramp's genitals in the kitchen sink she could not have looked less thrilled. We landed at Verona an hour later and Avi rented a car. We took the motorway to Trento, pausing only to have a furious row about my back seat driving in the forecourt of a petrol station. We arrived in Trento in a snowstorm, and found a cheap *Pension* overlooking the famous town fountain. The grim, high room had a cold parquet floor, dirty shutters and the smallest bath I had ever seen. A toddler, or even a large kitten, would have found it a squeeze. I felt like I was in a museum reconstruction of a Victorian bathroom. There was also a bidet, so continentals could clean their bottoms without getting the rest of themselves wet. I think this a vile habit; squeaky clean botties and armpits that reek of milk-curdling BO.

I hadn't seen snow for a long time, and I enjoyed slipping and crunching along the cobbled streets. Gay, festive lights decorated shop windows. We met Avi's friends and went for a cheery pizza together, followed by the usual struggle to pay the entire bill, accompanied by camp squawks of *"Ah, non Madonna, io paggo!"* This time we were joined by a seventy year old man called Sue Ellen, wearing just a hint of rouge and skin-tight leather trousers. The following morning Avi went to the Aliens' office to ask about his identity card. The friendly, plump man looked carefully at the card, listened to Avi's request and then regretfully shook his head. Italy had tightened its immigration rules under pressure from the EU, who were by now tired of honouring thousands upon thousands of easily obtained work permits granted to *extracommunatari* by the Italian authorities. If Avi could afford to set up a business then the card was valid for two years, but after that it might not be renewed. I toyed with the idea of discreetly shoving a few ten thousand Lire notes across the table, and then saying in a deep, gravely voice "Guido, maybe we can come to an 'arrangement' for the sake of the family." The refusal confirmed what we both suspected. There would be no future for us here. In a way, the news settled things and it forced us to make the best of it. After all I was now a legal resident in Israel. The decision gave me a sense of peace.

We began the ascent to the village where Avi had had the hotel. The journey would normally have taken just over an hour but on that day the snow was falling hard and the police were beginning to close some roads. By the time the main road had split at the entrance to the valley, we were forced to call at a service station in order to have chains fitted to the tyres; the police were stopping any cars that didn't. It was dark and the traffic was thinning. There was no light on the mountain road except that of the headlights and the snow was bending the branches of the pine trees to breaking point. We climbed slowly, often skidding, or sliding backwards when we attempted a hill start. It took two hours to arrive at the village. It looked magical. It was like a Fortnum and Mason's window display made real. We parked outside the chalet-home of Avi's ex-partner, and I was enchanted by its cosiness. After a welcome glass of thick, sweet hot chocolate we went for a pizza at a small riverside restaurant, before returning to the chalet to chat and watch TV. Avi's ex-partner showed me a surprisingly explicit collection of snaps sent by his numerous pen friends. In my day pen friends exchanged stamps, perhaps the odd postcard of each other's national dress. Certainly Vladimir from the Ukraine did not appear to be wearing any dress at all, national or otherwise. "Oooh, I say" I thought, fanning myself with a rolled up copy of *La Repubblica.* The following morning I awoke to complete stillness. I looked out of the window at the brilliant white village, at the snow-capped mountains and at the grey slither of the river. Avi's ex partner made a pot of fragrant, enamel-stripping espresso on the stove served with some buttery pain au chocolat. I settled down to read in the arm chair. We then went for a very cold and invigorating walk in the snow, stopping at the hotel for old times' sake.

    The next day we set off early, making the treacherous journey down the mountain before rejoining the motorway and making for Venice, which Avi was adamant we should visit together. We arrived at the port of Mestre, Venice's ugly sister on the mainland. Here we found a cheap but pleasant bed and breakfast. After a welcome shower and a snooze in the snug, well heated room we walked to Mestre station and caught the train to Venice. It was already dark as the train creaked and groaned its way across the lagoon bridge. We emerged onto the platform at Venice's Santa Lucia station, our cross faces pinched from the cold and caught a vaparetto to St Mark's Square. It was thrilling to sail down the ancient canal in the wintery moonlight. We disembarked and walked across St Mark's Square, stopping at a harshly lit café-bar where we ordered *trammazzini*, thin delicate sandwiches, and had a glass of red wine, partly as insulation against the cold. We wandered through the deserted, creepy alleys in search of a meal, Avi having decided we would push the boat out this time. We entered an ornate and glittering restaurant with plush red walls and chandeliers. Fortunately there was a fixed price menu, and it seemed I would not be needing to turn tricks at the docks after all. Pity. After eating an entire week's worth of calories and drinking a bottle of vinegary red wine, we made our way back across the Lagoon to our hotel in Mestre. Early the next morning we went to a bakery shop and had a cappuccino standing at the bar, eating sugary warm croissants before briefly exploring the delights of Mestre. The ugly little town fascinated me with its grim straight streets and industrial architecture. However there was little time to linger, as we needed to get to our last destination in Italy, Bergamo. In Bergamo we stayed at a slightly more upmarket hotel (i.e. one that wasn't frequented or indeed run by hookers, junkies or the mafia.) This was opposite the railway station and we spent the rest of the afternoon browsing the large shops and department stores. Avi decided to go to the sauna, for some 'relaxation' but I pleaded exhaustion and spent a quiet evening reading in the room. There was only so much unbridled promiscuity a girl could take. No, a nice hot *thé au lait*, the latest Jilly Cooper and an early night were what the doctor ordered.

On our last full day in Italy we caught a train to nearby Milan. I loved this bustling city, the grandeur of the huge glass arcades, and the massive Gothic cathedral. The following morning Avi drove me to Milan airport for my flight to Edinburgh via Stansted. On the way to the airport we were caught in a huge traffic jam which was probably visible from outer space. After the briefest of farewells I checked in and made it to the gate with seconds to spare. I was going home for Christmas and had two weeks of freedom to look forward to.

As soon as I got back from Scotland, I went to the Ministry of Interior, filled in a form and in three minutes became a citizen of Israel. My British passport was stamped, but I was still allowed to use it for six months, for entering and leaving Israel. Later I would be issued with an orange *Teudat Ma-avar* or Travel Permit, and then, in a year's time I would get a full Israeli passport. That was it. I was Israeli. *I was Israeli!* I was as Israeli as Golda Meir, Ariel Sharon, or Dana International.

Despite my ungrateful whingeing, and despite my culture shock and homesickness, I was tremendously proud. I loved my new state deeply. It felt like part of me. I just wasn't sure I could live there. Now that I was an *Oleh Chadash*, or a new immigrant, I was entitled to several rights, including free Hebrew lessons. This was for a period of three months. While I was doing this full-time intensive course, I would be paid social security. Once a month I was required to sign on at a depressing office off Dizengoff Street. I grew to hate it, almost as much as a visit to the Ministry of Interior. However, I found a bakery nearby and made it part of the ritual. Dole and plum tart, the perfect combination. I was given a *Teudat Oleh*, a small blue book in which my payments were inscribed, and which was stamped to within an inch of its life by an army of bored civil servants. Long, wooden benches ran the length of the Orwellian office and the wait was never less than an hour. I brought water and a copy of *Viz* which my mother sent monthly, and then sat back to wait. People often became distraught in these offices. One day an elderly French couple emerged from an office; the lady was sobbing and her husband seemed a broken man, his old face crumpled and humiliated. "*Vous etes mechant!*" screamed the less-than-thrilled woman, "you are bad, bad people!" I looked up from reading about *Felix and his Amazing Underpants* to see what was happening. "You bad, bad people!" she continued in French. The door slammed firmly on the couple's back, a move that strangely did little to calm the situation. I watched the elderly pair walk slowly down the corridor, wondering what awful set of circumstances had brought them to this place. I was glad when I eventually got out into the spring sunshine and bustle of Dizengoff Street.

Avi was keen for me to start using my rights. In particular there was a rather expensive fridge he felt would look nice in our kitchen.[3] It was so large it could have been used to store dead cattle. We made a trip to the incredibly depressing tax office in Jaffa, where I needed to present my British passport to a venomous clerk. Without a word she snatched my passport, the receipt from the fridge shop and brought up my alarmingly comprehensive details on a computer. Indeed, had she called up my primary school reports I would not have been the least surprised. She then stamped the word *fridge* into my passport along with

---

[3] New immigrants were allowed to purchase white electrical goods tax-free to help them get established in Israel.

the date and tutted, which I gathered was the end of the conversation. We spent the evening playing at houses, loading food into the various compartments of the gleaming fridge. I was delighted and felt like one of those women from 1950s American adverts, beaming a big smile, making pancakes and knocking back fistfuls of Prozac.

I woke up early on my first day of Hebrew school, or *Ulpan*, meaning studio. Although I was nervous, I relished the return of structure, and the challenge of learning. The *Ulpan,* or Hebrew school, was located off Ben Yehuda Street, in a white modern building. Inside was the indescribable luxury of air-conditioning, and there was a little refectory for students, with an urn, cups and a huge jar of cheap *Elite* coffee. For this we were asked to chip in a nominal sum every month, although I'd have preferred to scoop up some sand and put it in a glass of hot water. I was assessed, and allocated to *Kitta Bet*, the intermediate level. We sat at rows of desks facing the teacher, a very posh and mannered lady with big hair. The teaching would have killed the average British Ofsted inspector. I have seen Ragged School Museums with a trendier approach to class dynamics. I half expected to be sent to Sir's office for a jolly good caning, or at the very least to have a brutal run-in with the nit nurse.

"*Shalom*" said our teacher with a very large plum in her mouth. She asked us to say our names and it was clear that most of the class were Russian. I liked my classmates, and soon struck up a friendship with a well-spoken English woman my own age. It was the age-old story. Blond Western girl meets hunky tanned Israeli fresh out the army. Girl falls for boy. Boy persuades girl to stay in Israel. Girl's parents freak out. Boy's parents threaten to die on their own in the dark from a broken heart. Girl turns bitter and strange. Boy grows into overweight, seed-eating, spitting slob. We had a break after a couple hours of learning, and sat with cups of coffee and a chocolate bar, sunning ourselves like Anglo-Saxon lizards in the late morning sun. We formed comfortable cliques and exchanged life stories and tips for dealing with Israelis.

"Be as rude as they are!" suggested one woman. I tried it. It resulted in a fight.

"Be really polite to them. It freaks them out" suggested another. I tried that too. It also resulted in a fight. One of the students told me a joke about an American, a Russian, a Chinese man and an Israeli. A news reporter asks them a simple question.

"Excuse me, what's your opinion on the meat shortage?"

"What's a shortage?" asks the American, nonplussed.

"What's meat?" asks the Russian.

"I don't understand the word *opinion*" says the man from China.

"What's *excuse me?*" asks the Israeli.

Our teacher believed in grammar, and lots of it. I found this tedious and longed to speak in Hebrew about interesting topics, for example myself. However we often sang songs, and I enjoyed this, both for the cultural input and the novelty of singing. Sometimes this got off to a shaky start, as twenty five Russians, three Britons, an Irish woman and an American, all started singing *Eli, Eli*. Sometimes the teacher sang a song herself. As a result I often needed to replace my shoes, my toes having curled so far round they pierced the canvas. I enjoyed listening to the teacher's stories. She would tell us about her grandparents from Russia, and her son in the army. She also gave us useful advice on living in Israel, and once brought in a whole set of Sabbath dinner table paraphernalia. She then taught us the blessings over the candles and wine. Whilst some of us were familiar with this, many of the Russians were not. This teaching technique seemed appropriate in the context of Israel, although I cannot imagine such a subject going down well in a British ESOL course.

ESOL Teacher: "OK, I am going to teach you all how to say the Lord's Prayer in English! Mohammed, are you listening? 'Our Father who art in Heaven.....'"

One lady on the course was a Black American who belonged to a community of other Black Americans from Dimona. The group members were adamant that they were Jews, an assertion that seemed to bring the otherwise unflappable teacher out in hives.

"Well some people might think that, but it is certainly not a widely held view, nor one which is shared by any other body in Judaism" she would reply before turning to write a verb or two on the blackboard, her voice so cold it could freeze the Nile.

The American lady was very pleasant in a God-speaks-to-me-but-not-to-you kind of way, but she often came out with baffling statements such as "God intended us to live forever and we will, if we stop eating meat and fast on Saturday."

"Oh my!" chuckled the teacher, her tone patronising as though she were dismissing an alarmingly precocious child. That said, the teacher was not immune from the occasional bout of lunacy herself.

"There are no Arabs in Tel Aviv" she proudly announced one day.

"Yes there are" I retorted. "There's the Hassan Bek mosque."

"Well that's in Jaffa" she replied, her eyes shifting to see who was listening to this seditious challenge.

"Yes, but Jaffa's in Tel Aviv isn't it? It was annexed in 1949."

"Turn to page 16 of your grammar books please class" she announced shrilly.

Sometimes we had trips. Our first was a walking tour of old Tel Aviv, and involved an arduous trek to the south of the city, where we were shown crumbling old buildings from the time of the city's foundation. Our guide rambled on at length, next to small memorials and plaques. Meanwhile pale Russian students wilted in the sun, their peroxide blond hair fizzling. Another trip was a walking tour of Tel Aviv's splendid Bauhaus heritage, much of it marred by air-conditioning units, solar panels, and balcony extensions. Originally, these now drab apartment buildings had been pure white and streamlined. We walked through to the backyard of one such building and were listening with as much concentration as one can in temperatures of 35 degrees plus. Suddenly a hairy arm threw open a window.

"Ma at rotza?" enquired a gruff voice.

"We are merely looking my dear man" replied our teacher archly, maintaining her cucumber cool composure.

"Why don't you fuck off?" he yelled in Hebrew, adding references to inappropriate relations with animals somewhere in the family tree. The students stared open-mouthed and horrified.

"Well really sir! I think you are frightfully rude" she replied. "Come on class" she said, turning heel and heading for the street. Meanwhile the man threatened to drench us with a bucket of water. In the safety of the street the teacher explained that there are some people who are simply born rude, and that bad man was one of them. "Yes Miss Brodie"[4] I felt like saying in a lispy posh-Scot voice.

---

[4] *The Prime of Miss Jean Brodie* was a novel by Muriel Spark in which a megalomaniac school teacher in 1930s Edinburgh has a 'set' of girls whom she steeps in her own values such as good skin care and fascism. It was made into a wonderfully camp film.

A much longer trip, and one which involved the luxury of a coach, was our outing to Jerusalem. We piled onto the bus, eagerly taking seats next to our friends and nibbling chocolate. I felt like a child and made plans to moon drivers behind us. Our teacher took her place at the front, ominously checking the microphone. Soon we were crawling along the Tel-Aviv-Jerusalem highway. We learned the hard-way that there is nothing worse than a teacher armed with a microphone in a bus which is stuck in a traffic jam.

"Oh for fuck's sake" muttered the Irish woman with a pierced nose, as we received a ten minute lecture on rock formation. "Are we going to get a lot of this d'ja think?" After a few more minutes she added "Oy need a fag and a piss, so I do." Eventually the coach drove into the centre of Jerusalem, down the Jaffa Road and then skirted the walls of the Old City. We swept up the Mount of Olives, debussed and gazed out over the Temple Mount. The teacher delivered a not-so-potted history, whilst several of us ogled some rather attractive young soldiers sitting on a wall.

"Miss, Miss! How do you say "I don't have a gag reflex" in Hebrew?" I desperately wanted to ask. A bored Arab boy glanced at us, decided we would not be the type to buy his postcards, and sat back down. Once back in the bus we were driven to a cafeteria for lunch and then taken round some boring museum to look at bits of stones. Why is it that teachers think this will interest people?

Ulpan Teacher: "OK guys, we're in Jerusalem, some of you for the first time. Would you rather see some stones in a museum or go for a walk about?"

Student 1: "Ooooo stones please miss!"

Student 2: "Yes, and can we see some funny little earthenware pots in a cabinet too please!"

Ulpan Teacher: "Well, we were planning on seeing the third holiest site in Islam and the Church of the Holy Sepulchre, but hey why not!"

We were driven to the Western Wall checkpoint and separated into male and female groups. I enjoyed touching the rough stones once again. Next to me an elderly bearded Jew in a caftan was swaying violently, firing off words so quickly I imagine even God himself would have been hard pressed to catch them. Occasionally the word amen shot out at the speed of light, along with more swaying. I was reminded of a joke about an elderly rabbi. The man came to pray every day for fifty years, beseeching God to send the Messiah. Every day his prayers went unanswered. "Ach!" he exclaimed one day, packing up his prayer shawl. "It's like talking to a brick wall."

We were led briskly around the recently rebuilt Jewish Quarter, with its clean alleys and squares. This entire area had been razed to the ground and ethnically cleansed of Jews in 1948, a fact which was repeated several times in case anyone hadn't got the message. We were then bored to tears in the Cardo, an old Roman market. It was apparent that this was definitely a *Jewish* day out, and that we would not be exposed to anything smelly, tatty or Palestinian. I imagined the tour organisers desperately trying to keep it wholesome.

Ulpan Teacher: "Look out! There's an Arab selling tea from an urn. Get them into a museum quick. There's no time to lose!"

Guide: "Right you are Ma'am. Phew, that was a close one. Oh no! There's a nun, and gulp...a donkey having a piss."

We were driven up to *Yad VaShem*, the Holocaust Memorial in the Judean Hills and were then given a quick peek at the new Supreme Court Building. I loved this building with its elegant, modern-biblical marble corridors.

"This is where everyone's civil rights are safe-guarded" announced the teacher. "Even Arabs'" she added as a magnanimous after thought.

It was dusk by the time we were on the coach and driving homewards along the dual carriageway. Beyond the bus window the Judean Hills were soft and pink in the fading light. We passed olive groves, the shadows of the trees looking eerie and biblical. I imagined how it would be if the coach would drop me off and I could walk through the enchanted groves, breathing the cool evening air and running my hands on the bark of the trees. I felt a thrill as I realised I was living in the land of the Bible, that these hills and groves were the very ones which had witnessed miracles and revelations.

"Right! Who wants to sing *Halleluiah?*" asked the teacher beaming.

"God is not a woman!"

Living in the centre of Tel Aviv was expensive, and when the landlord did not allow us an extension, we decided to move further out, to the suburb of Neveh Sharet. This was a 1960s development on the north-eastern edge of the city, bordered by orange groves. We used the decrepit Simcha to move, making several trips and by the evening we were done. I loved the new flat, which was on the first floor of a three-story block. It was spacious and newly painted, and I had the luxury of my own room. From the living room was a balcony overlooking a green square with more blocks on three sides. At the back was a patch of waste ground. The kitchen was basic, but clean and cosy. I also loved the estate. There were few roads but several paved paths that wound between the blocks, overshadowed by Eucalyptus trees. At the heart of the estate was a so-called Country Club, basically a swimming pool with an area of grass and deck chairs.

Over the next few days I explored the area, taking long walks into the orange groves. I could reach these by walking to the edge of the estate and then cutting through a rough sandy field. Beyond lay mile after mile of citrus groves. It was possible to get lost in the shadowy, pungent orchards. Ripe and rotten oranges hung from the trees, and many more lay decomposing on the sandy soil around them. I returned with a plastic bag full of grapefruits and oranges which I had found on the ground. One hot Saturday when Avi was at work I walked as far as a small concrete hut in the centre of the groves. I lay sunbathing on the roof and looking over the acres of greenery. As I was walking through the groves, I discovered a man masturbating. As one does. Happens all the time in Israel.

"Morning," I nodded. "Nice day for it"
"Hello." he replied.
"Been at it long?" I asked conversationally.
"Oh, just an hour or so. Wife's at Bingo you know."
"Well, I'd best let you get on with it then. Cheerie pip."
"Bye."

In August the new Tel Aviv bus station was inaugurated, and Avi and I lost no time in going to see it. I enjoyed visiting places together, and the massive new bus station was pleasantly cool. There were five levels of shops and cafés, many of which were not yet open. However, many mourned the passing of the old bus station with its stalls and anarchy and there were even songs written about it. Only in Israel could someone write a song, grieving an old bus station.

Avi blanched as Israel awoke to news of the so-called Gaza and Jericho First agreement, which was reached in secret in Norway. The Israeli right-wing erupted into furious protest. Personally I was quite pleased by the outcome and was hopeful of its success. I learned not to voice my opinions about this though, as politics, like religion, is a passionate issue in Israel and tempers flare easily. Following the peace agreements more violence erupted, and I spent more and more time reassuring my mother over expensive long-distance phone calls.

"No, mother, Neveh Sharet is *NOT* on the West Bank. Yes, I am wearing clean underwear in case I get rushed to hospital. No, the Erez Checkpoint is NOT near the hotel where you stayed. Yes, I am wearing my bullet proof vest and eating enough fresh fruit."

Despite the best efforts of men with bombs, the peace agreements made Israel more attractive to outsiders, and various celebrities arrived, including Michael Jackson, Elton John, Madonna and the King of Spain. It was a hopeful time, though in retrospect it was a false dawn. In the Hebrew class I often clashed with the teacher over her how-wonderful-that-we-can-be-friends-with-that-nice-Mr-Arafat-off-the-telly attitude. In return she accused me of believing in the Greater Israel, referring to our expansionist compatriots and their ideology of pushing Israel's borders as far as Iraq. In fact I disliked the settlers. I loathed their ridiculous attitude that their unwelcome and illegal presence in the centre of Hebron was somehow doing us all a favour. Most of them were American, and were fanatical trouble-makers. Most secular Israelis loathed them, especially when their conscripted sons had to risk their lives to keep them safe. I wanted to hurl a brick at the TV when goofy teenage girls in braces and ankle length skirts appeared, telling the rest of us that they were doing God's work. Really? Was there a Biblical passage I had missed?

"And lo it came to pass that the Lord instructed American fundamentalist nutcases to leave the land of California and New York State and to build prefabricated villas on the outskirts of Hebron.

Verily I shall make of you a great people if thou willst get up at dawn to cut off the water supply to impoverished villages, that thou mayest build swimming pools therewith. Behold the daughters and sons of Knob did as the Lord commanded and saw that it was good in His sight. He then instructed them to take over a score of houses in the busy centre of Hebron and cause mayhem, that the sons of the Arabites mayest not go to buy their groceries without asking their permission first." Nope, I don't remember that verse.

I coughed back the laughter as another settler spokeswoman, oddly enough an American, tried to sound reasonable.

"All we want is peace" she began, surprisingly with a straight face, though I imagine she had her fingers firmly crossed. "We will find a solution for 'them' We can all live together in peace. We don't need this agreement. There will be a war." I could easily imagine her 'solution.'

"OK, listen guys. Here's the deal. We'll implant ourselves on what's left of your land, nick all your water and as a special treat you can come and do all our shit jobs for us. As we're reasonable folk we'll let you stay in your homes, provided you agree not to ask to vote or have your own state. Watcha say?"

I could see that the peace talks were doomed. The time scale was too long and extremists on both sides had ample time to derail it. I had a better idea. Why didn't we just get some bulldozers, a few buses and raze the settlements to the ground? Why should a hundred thousand people hold both the State of Israel and the Palestinian people to ransom? I was accused of wanting to ethnically cleanse the area of Jews. Aggressive bearded men ranted about making Judea and Samaria *Judenrein*, a term used by the Nazis to mean Jew-free. Meanwhile Israelis good-naturedly told their opponents what a pity it was that Hitler had not made room for one more.

As the Jewish holidays approached the teacher very kindly invited some of the Russians and I to eat at her house on Rosh Hashanah, the Jewish New Year. I was very excited by this prospect, and took the last bus before the onset of the holiday at dusk. I walked the last part of the journey to a neighbourhood of tall, exclusive flats in the fashionable north of Tel Aviv. It was the kind of area where twelve year old girls drove open top BMW sports cars and where people washed up their dishes with imported mineral water. The spacious flat was stuffed with European furniture, most of which was white and which in England would be termed as "gangster's wife" style. The tiled floor was covered with thick Persian rugs, and every wall was adorned with oil paintings and gilded mirrors. Our teacher made us very welcome and soon we were sat round her vast candle-lit table, as her husband chanted the grace before meals. When I was a teenager longing to become a Jew, this is what had fascinated me. I had longed to be in a Jewish home, eating traditional Jewish food on a *Chag* or on a Shabbat. The meal consisted of delicious gefilte fish, topped with a little piece of pickled carrot and followed by another fish course, along with potatoes and vegetables. Our teacher explained the symbolism of the fish head, as the hope for wisdom. To round off we ate apples dunked in honey to bring us a sweet New Year. This involved some embarrassing crunching and smiling, and a temporary pause in the conversation. Over coffee, I was introduced to the couple's twenty-one year old son and encouraged to ask about the army. His mother beamed patriotically, as my eyes were drawn like magnets to the lad's developed pectoral muscles. Was that a hairy chest I could detect? The husband showed me his study, lined from floor to ceiling with books on three and a half walls, leaving only enough space for a shuttered window and a desk.

"So how long has Daniel been in the army?" I asked conversationally, using a roll of kitchen paper to wipe the drool off my mouth. The teacher offered me advice about Neveh Sharet and the forthcoming festival of Yom Kippur. "Go to an Ashkenazi synagogue" she urged. "It's more European." In fact I did not consider myself Ashkenazi even though such ethnic labels have little relevance to a former gentile. I actually felt more at home with the culture of the Mizrachim with its haunting music, delicious Middle Eastern food and sense of fun. I also found them sexier. "And we dress better" Avi pointed out.

I walked the four miles home, enjoying the relative cool of the evening and the feeling of fullness and well-being from the meal. As the following day was a festival, we began with a pleasant breakfast of sweet *Cholla* bread, white cheese and eggs. We then had more bread with thick butter and *Silan*, a thin treacle made from dates. In order to continue getting the New Year off to a good start, Avi coyly produced some fresh yellow dates and some honey cake he had been hiding. I spent the rest of the morning reading from my *Reform Synagogues of Great Britain Festival Prayer Book.* I missed being surrounded by sane, liberal, or at the very least, rational people. I read the tradition passage about the Binding of Isaac. As always I found this passage deeply disturbing and felt it needed a lot of explanation and discussion, something which I was extremely unlikely to find in Neveh Sharet. The traditional message is that God tests Abraham and once assured of his utter willingness to serve him at any cost, replaces Isaac with a lamb. Well that's all right then! Were this to happen today Abraham would quite rightly have been sectioned under Section 2 of the Mental Health Act (1983), and Isaac taken into care. The only reason I could find for this story was as a warning against religious fanaticism. The God I believed in did not ever tell people to kill kids, not their own and not other people's either. I found the concept profoundly ungodly. To maintain that God needed men to slit lambs' throats in order to please Him struck me as both primitive and blasphemous. I felt lonely pondering these thoughts. I had no-one to share them with. I was reading from the new Reform prayer book, which contained inclusive language. I mentioned this to Avi which was a mistake, a fact which I realised when Avi turned a rather fetching shade of pink and muttered something incoherent about God not being a woman. I goaded him for fun asking why not.

"God is not a woman!" he gasped weakly before collapsing.

Ten days later was Yom Kippur, a holiday I have always disliked. As dusk descended I decided I really wanted to go to a synagogue to hear the *Kol Nidre* chanted, and so followed a steady stream of worshippers to one of the local synagogues, a large, 1950s building. Inside everything felt utterly alien. I have never taken to the gender divisions in Orthodox synagogues, and the chanting was masculine and harsh. As everything was in Hebrew I soon got bored and decided to leave early. Back home Avi had decided to fast. He was feeling superior about it and caught me making some hot milk in the middle of the night.

"What an easy fast you are having Miss Reid!" he exclaimed as I hurriedly wiped the white froth from my lips.

"I have a weak constitution," I replied defensively, sucking in my less than rock hard stomach. In the morning I awoke to total, utter silence. Not a car, not a bus or radio broke the spell. I dressed and walked to the main road. It was deserted and I enjoyed the novelty of walking slowly down the centre of a dual carriage way. Soon I was joined by packs of children on bikes tearing up and down and screaming, so I returned home to read, trying to feel religious.

The TV stations had shut down and there was no radio. No planes flew overhead. I sat on the balcony with my prayer book and noticed a little girl playing on a swing. She swung higher and higher, her pretty festive dress fluttering and her voice squealing in delight. Then an angry woman in a headscarf and long dress burst out of a flat opposite. She yanked the girl off the swing, smacking her harshly as the girl's delight turned to yelps of distress. I realised how people saw God differently, and how they would never understand each other. For me smacking a happy child and making her cry was sinful. It distressed God and separated that woman from her creator, and probably alienated the girl from religion. For the woman, God was a frightening King and his Holiest of days superseded anything else. If she had known me I imagine the woman would have considered my predilection for men's wobbly bits to be an abomination, and I am pretty sure she wouldn't have thought of me as a Jew anyway. And I am sure she didn't think God was a woman.

After dark we drove the few miles to Avi's parents house to break the fast. Avi's father very quickly blessed a cup of wine as parched family members told him to get a move on. We then sat down to a meal of steaming, fragrant rice with nuts and vegetables, and for the meat-eaters there was a bowl of thin stew. We rounded off with freshly baked Iraqi pastry, and Turkish coffee so thick you could stand your spoon in it.

The next major festival was Sukkot, and when we got home from breaking the Yom Kippur fast, the Orthodox Jews on the estate had already begun building their shelters in the green area between the flats.

I noted how elaborate some of them were. As Sukkot got underway some families were actually living in these huts; some had even stretched electrical flexes over so that they could watch TV. I hoped it didn't rain. I could imagine the terror of families watching children's TV together as the TV suddenly exploded. For the secular half of the estate however, the Jewish holidays were a time for relaxing, having barbeques and going to the pool, or for those with cars, the beach. The weather remained hot and I craved winter. Routine soon returned and I resumed my long, solitary night-time walks. One of my favourites was to the exclusive neighbourhood of Tzahala, which bordered the estate. The area had been built up for high ranking army officers in the1950s and the name is derived from the word *Tzahal,* an abbreviation of Israel Defence Force in Hebrew. Within the space of a few streets the flats gave way to massive detached villas with luxuriant tropical gardens the size of small safari parks. A short distance away, I discovered a minute park with incredibly tall trees and a thick succulent smell of lemon grass. This became my special place, and whenever I could I came here to soothe my soul.

Towards autumn Avi and I decided we needed a holiday and we both agreed that Eilat would be just the ticket. Accordingly we set out early one hot October morning in the car and took the road towards Ashdod and Ashkelon. This was a new route for me, and I was excited to read the exotic, Philistine names on the highway signs. At first the scenery was built up, but gradually turned to orange groves. Before long it became sandy, with dunes and weeds. We turned inland and headed for the biblical town of Be'ersheva. I imagined the patriarchs Abraham, Isaac and Jacob stopping for water but this daydream vanished promptly when Avi got lost on a busy roundabout. The town loomed large, modern and concrete. There wasn't a patriarch or a well in sight. Beyond Be'ersheva the landscape became rugged and desert-like. The sky was relentlessly bright, and I was glad of my strong sunglasses. I looked rather fetching in them I thought, giving myself a cheeky wink in the wing mirror. "*Dai,* stop looking at yourself. Look at the map" snapped Avi. Occasionally we passed Bedouins with herds of mangy looking goats but then all signs of life died out. The road stretched ahead for miles into the wilderness, black and shimmering. After a long drive we began to see signs for some Kibbutzim and I noticed signs for Yotvata.

"Ah Yotvata" sighed Avi, his eyes misting over at the memory. "It is an amazing place. Believe me. You've never seen anything like it." He was positively drooling as he recalled the Kibbutz café-shop with its rich selection of home produced dairy products. Strawberry yoghurt, vanilla ice cream made with rich whole-milk. There were shakes and malts and ices, all bursting with tropical fruit, fresh dates and creamy milk products. It was with something approaching spiritual rapture that we drew up, wallets at the ready. The heat hit me as I stepped out the car but never mind I thought, my mind already choosing from a range of dairy so rich that I was lactating. I threw open the door into the café-shop. A few plastic tables lay empty and strewn with uncollected cups. Behind the bar a miserable looking Kibbutznik was examining a broken nail, the Israeli equivalent of *Bella* open in front of her. There was a regular size fridge stocked with a few strawberry yoghurts and a selection of fizzy drinks. After a quick coffee we returned to the now baking car and sped off down the desert highway. The sun was getting tired and the Negev desert was turning golden. It felt so incredibly biblical and romantic. I longed to stop the car and just walk in the wilderness but I'd probably have got bitten by a scorpion or fallen into a ravine and eaten by vultures so we pressed on. Occasionally we passed the date groves of isolated settlements. I noticed a range of hills on my left.

"That's the hills of Moab" Avi informed me. "It's Jordan."

I looked more carefully and could make out the lights of trucks, travelling down a hillside road parallel to ours in the distance. What would it be like in Jordan I wondered? The sky was now pink and Avi turned on the lights. We began to see signs for Eilat and the traffic got thicker. We were there. Blocks of modern flats lined the road and stretched up into the hills. I tried to imagine living in Eilat but couldn't. Most of the year the town was hotter than a sauna, the heat breathtaking in its ferocity. In order to function you had to do everything slowly. How did people cope with things like shopping or walking to the bus or insulting each other in the street?

We needed to bypass the town and continue southwards on the last stretch of road in Israel in order to get to our hotel. On the way we passed one of the country's grandest hotels. This was carved into the desert rock and covered in a glass roof in the manner of a botanical garden hot house. After a couple of miles we pulled into the drive of the Orchid Hotel, and I stretched gratefully after the long drive. The reception was so cool the sweat turned to a thin coating of ice on my back. We were given keys to our hut then rode on the back of a little buggy, driven by a hunky porter called Dudu. Our hut was located on a hill, and from the window I could see the now dark Red Sea and the lights of the Jordanian port of Aqaba. The best view however was from the door of the hut, where the hills of the desert began to rise sharply from within a few feet of where I was standing. I instinctively went and touched the red rock of the hill, noting the glowing warmth of the surface despite the now dark sky. Shortly after nightfall the rock face was bathed in a green floodlight, adding to the drama. What lay beyond I wondered? I imagined walking there, exploring the rocky, wild desert. Unfortunately, as I wasn't Spiderman, there was no way up.

We ate at the very posh Thai restaurant in the hotel, sitting by the illuminated outdoor pool. As we were both tired after the long drive we decided to stay put but the following morning we were up early to enjoy the massive Israeli buffet breakfast. After demolishing plates of watermelon, various kinds of cheese and a variety of eggs we staggered to the car, hot from the blinding early morning sun and sated from too much food. We drove the short distance into Eilat and parked. We decided to take a boat trip up and down the Gulf of Aqaba, and I was struck at how close Israel, Jordan and Saudi Arabia are to each other. Every few minutes jets roared by, bound for the small city centre airport. We spent the afternoon on the beach where I made an elaborate sand city. We were too full for any lunch, but on the way back we stopped at the Princess hotel for coffee and cake. I was awe struck. Was this a hotel or a palace? There were luxurious leather sofas where we could sit and enjoy incredible views over the Gulf or over the rocks. Above and behind us, was the tinted glass ceiling and the red rock of the cliff. To pass the afternoon we splashed around in the pool, eyeing up a stocky, middle aged man in black trunks who was showing off his diving. "Yum" I thought to myself, then caught his wife looking at me curiously.

"Don't worry" I wanted to say reassuringly. "We are *homosexuals* and we were just admiring your husband's body."

"Oh I see!" she would laugh. "Quite something isn't it?"

I yelped from the cold shock each time I lowered myself into the pool, finding it hard to see because of the glare. Back in the room, I enjoyed the warm after glow of my tanned body under the shower. It was time for dinner. This time our budget demanded something less extravagant, and twenty minutes later we were on a bench in Eilat, eating falafel and looking at the sea.

After our meal we walked along the front, Israel's answer to Las Vegas, with enormous and kitsch hotels, vying to outdo each other. We walked through the lobbies of several of them, marvelling at the faux Egyptian columns and at the sheer scale of it all. Afterwards, we returned to our hotel to enjoy our own hotel's lobby, with its Thai ceiling of bamboo and whicker furniture.

The following day was dedicated to exploring the desert near Eilat and our first stop was Timna. As soon as we had pulled up I made straight for the artificial lake and, quite illegally, jumped in to cool off. We then drove around the sights of the desert park, including the entrance to the famous mines, and the Pillars' of Solomon. Our next stop was *Chai Bar*, the famous Biblical wildlife park. Here the government had set out to reintroduce every species of animal mentioned in the Bible and there were reputedly over 450 different species, including some beautiful antelopes, along with wolves, hyenas and wildcats. Some ostriches came close to us, before making off.

We left the next morning, returning along the same highway as the day before, passing once more the Timna Park and the Chai Bar. We then forged ahead, through Be'ersheva. We stopped for petrol and lunch at a desert service station, where a weathered, leathery man in overalls filled up the tank whilst smoking. "We're going to die, we're going to die" I repeated silently to no-one in particular as I watched the ash fall like snow over the fuel-soaked concourse. By mid-afternoon we were approaching the south of Tel Aviv. This was a truly depressing sight after the beauty of the desert and the luxury of the hotel.

The summer passed. November brought a new mayor for Tel Aviv and saw the arrival of a new TV station, *Arutz 2*. Then it was December, and time, once again to go home for Christmas.

"Israel is a hot country!"

It was a bitter, raw January night and rain lashed against the windows, making them rattle and shake. Around ten in the evening I heard Avi's key turn in the lock and went to greet him. He was smiling strangely and then I noticed a kitten in his arms, wrapped in a coat. Avi explained that he had found her abandoned at the airport. I took the shivering soaking kitten in my hands. I could see her pink skin through her wet fur and even in the gloom of the hall I could see the flees jumping off her. Avi was adamant he was going to wash her in the shower, and although I protested, he did so anyway, making the terrified cat miaow even more. We then dried her roughly with a towel. We had not planned to get a cat that evening and were completely unprepared. I got a cardboard box and filled it with sand from the plant pot in the communal hallway. We then mixed some bread with milk and I found a tin of tuna for the ravenous animal. I slept uneasily, worrying if the cat was OK. "What shall we call her?" I asked Avi, whispering in case I woke her up.

"What about Lola?" suggested Avi. It was just the kind of vampish name he would choose but it suited the feisty kitten perfectly.

A few days later we drove to the Israeli Society for the Prevention of Cruelty to Animals. This was located in a poor area of south Tel Aviv, near Jaffa. I was surprised to see a church tower, a sight I missed. It would be nice to hear church bells again I decided. We carried the struggling cat into the vet's surgery and returned a couple of hours later to collect her. I was shocked to see her tiny, unconscious body in a box.

"She's been spayed" explained the vet in Hebrew. "She also has a chest problem, probably because of being left in the rain. She should be OK." We bought a proper basket and a small collar and took her back to the car. I anxiously looked through the grill at her every few minutes as we sat stuck in a traffic jam.

She came around in the late afternoon and then went back to sleep. During the night she crawled into bed with me. "You poor little baby" I whispered. She turned out to be a real handful and was in fact partly feral, a trait which was not helped by Avi's insistence that she remain a house cat and not go out. It was as though he had brought home a particularly vicious and hormonal fox and tried to make it wear ribbons and a coat. Although I didn't like to keep her prisoner, I could see his point. The estate was infested with dozens of feral cats and I didn't fancy her chances. Lola then began her campaign of terror, climbing onto shelves and looking to see if I could see her, before deliberately pushing ornaments onto the floor.

Later that month I watched a developing news story with horror and revulsion. Two spoiled teenage boys had killed a taxi driver "to see what it would feel like." A few weeks later, in February, a Jewish settler, Dr Baruch Goldstein opened fire on hundreds of Palestinian worshippers in the contested city of Hebron. He killed twenty-nine people then himself. The incident was revolting, and I was horrified to the reaction by many on the Israeli right. They muttered remarks such as "they deserve a taste of their own medicine." Within hours of the massacre, riots erupted all over Israel in those areas where Arabs lived, including nearby Jaffa. This was deeply frightening to many Jewish Israelis who were accustomed to a docile Arab population in their midst. In a truly perverse twist of events the local settlers decided to erect a memorial tomb to the killer. In the years following the shooting it became a shrine and a sick place of pilgrimage. Why the hell were they allowed to do this I asked angrily?

Spring was coming. As the weather heated up we were constantly plagued with *jukkim* or huge flying cockroaches. To the delight of Lola, these flew noisily into the kitchen, where, with the quickest of reflexes she had them pinnned down with her paw, allowing them to escape briefly. Knowing what was coming I closed my eyes just in time to hear the nauseating crunching sound. When I opened my eyes again, all that was left were some wings, which I had to sweep up. Invariably the rest surfaced later in a protein-rich pile of cat sick, usually in one of my slippers. When the time came for Lola's inoculations I was filled with dread. The cat was dangerous. If she had been a dog she would have needed a muzzle. Indeed I'd met more docile Japanese Tosas. The vet was not worried however, laughing gently at our warning.

"Don't worry" he chuckled, beaming "cat's love me, don't they puss?" Suddenly he screamed, the blood draining from his face, and also from the five seven-inch cuts in his arm.

"*Elohim!*" he exclaimed in pain and horror. Minutes later he returned with industrial rubber gloves, and a pair of what looked like wire clippers. Lola's claws were unceremoniously cut off and the animal then injected, rather roughly I thought.

One tragedy which shook Israel that spring was the savage car bombing at Afula. Eight civilians were killed; dozens were horribly injured. This resulted in a long closure of the Occupied Territories, plunging Gaza and the West Bank into crisis, which was precisely what the terrorists had set out to do. A few days later a second bombing occurred in nearby Hadera, killing five more. The attacks were becoming ever more brutal and regular. Avi blamed the government for loosening its grip over the Occupied Territories; the military's hand was tied for political reasons, and this frustrated him. When he saw footage of jeering mobs in Gaza celebrating the attacks his frustration turned into rage. I tried to stay calm. In May 1994 the PLO and the Israeli government reached an agreement in Cairo. This was hailed by Israeli left as a major breakthrough; the right dismissed it as a gesture without real peace or security. I agreed.

As history was made around us we continued with our day-to-day lives, watching *I Love Lucy* and enjoying our meals and outings together. Avi bought a new car and we bade farewell to the Simcha. Two days later I found its burnt out shell in the orange groves. I was alarmed. Why would someone buy a car and then torch it? I thought sadly of our outings in it; it was like an old friend. The weather was now getting unbearably hot and one day a lady from the government came to the Ulpan to give us a lecture about hygiene.

"Israel is a *hot* country" she began tactfully, taking a range of deodorants out of a bag and laying them on the table.

In June the Hassidic Lubavitcher rabbi died in New York, and a series of ridiculous posters appeared lauding him as the King of the Messiah. That same month Yassir Arafat arrived in Jericho. Avi warned of dire consequences and became more and more alarmed at the unfolding events. A new joke about Arafat began doing the rounds, the usual Jewish response to adversity.

Arafat was ill and consulted a clairvoyant, wishing to know when he would die. "You will die on a Jewish holiday" she told him, her eyes closed in concentration.

"Mmmm. Interesting" replied the cuddly militant rascal. "Which one?"

"Any day you die will be a Jewish holiday" she clarified.

This country was seriously nuts I thought, not for the first time. Within an hour's drive from our flat we had the mastermind of the Munich Olympic massacre setting up a quasi government. The Israeli government was arming him, hoping he would do their work in maintaining law and order. A few streets away were people who thought a geriatric rabbi in New York was probably the Messiah. An hour and a half to the north rockets and missiles were crashing into Israeli towns and villages, and in the neighbouring town of Bnei Brak gangs of Ultra Orthodox Jews were stoning cars for driving on the Sabbath. In Tel Aviv, a short bus journey from Bnei Brak, there was a thriving youth culture, a red light district and a gay park. The government was a hotchpotch of Labour, a radical left wing party called Meretz, and a bunch of fundamentalist opportunists called Shas, whose leader was being prosecuted for corruption. Even the architecture was crazy with European Bauhaus, Arab and Ottoman buildings and 1960s functionalism all thrown together.

I was glad to be returning home for a welcome dose of sanity and in July I was once again on a Monarch Airlines charter flight bound for London and then Edinburgh. I enjoyed the usual treats of home cooking, socialising and drink fuelled visits to Edinburgh's gay pubs and clubs. My parents also took me on a short holiday to the Highlands where we stayed at a peaceful and graceful hotel near Oban. I loved the atmosphere of the hotel with its reading room, manicured lawns and ticking clocks. I had my own room, and it was lovely to sit and read and not have anyone bother me. In the evenings I met my parents for pre-dinner drinks in the lounge before sitting down to a four course candle-lit meal. The peace of the holiday was broken when we returned to Edinburgh. I came downstairs to the living room and noticed my mother quickly and guiltily turn the TV station.

"What's happened?" I asked instantly on guard. It was either bad news or she'd been watching porn. It was bad news.

A huge car bomb had exploded outside the Israeli embassy in London and other attacks had been foiled on Jewish targets in Golders Green. Some people bring bad weather with them. I was bringing terrorism with me.

To celebrate the new peace between Jordan and Israel, or rather between King Hussein and the Israeli government, Jordan's monarch, a keen pilot, personally flew a Jordanian airliner over Tel Aviv. I was convinced I could hear Avi retching in the bathroom.

"What's wrong with Israel making peace with Jordan?" I asked Avi, surprised at his lack of enthusiasm. The gist of his reply, minus references to our Prime Minister's paternity and mental health, was that Jordan had neatly avoided any involvement in the issue of Palestine. Until 1947 Jordan had been part of Palestine. Most people who live in Jordan were Palestinian. Many argued that Israel took up only a small percentage of 1947 Palestine, but if Jordan were removed from the equation then the percentage was much larger. A Palestine that was squeezed into Gaza and the West Bank would not be able to accommodate the return of the three and three quarter million Palestinian refugees. It was highly likely that the Arab countries where the refugees lived would expel them into the West Bank, deliberately destabilising it and provoking civil war.

Peace or no Peace I still needed a job, and naturally I was looking for a career in teaching English. Large groups of children scare me. I am basically infantophobic. It is unfortunate then that I found a job teaching an innovative new programme for children. This involved following a training programme for a week at a flat in Holon. Incidentally, if you want to pronounce this name try brining up phlegm and add the suffix-*lon*. I had never taught children before, but how hard could it be I thought? I was game for anything, and I enjoyed the training, which involved lots of nice songs and using little kits of stickers and colouring in. I met a young English man whom I liked and who looked slightly camp. This was not helped by the Burberry case which he carried round with him. It looked more like an accessory for a *petite* Japanese lady, rather than a suitable bag for a strapping young Englishman. We both enjoyed slating the trainer as soon as her back was turned. This was justifiable as the woman was unpleasant in a I-can-smile-and-hate-simultaneously kind of way. Her sunglasses were surgically implanted onto the top of her head and she always had an expensive headscarf tied so tight around her neck I thought, or indeed hoped, she would choke herself.

After the training finished I was sent, quaking and against my better judgement, to a school in a satellite town of Tel Aviv for my first lesson. I was invited into the teacher's room, where the all-female team were drinking weak coffee. My attention was drawn to the 3 Shekel a term coffee levy and I was introduced to the scowling, cross looking women. They were so sour one drop of their sweat would be enough to preserve a vat of vegetables. One of them looked as though she chewed broken glass as a hobby. Another was picking her teeth with a rusty Stanley knife. If I was a child they would have scared me, which is probably why they had been employed.

As soon as the bell rang a boxer dog wearing rouge and lipstick led me down a poorly lit corridor teeming with screaming 7-11 year olds. I was shown a classroom. This was bare apart from a large map of Israel on one wall, a picture of Yitzhak Rabin on another and a few pictures of animals. Little devil-children began to pile in and the teacher explained who I was and that I was going to be teaching them English.

"Isn't that nice boys and girls?" she added to a roomful of stifled giggles. She left and I was alone with them. "Shalom" I said, trying to remember a saying my school teacher friend Graham had once told me. "Never smile until the second term." I tried to look stern.

"A song, a song" I said to myself, trying to get them to sit in a circle. I felt ridiculous as I began singing a little ditty about "hands, fingers, nose and ears" or some such nonsense. A few of them gamely began touching their ears and noses etc but many had returned to whatever they had been doing in the break, for example vomiting or worshipping Satan.

"Ayyyyy" screamed a little boy. "*Hu mabitz li!*" which I assumed meant "Hey that little rotter gave me a bunch of fives," upon which he burst into tears, snot and drivel running down his puffy little face. The few children who had been joining in with the song now wandered in all directions and I felt like a geriatric, toothless sheepdog as I tried to scream at them in broken Hebrew. "Fuck, fuck, SHIT!" shouted one of the infants, triumphantly. "I thought you weren't supposed to know any English you little imp!" I cursed. At that moment the door flew open and the organiser of the programme stormed in. There was a silence so pregnant it needed a midwife and some hot towels.

"*Ma kara?*" she hissed. "We can hear you down the corridor where the other good children are all doing their songs and learning how to touch their ears and noses." The children all looked at their feet, looking suitably repentant and waiting until she had left, before bursting into life again. I was starting to feel like the pig in *Lord of the Flies* and expected them to hunt me down with a pointed stick at any moment. Somehow I made it to the end of the lesson. The following day I was back. Once again the lesson was chaos. At the end an irritating parent arrived, pestering me and asking if their little angel had mastered any Shakespearian plays in English yet.

"How is Yossi? Yossi make progress?" the woman asked, ignoring my four foot exclusion zone and getting into my face. She was so close I felt we should broach the subject of contraception.

"Erm, which one is Yossi?" I asked apologetically. What I really meant was "I don't know their names, they all look the same and they are horrible."

I returned to the class for the next lesson, and shortly before the end the headmistress of the school came in.

"Children, you need to stay in the classrooms. It says on the news there is a car with terrorists in our town and the police haven't caught them." The children gasped. For heaven's sake, I thought. They are seven year olds. Why on earth was she telling them about terrorists in cars. One child became tearful. "My mum's outside" he began to wail, his tonsils flapping.

"Oh, don't worry. It said that they are in Beit Masreach" giving the name of an industrial estate nearby.

"My daddy works there!" screamed another child.

"I am sure he's fine" she snapped, and then turned to me. "You must keep them here till I say." I was furious as I was due to go home. All I wanted was a cup of tea, a Custard Cream and a nice episode of *The Streets of San Francisco*. Moreover I didn't want to get caught in the rush hour. Still, I didn't want twenty dead children on my conscience so I tried to keep them happy, giving them pens and paper to draw on. This did not quite work, with the children thinking that their parents, grandparents and pet kittens were being strafed with machine gun fire at that very moment.

The next day was a Friday and I was not due to teach, nor was I being paid to. Nevertheless the programme director wanted to have a teacher's meeting and insisted everyone travel out to where she lived, which for me involved two buses. I noticed one of the Russian teachers was not there so I asked where he was.

"He is no longer working for us" she snapped. Later on I heard the full story. During his lesson one of the children had cheeked him so he did what any self-respecting Soviet teacher would have done and had given the lippy urchin a resounding slap around the face. I could picture it. The slap. The stunned silence and looks of horror from the other horribly spoiled children. Then the air raid siren-like wail as the child burst into tears. The pounding of the head mistress's feet on the stairs and finally the incomprehension on the face of the unfortunate teacher mouthing "What did I do wrong?" as he was bundled into the back of a police car. The following week my camp English friend had gone. It was like some nightmarish South American junta with people vanishing into thin air. The following week it was my turn. When Avi returned from work he found me crying at the kitchen table.

"*Dai!* What happened?" he cried out.

"They fired me!" I roared indignantly. Mind you, I suspect they were probably quite right. I vowed there and then never to teach children again. Never. Ever. Ever.

"If you turn right here we'll end up in Palestine!"

"Perhaps Lola would like to go next door?" suggested my mother, suspiciously sniffing an expensive Jaeger jacket and putting it on a hanger. I shooed her away; the cat, not my mother. Not having any of it, the obstinate little darling returned frequently to the spare room, deftly opening the flimsy door with her front paw. She had a strong attraction to my mother's case. We soon discovered why. She had pissed in it. Once again, the cat, not my mother. It was October 1994 and my mother had just arrived from Scotland, bravely flying alone with British Airways, treating herself to Business Class as this made her feel safer. I am not quite sure why. I can't imagine terrorists saying "prepare to die infidels! Except passengers in rows 1-15. You are free to go!" We planned to have a few days in Tel Aviv and then have a short trip to Eilat.

I was very excited by this prospect but the visit was already being overshadowed by an ongoing tragedy on TV. A few days earlier, a young conscript called Nachson Wachsman had been abducted by terrorists disguised as Orthodox Jews. His mother, a devout Jew, had been on TV pleading for his release but to no avail.

One evening we were all having dinner when the news broke that a rescue attempt had gone wrong and Nachsom was dead. I was deeply upset by this particular story, although why this particular tragedy should affect me more than others I don't know. Avi furiously blamed the government for dealing with the corrupt Palestinian Authority and I agreed with him. There was no attempt by the PA to clamp down on the group responsible, nor did they stop the sick 'plays' staged in Gaza, re-enacting the killing of Wachsman, during which he was portrayed as a sobbing bespectacled victim.

A couple of days later I went to work for a few hours. I was teaching English at an office in the south of the city. On the bus to work I became aware that something was wrong. The bus driver turned up the radio. I heard the dreaded words *pegua chazaka* and *harbay harugim*, meaning a 'massive attack' with many 'feared dead'. I then made out the words Dizengoff and bus. With a heavy heart I called Avi from a public call box near the office. Then I went to teach. There was a misunderstanding. When I phoned Avi I assumed he would tell my mother I was safe. He in fact thought he should not tell my mother anything about the attack. He was due to go out for a couple of hours, leaving my mother safely in the flat. Becoming bored she switched on the TV and saw the carnage. The scene was awful, with the number 5 bus's roof completely ripped off and the dead littering the familiar street, sheets hastily thrown over their lifeless forms. It was one of the most savage attacks yet, with a horrific 24 fatalities. It was only several hours later that my mother found out I was safe.

Despite the news, we decided to spend the evening in Old Jaffa, and set off just after the evening rush hour. The air was sweet and smelt of the sea and of flowers and pizza. The sound of the sea was audible as we strolled around the pleasant, Ottoman square and alleyways. The old Arab houses were now home to quaint shops, selling crafts and ceramics. On the square was the beautiful old church of St Peter's and several restaurants, with outdoor terraces. We chose *Aladdin*, a restaurant housed in an ancient building, which seemed to hang off the cliff. The first room was reminiscent of the *Thousand and One Nights*. Carpets and rugs seemed poised to take off. There were various *hookah* pipes and coffee urns, as well as sofas with thick, satin-covered cushions. The focal point of the room however was a huge, mysterious mirror. We passed through the room and sat at an outside table. To one side were the domed, stone roofs of Jaffa, and to the other was the wide sweep of the Tel Aviv coast. Meanwhile the sea continued to break over Andromeda's Rock. According to legend Andromeda's mum had been boasting about her daughter's great beauty. She even went so far as to say that Andromeda was prettier than the Nereids. I had no idea what the Nereids actually were, but apparently they were not happy and persuaded the Greek God Neptune to chain Andromeda to a rock as a tasty *amuse bouche* for a peckish sea monster. Perseus then came to the rescue, married her and quickly dispatched his competition. All this happened on the rocks which I could see from the terrace. Our meal consisted of a *mezze* of stuffed vine leaves, chips, and little plates of fried aubergine, houmous, and mashed avocado. All this was served with large, warm pitta breads. We stayed late, drinking wine and then sweet mint tea served in glass cups.

The next day we prepared to set off on the long hot drive to Eilat in our little red Seat. This was a nice car, but did not benefit from air-conditioning. We were soon on our way, my mother nervously anticipating the drive through the desert. For me this was routine. I knew it was one of the busiest roads in Israel but for a stranger, I understood it could be daunting. We followed the Be'ersheva route and after a long drive, we finally came to the Negev desert, arid and simmering in the autumn heat. All the windows were open but I was still stuck to the plastic seat, my underpants soaking wet. From sweat I hasten to add. After a brief lunch of stale vegetable oil and E-coli at a service station we were once more on our way. The road ahead was straight and black, and for once there was no traffic. Avi's speed was creeping up and I told him. Like most Israeli drivers there was no way he could ever go too fast. Of course not. Fast drivers were good drivers. Nevertheless as I didn't fancy being involved in a serious car accident in the desert and left wounded and stranded, possibly eating my mother in order to survive, I broached the subject once again. "I am not going too fast" protested a now cross Avi, the g-force pinning back his cheeks. I glanced in the rear view mirror, feeling like I was winning the Paris-Dakkah car race, when I noticed a very faint but noticeable flashing blue light.

"Avi?"

"I am not going too fast. Everyone knows 150 KM is the unofficial speed limit."

"No. Look behind you."

"*Ach*" he dismissed. "They are going somewhere else."

"Quick" I said to my mother. "Put your seatbelt on."

"But it doesn't work" she protested, images of her new life in an Israeli women's prison flashing before her eyes. She would need to find herself a queen bitch on G-Wing to protect her, trading cigarettes for toilet paper. The police car was now on our tail, its headlights flashing. I felt as though I were getting a lift from OJ Simpson. After finally getting the message that, yes, they were after him, Avi pulled up. The yes-I-have-got-a-gun-in-my-pocket-and-no-I-am-not-pleased-to-see-you police woman approached the car, as Avi resignedly got his identity card ready. Without even glancing at my mother in the backseat the officer said curtly "You can tell her to unwrap that seat belt from around her neck. She isn't fooling anyone. Just get it fixed." There then followed the have-you-any-idea-how-fast-you-were-going-sir, routine, followed by the standard Are-you-sure-I-was-going-that-fast-officer reply. Noticing that Avi should have been wearing glasses but wasn't, the officer demanded to look into Avi's eyes with a torch to see his lenses, or 'lentils' as Avi insisted on calling them. After issuing an on the spot fine and giving my mother a filthy look, the police car drove off in a cloud of dust. Avi got back in, and feeling smug that I had been vindicated, I suggested we get a move on and not waste anymore of our trip. Unfortunately the car had different ideas. Avi turned the ignition key. Nothing. He tried again as three very hot people held their breath. Nothing. A vulture circled high above us, licking its lips and tucking a napkin under its chin. The busy road was suddenly not that busy. Not a car in either direction was to be seen. Jackals cracked open a bottle of pre-dinner Sherry. My mother and I exchanged I-am-going-to-kill-him-with-my-bare-hands looks. Avi lifted the bonnet, trying to convince everyone he knew what to do. After ten minutes a car pulled up and an affable Swiss tourist got out.

"Let's get in his car, and leave Avi here" suggested my mother, making for the car. A group of angelic blond children looked out of the back window, obviously enjoying our distress and giggling.

"Mummy, why don't those financially-disadvantaged people buy a better car, perhaps one like ours?" I thought I heard the child ask. Against all the odds the Swiss man managed to start our car, and then drove off. Each thanking God silently, in our own ways, we pulled out and completed the last stage of our journey to Eilat. We checked into our rooms at the Orchid Hotel, where we had stayed the previous year. My mother was fascinated by the red rock of the desert just beyond our rooms, and took great delight in touching it. We had a refreshing pot of tea in the huge, wooden lounge of the hotel overlooking the Red Sea.

"Do you have any biscuits?" asked my mother in English.

"*Bisqvuitim?*" asked the scowling and premenstrual member of staff.

"*Ugiot!*" barked Avi, filling her in.

"*Lo*" she replied, which was Hebrew for "I am terribly sorry sir. We seem to have run out. Would *modom* perhaps like a slice of cake?"

We had dinner at the hotel's Thai restaurant. This time I didn't need to choose the cheapest thing on the menu, which was a welcome treat, so I ended up devouring a huge piece of sweet and sour fish. We returned to the lounge where there was live entertainment. This took the form of a lone female singer, and a handful of guests. We ordered extravagant multicoloured cocktails with umbrellas and cherries in them, and sat back to relax.

"It's nice that the cocktails have normal names here" said my mother, sipping her nicely named Cosmopolitan. "Back home they all have stupid names like *Slippery Nipples* and *Sex on The Beach*." Avi looked like he didn't quite know what to say so he smiled politely and said *chin, chin*. Unfortunately the now desperate woman on the stage needed some input and was making grab raids, rushing off the stage and seizing members of the audience. I remained firmly in my whicker chair but Avi and my mother ended up on the stage, singing a resounding chorus of Halleluiah. It was so embarrassing I wanted to die there and then.

The following day began with a huge breakfast, and then a drive up to Eilat, which was blisteringly hot. We had an expensive coffee and cake at the Princes Hotel, served by a scowling, scruffy, teenage girl called Ruthi. Ruthi then handed us a bill with more digits than an American toll-free telephone number and stood around aggressively, waiting for a tip. In the afternoon Avi and I hired bikes at the hotel and cycled slowly up to the Egyptian border and back, whilst my mother slipped in and out of consciousness in her room.

The next day we set out early. At the first main junction we got slightly lost. After this, the journey did not go according to plan. As we eventually cleared Be'ersheva and headed north we ended up clashing over which route to take.

"Avi" I exclaimed with exasperation "if you turn right here we will end up in Palestine."

"I know what I am doing" he replied, using moderate language in consideration of my freaked out mother in the backseat. We were all feeling hot and thirsty, and the last thing I felt like doing was straying into the outskirts of Hebron with Israeli number plates. We were definitely not on the right road and there were no longer any signs for Tel Aviv.

"Just do as he says Avi please" snapped my mother, her voice arch and clipped, and a suitably chastened Avi did a U-turn back to the main road. As we approached the outskirts to Tel Aviv I got my usual feeling of post-holiday blues. I wanted the wide open spaces of the desert. I imagined, not for the first time how it might be nice to live in a small Israeli town in the north of the country, close to nature, or even in the desert.

I spent the next day in Tel Aviv with my mother, being treated to nice things such as new books, coffee and cakes at Kalpulskys, and a slap up lunch. In the evening I took my mother to the British Airways Advanced Check in the north of Tel Aviv. Here she would check in her luggage and go through security clearance before getting her boarding card to be used the following day. This meant she could turn up at the airport an hour before the flight and go straight through the passport control. It was a good idea but unfortunately my mother froze.

"Did you pack this bag yourself?" asked a diminutive, teenage girl with a clipboard and B.O that would offend a camel. Or even kill one.

"Erm, Andy?" my mother replied, looking at me, a panic-stricken grin spreading over her face.

"Talk to her yourself!" I replied none too graciously.

"Do you know anyone in Israel?" asked the girl.

"Sorry darling?" replied my mother. I was pleased to get out of there before we both ended up having a chat with two lovely gentlemen from Mossad.

The following day Avi drove my mother and I to the airport. Afterwards I felt sad and empty. It was horrible being so far from home and family. I wanted to go home. On the way back to Neveh Sharet we passed a garage which was used to repair buses. Sat in the middle of the yard was the shell of the bombed number 5 bus. I stared in horror at the roof; it looked like a half-opened tin of sardines. The next day it had gone.

Although autumn had arrived the temperature remained high, and the coastal plain continued to be sticky and muggy. People were craving the onset of winter and were washed out after the long summer.

It was approaching the *Yom HaNoraim* or Days of Awe, and as usual there was a frenzy of shopping, cleaning and cooking. My private lessons began to dry up, and students promised to resume their studies after the Festivals were over. We were to spend our *Erev Rosh Hashanah* with Avi's parents, and I was looking forward to it. I ironed a clean white shirt and shaved. I carefully applied a generous dollop of my rationed *Crabtree and Evelyn* face balm, before carefully hiding it from Avi and his voracious appetite for my luxuries. We then drove to Givatayim. It was pleasant to be in a family environment, even if it wasn't my own family. Avi's brothers and sisters were there, and the house was buzzing. We spent time chatting but the older females remained in the kitchen, getting the meal ready. It smelt delicious and I was so hungry I could have eaten a nun's arse through the convent gate, as Lily Savage would say. I was finding it hard to concentrate. Avi's father stood at the head of the table and chanted the grace from a small, disintegrating prayer book, well used over several decades of family *Shabbatot* and *Chaggim*. We sat down to a noisy meal of baked fish, served on a mountain of fragrant rice, sprinkled with juicy raisins and oily nuts. After this, we were treated to a huge portion of baked, spiced apple. I began to feel uncomfortable. I sensed a rip-roaring-curtain-lifting fart might not be socially acceptable.

The women went into the kitchen to clear up and I asked in Hebrew whether I could help. Avi's mother looked at me oddly, a touch of confusion mingled with pity in her voice. "*Lo, todah*" she said, shaking her head slightly and obviously deeply confused. I shrugged and sat down with the men folk. Avi's father had cracked open a dusty bottle of that ghastly Israeli liqueur known as *Sabra*. Tasting like a Victorian laxative laced with alcohol and orange chocolate, the drink is drunk on special occasions and then, sensibly, returned to the cabinet until the next time guests come round. Gagging, we toasted each other's health and wished each other a happy New Year. A nice refreshing glass of Toilet Duck would have been preferable. After an hour or so of washing up Avi's mother returned with a tray of Arabic coffee and a huge plate of hot, sweet, cheesy pastries. Replete, and in my case slightly bored, we left at around midnight and drove home.

In November 1994 sending my CV to language schools paid off. I got a phone call from Berlitz, the upmarket language school near *Beit America,* the grim 1970s home of the American Zionist organisation. I loved the school as it had air-conditioning, potted plants, and toilets so posh that little plastic covers were issued from an electronic dispenser. I enjoyed this experience so much that I used to save up and go to the loo at work. It felt good to be working again, especially in such nice surroundings. Before being allowed to start teaching however, we had to follow a special week-long course in the Berlitz Method, which consisted mainly of getting people to say "This is a pen"(holding up a pen.) "Is this a pen (yes)?" "Is this a pen?" (holding something else, like a pencil, a grapefruit or a used condom and shaking your head emphatically.) When the student was deemed ready, and if they hadn't walked out the door laughing, or if you hadn't walked out the door laughing, then you asked really big questions like "what is this?" If you deviated from this order our trainer, an amply bosomed American *Haredi* Jew from Bnei Brak, would smile indulgently and shake her head. And also her breasts.

"No Andrew. Is this a pen?"

"Erm, yes" I'd answer slightly nonplussed. I silently added "Of course it's a bloody pen. What do you think it is, you daft mare? A rabbit?"

"No" she added, shaking her head and still smiling sweetly. "You say "Is it a pen? See?"

Students were always assessed using this tried and tested format. On one occasion the assessor in question was somewhat distracted.

"Is this a pencil?" she asked.

"Yes" answered the student, a high-ranking officer in the artillery corp.

"Is this a pencil?" she asked holding up a staple gun.

"No it isn't, but ..."

"Just a moment" she interrupted, lest the flow be broken before asking "What is this?"

"It's a pencil. The thing is I am here to learn Spanish."

Like Cynthia Payne, my clients were mostly successful business men. One-to-one lessons usually lasted for an hour, and unfortunately they often began at 8.00 a.m. At 9.30 we then taught classes of up to eight students, mostly women, many of whom were a bright you've-been-Tangoed hue of orange, a result of the over-application of foundation. There was absolutely no way that the Berlitz method would last more than a minute in one of these classes.

"Is this a pencil?" I'd begin bravely.

"You Jew?" asked an elderly lady from Bat Yam, her body shimmering with gold accessories. She was obviously a stranger to the old adage 'less is more.'

"Yes" I answered.

"You don't look like Jew" she replied. By now the other women were poised like birds of prey.

"You married?" asked another doubtfully, a plump and powdered widow from Herzelia. "Why you not married?" she asked me when I shook my head. "You want help to meet a nice girl? How much you earn?" And the sad thing is no one learned how to ask if a pencil was a pencil.

From time to time we were given an all-day Total Immersion course. This was not a course in preparing for baptism. It was in fact an ordeal which consisted of being closeted in a cubby hole for an entire day with a sullen business man who kept being interrupted by a mobile phone. Each time this happened he would make a strange sucking-clicking sound and hold his ring-finger to his thumb, which is Hebrew for "One moment please me Old China." I then put down the pencil I was holding and sat listening to a series of grunts followed by a terse "bye" which is Hebrew for bye. Were this not ordeal enough we then had to eat lunch together. This took place at the cafeteria at *Beit Amerika* and although the food was good this was the point at which the infernal man would start to talk. Every time I had a tasty morsel poised to my mouth he would ask me some involved question about English grammar. I asked the waiter if he could stick my food in a blender and bring it to me in a glass with a straw.

Despite the pencil talk, it was a great feeling to be working in a proper school and to be able to use a whiteboard and proper resources.

I enjoyed the camaraderie between teachers and met several new friends. We would bitch mercilessly about the students over cups of instant coffee. After a few days of this I noticed I was getting headaches and a curious buzz and decided to avail myself of the herbal teas instead. One object of derision was a vacuous woman from Holon. With considerably more money than brains she responded to every single word I said, even if it wasn't to her, with a whiny "*ani lo mevinah*!" meaning "I don't understand." It wasn't this that bugged me so much as the I-don't-think-I-can-live-if-I-don't-understand-everything-right-this-second way in which she said it, drool hanging from her chin, and a whine that would attract stray dogs from miles around. The woman once complained to my Australian colleague that although she was rich and could afford lessons, she wasn't making progress. The unfortunate woman was decidedly one Matzah short of a Seder. "Money doesn't buy you intelligence" my friend allegedly replied although, as she still had a job, I took this with a pinch of salt. One customer was named Tzippi. Her name, and face, reminded me of Zippy, a character from one of my favourite childhood shows *Rainbow*. This old darling believed that the lesson was for her benefit only, but unlike the real Zippy I wasn't actually able to zip her mouth together. Had this been possible I would most certainly have done so, for my own benefit and for the benefit of all around her.

"Hang on a second Rivka." Zipppppppp. "There, that's better. Now, what were you saying? Is this a pencil? No, it's a pen." I used a variety of techniques for keeping Tzippi under control. One method was never, ever looking at her or asking her a question. Another was holding a hand up to her face, whilst addressing someone else. The most effective however was to bang her head repeatedly against the wall shouting "For the love of all that is sacred, will you shut up" whilst stabbing her with a pencil. "Is that a fucking pencil then? Is it? A fucking sharp pencil? Eh? Eh?" One student summed it up neatly when she said, quite reasonably "I didn't pay 500 Shekels to hear you talk. Now shut up."

Our lessons were booked and allocated by an absolutely stunning young Israeli woman whose smile was warm enough to thaw ice caps. If I had been straight, which you may have gathered I am not, then I would have worshipped her. She could certainly charm me; I was putty in her hands. She was just so heart-stoppingly *nice*.

"Andrew" she asked, smiling coyly, her almond eyes sparkling. "Can you give Mr Frogstein a private lesson at 5.00 a.m. tomorrow morning? In Haifa? Wearing panties and suspenders?"

"Yes of course!" I'd gulp, my sexual identity worryingly blurred.

"Thanks" she purred like a kitten, winking at me in a I'm-not-wearing-any-knickers-and-it-feels-nice kind of way. I pitied the straight male teachers, some of whom were working twenty three hour days.

Apart from teaching, I was also learning how to cook. One of my dearest possessions was a copy of Rose Elliot's vegetarian cookbook. It represented a lot of things for me. It represented independence, and from her recipes I taught myself not only to cook but to cook well. It also represented continuity with home. I often stared at the photo of the writer who was sat at a huge kitchen table whipping cream for a bowl of ripe, sliced strawberries. I promised myself that one day I would have a kitchen like hers and I would be back home.

In the meantime whenever I had time I walked through Tzahala to the curiously shaped round supermarket there. Here I would buy the ingredients for one of Rose Elliot's lentil bakes, nut rissoles or a vegetarian Irish stew. I loved Rose Elliot so much that I wrote to her. A few weeks later a rather surprised Rose Elliot wrote back. Equally surprised, I decided to write to other famous people asking them to send me signed photographs. Soon a bizarre collection of British B-List celebrities were popping through my letter box, some with charming little notes or restraining orders attached.

However it seemed my new career was about to be interrupted. One morning, when I returned from the *Mecholet*, or corner shop, I found a letter in our letter box, along with some bills and a slightly confused note from Valerie Singleton. Unusually, the official letter bore my name in Hebrew along with an official triangular stamp in the corner depicting a sword motif. Putting down the carton of milk and loaf of bread, I tore open the envelope but frustratingly I couldn't understand it. Only when Avi got home did I get my answer.

"It's from the army" he said. "They want you to go for a medical examination." I was surprised at the speed with which they'd contacted me; after all I had only become a citizen a few months earlier.

On a warm winter afternoon, I took the bus to the large army depot at Tel HaShomer, on the outskirts of Tel Aviv. It felt utterly strange to stand at the gate of the huge, sprawling base. I was tremendously excited and I visualised myself as a soldier, wearing a white T-shirt under an olive green crumpled shirt. I would be tremendously handsome, a soldier of Judah, a hero of the Jewish people. Old ladies would gulp back tears of pride upon seeing me. I showed the teenage guard my letter and walked through, my head held high and my jaw set heroically and manfully. The base was bare and paved. White huts and concrete, modern buildings stretched for acres. An Israeli flag fluttered noisily in the warm breeze. Young female soldiers were busy shepherding groups of middle-aged men along with some younger men in their late twenties. I soon got used to waiting. Eventually, I heard my name yelled out and was shown into a medical office where a female soldier took my blood pressure and weighed me. Then I was asked to piss in a cup and pass it to another extraordinarily grumpy female soldier. Mind you, it can't have been the nicest job in the world so I couldn't blame her for not slapping her thighs and roaring with uncontrollable laughter. I imagined her talking to her significant other when she knocked off duty.

Partner of female soldier: "Hi darling. Nice day?"

Female soldier: "Oh you know, the usual. Collected piss from several dozen middle aged men. And you?" After this compulsory tinkle I was told to wait again, which gave me time to absorb the strange atmosphere. I noted the drab brown walls and the posters in Hebrew. Then I noticed the small police station, whose sole function was to follow up draft avoiders. An excuse-me-aren't-you-too-old-to-be-a-policeman policeman was sat doing a crossword and eating *pain au chocolat.* In the psychologist's office I was asked to explain my teenage depression, which I had felt it my duty to declare. As I was really fired up, I put a gloss on it and told them what they wanted to hear. It would have been easy to get out of the whole thing had I wanted to, at that stage, especially when they asked me if I ever heard voices. "Who said that?" I could have responded looking round. "God, is that you? What, you want me to kill again? That's the third time this week! Sorry doctor, where were we? Voices? No. Never."

Next came some psychometric tests, at which I did well. I finished early and stared out the window. I could see life beyond the camp.

There were some rigid square blocks of Israeli flats in a *Shikun* or estate. Cypress trees towered over the barracks, and the solar panels of the flats reflected light back at me. It was a bizarre mix of ugly and beautiful, normal and strange. Next we had a battery of Hebrew tests which I found easy, and then we were free to leave. For now. The last words the female clerk uttered were "Don't bring your cars when you next come as you won't be going home."

Still filled with the military bug, I launched myself into a Jane Fonda fitness routine. Soon I was running further and faster than I had ever run before. In fact I could have outstripped the Bionic Woman I was that fast. I ran to beyond the orange groves, I followed the stream to the dual carriage way, way beyond the municipal boundary. I was getting fitter and fitter, listening to rousing Hebrew songs as I pounded mile after mile. I was going to be a soldier! This was really going to happen. I could scarcely believe it. I would grow, discover myself, become a real Jew, a real Israeli. I would finally be proud of myself.

Even though I had found a job at Berlitz, and though I knew that I was going to be in the army for three or four months, I continued with my private lessons, which was a useful way of supplementing my income. One of my local clients was an unusual Turkish-born Israeli who lived in a very pleasant villa in Ramat Gan, a short bus journey away. He was mad. However his insanity was the pleasant kind, rather than the chopping-up-kittens-and-eating-them kind. He lived with his equally insane wife. I only ever taught them in the evenings, and I enjoyed the walk there, through the tree-lined streets enjoying the pollen-scented silence. As soon as I arrived at the couple's envy-inducing villa, I was plied with Turkish coffee and a plate of honey-dripping-gut-busting baklava or Arab pastry with nuts. We went through to the living room where I then asked the man a couple of open questions to get the 'lesson' started. He talked for an hour without pausing for breath. I interjected with the odd correction, which he of course ignored. At the end of the hour I received a crisp twenty Shekel note and a doggy bag of cake. Then he and his wife crowded around me in the marble-floored hallway, cooing over me. Some of the things the man said were fascinating and I loved listening to his stories. He often talked about his holidays to London and I experienced a vicarious pleasure in hearing about my former home through his eyes. He and his wife loved London and went nearly every year for shopping and to watch his beloved Tottenham play football. He described in loving detail his meals at *British Home Stores*, making them sound like a particularly succulent dinner at the Savoy. He also talked about growing up in Turkey, his sporting career, and his time in the Israeli army where he was something terribly important, with lots of pips on his shoulders. He was very tough and boasted about never having an anaesthetic at the dentist.

"Is waste of time!" he half yelled in the manner of the hard of hearing. I listened in horror to his accounts of various fillings and drillings without so much as an aspirin, and I decided he really was mad. I mean seriously barking, stark raving mad. Often his wife would shout things from the kitchen as he was having his lesson, upon which he would produce politically-incorrect gems such as…

"Shut up stupid woman. Bring our teacher coffee."

"Milk, no sugar please" I added.

I talked to him about the army. I was desperate for information about what to expect. All I learned was that I should practice running on the beach as it was good for fitness, along with something incoherent about shooting people if you could see the white of their eyes.

One night it had been raining heavily, and the lesson had gone on slightly longer than usual. This was due to an in-detail account of a particularly toothsome fruit scone which Mr Loonystein had eaten at the café in John Lewis in Oxford Street. Not wishing to miss the 23 bus I decided to run. As I got to the kerb I pressed my foot to the kerbstone but slipped on a wet leaf, bending my foot painfully.

"Shittingfuckinghellbells" I winced as the pain shot through my foot. Nevertheless, I continued to run and caught the bus. I took off my shoe and rubbed my foot. The following morning I woke up to discover that my foot was a) twice the size it should be and b) black. I stared in horror and gasped for Avi to come and look.

"Ooowa!" he exclaimed which is Israeli for "cor that's a beauty and no mistake." Minutes later we were driving through the rush hour on our way to the Medical Centre in Basel Square. Here Avi helped me upstairs but he had to leave me to go to work so I waited patiently for the doctor. One look at the foot was all it took for the doctor, a pleasant modern Orthodox Jew from South Africa, to write me a chit for an x-ray.

"Ooowa, it looks rother nosty" he added, sounding like Eugene Terre-Blanche in a skull cap. The snag was that the x-ray place was the other end of town and I couldn't afford a taxi. I therefore had to hop to the bus stop, my foot so fat it would no longer fit into a shoe. Feeling like a rather scruffy kangeroo I eventually arrived and was soon laying on a bed with a huge x-ray machine positioned above me.

"*Yesh lecha shever*! Is broken" announced the doctor.

"A bit like your English then" I wanted to reply, crabby from pain.

"You go back doctor yes?"

"No" I thought "I'll sort it out myself with a fucking splint, shall I?" I agreed a return visit to the doctor, might indeed be a good idea. I then had to hop back to the bus and back to Basel Square where I was referred to another doctor.

"The doctor busy. No see you now. Afternoon you come. Maybe see you." The receptionist was engrossed in her nails and was reading an article about how to make the most of your breasts.

"I have a broken foot!" I hissed. "I am not going away and coming back again." What did the woman expect me to do? Go to a café for lunch, have a stroll in the park and then do some last minute groceries, before nipping back to have my broken bones put back into place?

She shrugged. "*Hu asuk!*" she repeated. "Busy." Not for the first time in Israel I felt tears of frustration well up, and burst into tears. This seemed to do the trick. I was ushered into the foot doctor who smiled and began looking at the x-ray.

"Oooha!" he exclaimed. "Is broken." He then explained how I could either have an operation to straighten the fracture or just have it plastered and let it heal slightly crooked. I chose the latter. By now I was sick and tired of hopping and taking buses and, money or no money, I was soon ensconced in the back of taxi heading for the place where they put plaster on. I strangely enjoyed this, and the nurse had a sense of humour. Either that, or she'd been tipped off by the receptionist that I was a nutter. Soon my foot was encased in my very first plaster cast. I was told I would need crutches.

"You need sticks!"

"Oh do I? Crumbs. I had kind of just expected to hop everywhere" I wanted to answer. I was referred to a charity which loaned crutches and wheelchairs to the poor and needy, a trip I needed to make by taxi. A suspicious and bitter-looking receptionist put down the lemon and vinegar smoothie she'd been sipping in order to size me up more effectively. After a moment of squinting at me she grunted unpleasantly and went to get me a pair of First World War crutches, but only after getting me to fill out forms. The whole office gave me the willies with its frosted glass and teak furniture. The selection of crutches reminded me of a church I had once seen in Marseilles, dedicated to healing. There, those fortunate enough to be healed left their sticks and crutches and presumably skipped home like Spring Lambs to the shouts of "it's a miracle!"

It felt very strange to walk with crutches. Actually it was good fun. I enjoyed stepping on the toes of unsuspecting pedestrians and then shouting "*SLICHA*!" at them, which means excuse me, but really means "Watch it!" Soon this novelty wore off and I made the slow journey home by bus. Within days I was developing some cute little man breasts and, a novelty for me, some muscles on my arms. Soon I would begin to look like the lady at the swimming pool.

The next day I had the fun task of travelling to Ramat Gan, where I had to teach a private lesson to a group of Russians. I had to leave the house earlier in order to compensate for my slow progress. On my return I had a problem as I could not finish the lesson early. I had to try and run with crutches to catch the half-hourly bus service. As soon as I left the house a dark, silvery rain cloud burst, complete with biblical thunder and lightning. The deluge was so powerful that the water was bouncing off the pavement. It was soaking me. I turned the corner and saw the illuminated driver's cab of the bus about thirty yards away. I began to half run on my crutches, waving frantically to the driver. I then felt myself falling and landed face first in a deep puddle. The last thing I saw as I fell was the driver's smirk. The bus pulled away from the stop, splashing me as it sped through a pot hole. I staggered to my feet, picking up my crutch and staggering to the bus stop, resigned for the wait. Because there was no shelter I was getting wetter and wetter by the second. However I fancied my luck was about to change as I noticed an elderly man holding the largest umbrella I had ever seen. In fact it was so big it was more like a small tent with a handle. Under the umbrella I could see how blissfully dry the man was. Surely he would see my plight and say the Hebrew equivalent of "Here ya go pal, come an' share this wi' me." To which I would of course say "Oh really! Are you sure?" "Och aye, nae trouble pal" he'd answer. Well that isn't what happened. As the ground around the man remained so dry that the grass began to wither I stood in the torrential rain, the expectant smile frozen on my face. He stared away from me, and I began to utter a series of expletive curses about the parentage, manners and general lack of breeding amongst the people with whom fate had decided I should reside.

"You fuckin' bunch of fuckin' little...." I grumbled, sounding like a Glaswegian tramp embarking upon his fifth can of White Ace of the day.

"Toto, I don't think we're in Golders Green anymore!"

Over the next month my foot healed slowly but surely, and I returned to the doctor so that he could cut off the plaster. To do this he selected a small circular saw of the kind used to scalp corpses in *The Silence of The Lambs*. I cringed, and braced myself as the saw screeched closer and closer to my flesh. Meanwhile the doctor seemed unaware of what he was doing. In fact I think he might have dozed off for a while. And then suddenly it was off, the plaster that is, not my shrivelled, purple foot. At first walking was painful but soon my foot grew stronger and stronger, to the extent I could run on the wet sand of the beach.

That Christmas I returned home to a testicle-freezing-blood-vessel-crackingly cold Edinburgh, using my orange Travel Document, or *Teudat Ma-avar* for the first time. I enjoyed the holiday with my family, and enjoyed showing off about the army to my friends. I decided to keep it secret from my family however. They would worry, and that would spoil the fun for me. During the break I found my excitement and curiosity rising. I was on the threshold of a life-altering experience, one that would make me a man and an Israeli. I visualised long runs, proud looks, camaraderie and who knows, perhaps the odd commando raid, maybe even medals. I began pushing myself to jog, despite the ache in my healing foot. It was odd to be jogging through Edinburgh, getting ready to serve in the Israeli army. I passed elderly Edinburgh citizens with their frozen December faces and panting dogs. I felt oddly smug. How much more exciting my life was than theirs. After New Year I returned to Israel, for once with a great sense of excitement and humming the tune of *You're in the army now* to myself.

However, the good mood did not last long. Soon after getting home I received the now routine phone call from Avi to say there had been a particularly brutal bombing. I turned on the news. This time the bombers had worked as a team, with a second explosion coinciding with the arrival of the emergency services. The target was Bet Lid junction near Natanya, and most of the dead were young soldiers returning to their bases after a Sabbath at home. The news was filled with funerals for the next two days. Israeli funerals are harsh and raw. They occur almost immediately after death, and mourners wail and scream, often ripping their clothes. There is no bitter-sweet wake or comforting words from a country parish vicar, just bare grief, and often rage and shouting. With the military burials there were always a lot of young people present, often breaking down with shock and anger at the sudden death of their friend. Israeli soldiers are always buried in coffins, rather than the usual Jewish shroud. As many of the casualties are horribly mutilated, all military dead are buried in coffins with no exceptions. This way no one can know, and mourners can hope that their son or daughter escaped this final degradation.

On the eve of my draft date, Avi had to work a night shift, which meant I would be alone. Outside the rain lashed down and the cat cringed from the loud roar of the thunder. I sat in bed and tried to read; sleep wouldn't come. At five a.m. I got up and had some toast and *Silan*. I packed a few things into a bag, including a copy of *Brideshead Revisited*, although quite when I was going to have a chance to read I wasn't sure. Would I be sitting in a ditch in southern Lebanon reading about Sebastian's experiments with homosexuality? Would there be a little book circle?

Samal (Sargeant): Okay, now I would be interested in us all sharing our thoughts on Jane Austen's use of …hang on a second guys. KILL! KILL! Argggghhh." Gouge. *Rattttaatttat*. "Yes, where were we? Ah, yes. Jane Austen. Now Moshe you had some interesting thoughts you were going to share?"

In the darkness of the pre-dawn I took a local bus to the railway station where I changed for Tel HaShomer. On arrival at the guard house we were told to board another bus, which drove us straight into the heart of the base. We were shown into a large room with fixed plastic seats, reminiscent of a passport office and a female soldier switched on a huge TV. The video described what would happen next. We would be examined, kitted out, and all have a jolly hard but rewarding three months after which we'd emerge as fully fledged card carrying Israelis with loads of new friends. How super I thought to myself. It was like an adventure at the *Swiss Chalet School*. Perhaps there would be midnight feasts, or some harmless and resolutely heterosexual bottom slapping in the showers. Heavens! It was all going to be an absolute scream.

We were taken to another room and told to strip down to our pants, and then we queued up. One by one we were shown to a door and as soon I stepped through, two doctors simultaneously injected me. Still confused, I was told to bend over and a third doctor did my *tuschic*. I hated the experience. It was humiliating and brutal. In another room a medic ordered me in broken English to "take down my panties" by which I think he meant my underpants. There was no hint of irony, and the poor man had been obviously been making the same mistake for years. Panties indeed! By now I was not quite as excited as I had been. We had our finger prints taken, making me feel like a criminal, and then we were told to line up again. I was too depressed even to ogle the other recruits. Our next ordeal on this ghastly military *Via Dolorosa* was to have a camera shoved into our mouths. This was so that the army could identify us from our dental records if it needed. It creeped me out. I at least hoped I'd be dead if it came to establishing my identity in this way, although there have been cases of Israeli soldiers being used as bait and held captive for years. It seemed odd that fillings given to me at the Barnton Dental Practice could be used to identify my mutilated body by the Israeli army. I was given two dog tags, one for my boot and one for around my neck. I was handed an identity card in French and Arabic, requesting that I be treated according to the Geneva Convention if captured alive. Why French I wondered? Is that what Hizbollah generally spoke?

"*Ah, oui monsieur. Salaam aleikum. Je suis un soldat d'Israel*. Oh, blast. What's French for I am too young to die?"

We were shown into a yard and, wait for it! Told to wait. The sky was light brown and heavy. Cypress trees and olive trees dripped following an earlier shower and above us a plane roared as it took off from nearby Ben Gurion Airport. How I longed to be on it. I felt trapped. I wanted to be able to leave the country whenever I wanted. For example right now. Next came the stores. We went through a tunnel-like corridor with booths all along one side and were ushered towards the counters. Expressionless male soldiers began piling clothes on the counter and soon I was laden with a new uniform. We put our civilian clothes into our luggage and sat in a changing room to get dressed. By now everyone was sullen and dispirited. I fiddled trying to insert the dog tag into my new boots.

Lunch consisted of pitta, humous and water and was served standing up on the steps of another office building. Here we were to be selected for various units. I wanted to be allocated to the unit that dug people out of rubble, this seeming a fairly non-violent and worthwhile task, and hopefully one that didn't involve going anywhere near south Lebanon, delightful though I am sure it was. I was gutted when I was told that I would be in the *Totchanim* or artillery corp. Perhaps the pupil-dilatingly-lip-lickingly gorgeous clerk had misunderstood me when I had told him that I wouldn't mind loading *his* high explosives into *my* artillery shell.

Shortly after being shown photographs of wounded and dead bodies a wave of fatigue overtook me. There is a wonderful scene in the American Sit-com *Will and Grace* where one of Will and Grace's friends looks distressed and says simply "I am not having fun." I had reached that moment. I wanted more than anything a nice cup of hot tea and a sandwich. I wanted to be in charge of my life enough to make myself a cup of tea and say to everyone "hang on, I'll be with you in two shakes of a lamb's tale but I need a quick snack." Somehow I got the feeling that wasn't going to happen. There was no tea in the offing and what was worse there was no indication of when there would be. I overheard one of the Americans telling his friend that we would probably be sent home after the selection process, as this is what had happened to his friend. Well, that would be nice I thought. I really wanted to be home.

I began to feel restless; night was falling and there was no further mention of going home. I began to feel tearful. It was also impossible to use the phone, and I really wanted to speak to Avi. Cold, miserable and with a rapidly decreasing blood sugar level we were shown to a large, draughty tent where we would spend the night. The flaps didn't even reach the ground and the night was raw and windy. Some of the younger Russian soldiers played cards by torchlight. I chatted to a Canadian guy, trying to hide my misery before crawling fully dressed into my sleeping bag. I didn't even know where to clean my teeth. For the second night in a row I had no sleep. Around dawn we were told to get up and were taken to a parade ground where an officer addressed us using a megaphone. He threatened that unless we tried hard we would not be allowed to go home and see our families that weekend. His whole manner was vulgar and aggressive and I hated him just as I hated that place. I also hated the boots which were beginning to hurt my shins.

We were boarded onto buses, according to our names. I enjoyed being in the warmth and although I knew we were going somewhere even worse I was glad to see the back of Tel HaShomer. We took the coastal route and began heading south, getting stuck in early morning traffic. I tried to snooze but the more I tried the less I could. The sky remained brown and overcast and I prayed it wouldn't rain. I envied the care free existence of all I saw out of the window. The commuter in his car. The school children waiting for their bus. The backpackers on holiday. How I wished I could swap places with them, to be free and in control. As much as I wished it wouldn't, the bus continued south and I noted with alarm that the road signs began indicating Gaza. Outside I noted the sand dunes and signposts to a nearby kibbutz, built by the beach. The bus stopped briefly at a check post, and then drove up a driveway to a collection of huts and tents. We disembarked and I became aware of a group of po faced sergeants looking down their noses at us. "*Maher, maher*" they barked which is loosely translated as "I say chaps, do you think could perhaps step lively, what, what."

I was immediately handed a brush and told to start sweeping up outside a tent. Other soldiers were dispatched elsewhere. I actually quite enjoyed the safety of doing the sweeping. Nothing bad could happen to me whilst I was sweeping I reasoned. After a quarter of an hour I was told to go to the kitchen where I was needed. Meanwhile the others were to go and get their guns. This meant I didn't get a gun but rather a Brillo Pad, and was told to start scrubbing an enormous pile of pots. As the morning dragged on I started feeling sullen again. One of my jobs was to pack food into large fridges, including enormous chunks of Edam cheese. I craved a big slice of this, not having eaten since a slice of teeth-crackingly stale pastry, handed out by elderly volunteers at Tel

HaShomer. A few very skinny cats gathered around, hoping for some scraps of food, and I instinctively made a clucking noise at them. A moment later, one of the sergeants appeared and threw stones to chase them off. One torment was not being allowed to take off my sweater, without first removing the epaulets on the shoulder and transferring them to my shirt. I found this incredibly fiddly and therefore didn't bother, with the result that I soon felt hot and sticky. I was told to mop the canteen. I felt I had returned to the kibbutz and all my feelings of doubt and regret about not joining Sussex Police flooded me. What was I doing here, scrubbing floors for foreigners and getting treated like scum? Why had I thrown away my career? What would happen next? A female soldier sitting at a table asked me the same. "What are you doing here? Why did you come here?" she asked, a question to which I had no answer anymore.

At lunch time we were given ten minutes to eat. We were not allowed to start until the sergeant told us so and it felt like a race. The food, some sausages and soggy pasta, was disgusting; it looked like a monkey's penis and I decided not to eat any, as it was meat. I had some greasy cold chips and a yoghurt. Another problem was becoming apparent; I hadn't been for a poo in two days and there was no way I was going to have one any time soon. My blood sugar level was falling and I really wanted some fresh fruit and some caffeine, perhaps a nice cafetiere of finely ground Columbian with a biscotti. After lunch I was sent back to the kitchen where I started cleaning pots so big you could rustle up a couple of well-built missionaries in them. An officer I'd never seen before arrived and yelled at me in Hebrew, telling me I had 20 minutes to get the kitchen spotless. I stood rigid by the sink. One of the sergeants looked oddly at me.

"*Ata beseder?*" he asked me. "Are you OK?" I couldn't look at him. I couldn't move. He put his hand on my back. I tried so hard not to, but red hot tears welled up.

"*Ma cara?* What's wrong?" he asked genuinely alarmed. The warmth in his voice only made it worse and I began to sob. He sat me down at the table and gave me a glass of water. A moment later he returned with another sergeant. They spoke about me in Hebrew and told me to breathe deeply. Israelis pride themselves on their prickly, tough exterior. However when someone was in genuine distress they could be warm and kind and sensitive. When I had stopped crying they let me get back to work. I wondered if this would have happened in the British army.

"There you go you 'orrible little man!" the regimental sergeant major would boom. "'ave a bloody good cry. Let it all out!"

After a quarter of an hour or so my misery bubbled over once more, and I started to sob again. This time the sergeant walked me back to the tent. Two of the Russian soldiers saw us and asked what was wrong. "Leave him in peace" said the sergeant, rubbing my back, then putting his arm over my heaving shoulders. *"Ata beseder?"* he asked softly. I sat on a fold up bed. I didn't know what to do. The wind howled and lifted the flaps of the tent and then let them drop. Hours passed and I tried to stay warm. In the evening the other soldiers went for a lesson in a portacabin but I refused to go. I walked to the phones and told Avi. He tried to encourage me but I was stuck in a hell of my own. The landscape was bleak. I could make out the huge chimney of a power station and on the other side some red roofed cottages of a nearby kibbutz. I was shivering and dry sobbing as I walked around. A female soldier told me to run if I wanted to stay warm. I went to the shower block, which was housed in another portacabin and tried to wash myself warm before returning to the tent and getting into my sleeping bag, fully dressed. I missed the routines of home, breakfast, lunch, dinner, *The Bold and The Beautiful,* a hot shower, bed.

All night long I lay awake listening to the wind and the snores of the others. When I needed a piss I pulled on my boots to walk to the portacabin. I half expected to be shot between the eyes. How on earth did people cope in situations far worse than this, for example in prison, in the trenches, or even in a concentration camp? Before it was light a sergeant opened the tent flaps and shouted that anyone wishing to pray was to do so now. This was a thousand miles from the Judaism I had been used to, with nice lesbian rabbis in Notting Hill or delightful organ music at West London Synagogue. This was not Rabbi Lionel Blue on *Pause for Thought* or Julia Neuberger *On Being Jewish.* "Toto, I don't think we're in Golders Green anymore" I said to no-one in particular.

I lay in bed. Minutes later the non-prayers were ordered up for a run and I made up my mind. I was getting out of there. The dream was over. I said I wanted to see the doctor. I was told I could do so after breakfast, a miserable affair served in the canteen with a time limit of seven minutes. I managed to eat some cold scrambled egg and a piece of stale sliced bread. I was taken to see the camp commander in a tent nearby. A huge Israeli flag hung on the wall of the tent behind his desk. He looked at me sternly over his glasses, looking like a military Anne Robinson from *The Weakest Link*. I sniffled an explanation.

"Stop crying" he said coldly, "it's not appropriate."

I had to wait outside the medical hut for the doctor to arrive. Initially he tried to persuade me to get a grip, to try to get Avi to support me but after a while he relented and decided to refer me back to Tel HaShomer. He asked if I had any issues about sexuality and for once I wished Israel could be less progressive. After all equal rights meant equal responsibilities. However, I did not want to use sexuality as an excuse as it had nothing to do with my present state of mind. I would need to make my own way to Tel HaShomer, so I phoned Avi. I collected my things and went to wait by the gate, where I needed to explain myself to the two women and one male soldier on guard.

"There are some people like that, who can't make army" said one of the women to her friend and shrugged. After a couple of hours staring at the sand dunes beyond the gate house my spirits lifted when I saw our familiar small blue car appear. Avi, still wearing his driving glasses, saw me and grinned. We hugged and both got into the car. It was the first time Avi had seen me in uniform. His pride left me cold now. It was unwelcome. There was nothing to be proud of. We drove off towards Tel Aviv. The heat of the car and the feeling of safety lulled me into a light snooze, and we soon arrived at Tel HaShomer. We sat waiting to see the doctor. Next to me was a middle aged reservist handcuffed to a young military policeman, and a younger reservist with long hair in a ponytail who stared at his feet, talking softly to himself. Avi suddenly became emotional. "I should never have brought you here to this country" he wailed, "We should have stayed in Italy. Why, why, why did I do it?"

We were told that I would be seen later and that Avi should leave. I told him I would OK by myself so he reluctantly left. After a few hours it became dark and still nothing had happened so I asked a spotty and snotty teenage girl in uniform what was happening. She went to find out and then told me I would spend the night in the army hospital. She directed me there, but I arrived to find a confused receptionist. She said

I could not stay there, and had no idea where I should be. I felt utterly lost. I was in a huge base. I was exhausted and scared. All I wanted was to sleep and be safe. Then it became too much and I was sobbing again. I cried so much I can barely remember what happened next, but I was given pyjamas and shown to a bed in a small ward. There were just five beds, all empty. I climbed between the sheets and a female doctor gave me a sedative strong enough to relax a very highly strung Rhino. I awoke around three o'clock. The doctor was taking my blood pressure and I must have slept even as she had put the device around my arm.

"Is it high?" I mumbled in Hebrew.

"A little" replied the doctor. I awoke again around five with the same procedure. At seven I was told I was going to the army court in order to be dismissed on medical grounds. I was also told that I was to wear my army shirt and boots but I was to wear my pyjamas rather than trousers. I waited in a small room near the door with two others. One was a young woman, with puffy red eyes, and the other was a young man who seemed hysterically happy. All of us were in our pyjamas, boots and jackets. We were driven across the base in a jeep, and I was shown into a room with five stern officers behind a desk. I was asked about what had happened and they listened with a vague look of distaste, as if there was a particularly rich and fruity fart in their nostrils. They looked at each other meaningfully and one of them began writing a chit. I hate it when people write without telling you what they are writing. What was it? A shopping list? A prescription for Prozac? A death warrant?

Outside I was told I would be returned to the ward to collect my things and then there would be paper work to complete. I was going to be discharged. A couple of hours later I left Tel HaShomer and stood bemused by the local bus stop, waiting for the 55 bus which would take me to the railway station. It was odd being in the real world again. On the bus I felt ashamed when an old man offered me his seat. There is a tradition in Israel for civilians to offer soldiers in uniform a seat. I shook my head. I didn't deserve it. After a long bus journey across town, I arrived back at the flat. It was a bleak, overcast day and I knew Avi would be at work. As I looked up at the window of the flat I saw our cat Lola looking down at me. I opened the door, and was surrounded once again by the familiarity of home. I went to the kitchen and made myself a sandwich, a cup of milky coffee and then I sat and cuddled the cat. Outside rain began to fall heavily, turning the dust into a thin mud and rattling the windows. I turned on the TV, saw the first five minutes of *Murder She Wrote,* and fell sound asleep. I was able to rest for a few hours until Avi returned home, and then we set off in the car, headed for the same base I had left the day before. I felt sorry for Avi, who after a long double shift had to drive all the way to the edge of the Gaza strip and back. I needed to return my uniform whilst Avi waited on the other side of the perimeter fence. I waited for the female soldier in the stores to help. At first she ignored me. Then she told me she was on her break and I would need to wait for an hour. Fuming with frustration and anger, I shouted to Avi across the barrier at the gate house. With a feeling of profound relief I eventually handed back my uniform, item by item. When I got to the boots I was told I could keep them, and to this day they remain as a memento to my long and glorious war service. As soon as Avi put the car into gear and drove off, I fell sound asleep again.

"You like Tottenham Hat Spirs?"

After my brief spell of military service, life returned to normal but a little part of the dream was gone. I was never going to be truly Israeli now. I hadn't served in the army, I didn't like olives and I didn't have a hairy back. Thankfully I had my job at Berlitz to go back to and I meekly explained to my boss that I'd failed my medical, which was technically true but I left out the bits in between. I was glad it was over and I settled back into my routine of work and home life. I still continued at the Ulpan, but this time I only attended part-time in order to work. I had moved up a level too, to the giddy heights of *Kitta Gimmel*. This was taught by a pretty but nasally congested woman, who was always suffering from colds. The class had less camaraderie than the first full-time class. It was shorter, later in the day, and the students were too busy to stop and chat. I sat next to an unpleasant New Yorker with eye-watering-taste-bud-numbing B.O, who picked up on my grammar. My crime had been to say *if I was* rather than *if I were*. I told her I believed language evolved and if most people said *was* then why was it wrong. After all, we no longer went around saying words like *thou* or *verily*.

"And you call yourself an English teacher!" she exclaimed, looking around for people to back her up, smiling in disbelief. Not getting the attention and vindication she obviously craved, she then talked *about* me rather than *to* me.

"He's an English teacher and he doesn't know grammar!" she announced to anyone willing to listen.

"Oh, why don't you just f…"

"*Shalom!*" the teacher announced, sitting down her usual six minutes late, mucus cascading down her chin.

One hot topic early in 1995 was the start of campaign to keep the Golan Heights. Shimon Peres had hinted at giving it to Syria, though the Prime Minister Yitzak Rabin had not gone that far yet. I was not in favour of returning the Golan to Syria. It would not bring peace. It had catastrophic military implications. It would allow Syria to turn off Israel's supply of water at will and, unlike the West Bank and Gaza Strip, it was sparsely populated. The Heights had been annexed years earlier and the Druze population there had been given full citizenship. Syria had twice attacked Israel from this point and I was convinced they would do so again. It was naïve to believe that the fascist Ba'ath party of Assad would ever recognise Israel. Indeed the Syrians would not even recognise Lebanon; if Israel were replaced by Palestine, Syria would claim that too. Syria had never recognised the carving up of the area by the French and British. It was an expansionist and ruthless regime. I am sure they probably thought the same about us.

I was however desperate for Israel to end its occupation of Gaza and the West Bank. Another people lived there, and the occupation was destroying their lives as well as ours. What possible benefit could be gained from keeping three million Palestinians under foot, degrading them daily and stealing what little they had left? The occupation was a festering cancer in the heart of Israel. It was destroying Israel's standing in the world, it was prolonging conflict and it was bringing Israel to the point of destruction as a Jewish shelter. What would happen when the Palestinians became the majority, as they surely would? How long could an Israeli Apartheid continue? What would happen to the Israelis when they were outnumbered? I couldn't bear to think.

The news also remained dominated by the issue of Russian immigrants and their perceived lack of gratitude or willingness to integrate. This often rebounded on me, as I apparently looked Russian. I made every effort to integrate however, making a point of always speaking Hebrew in public. Some Israelis have an annoying habit of replying in English (so they can show off and also belittle you in one move) and then reviling you when you yourself don't speak Hebrew. In order to help make you feel part of your new home and a welcome addition to the State, they ask in English "where you from?" when you ask to pay, or otherwise state your business.

A conversation might run thus.

Me: "*Shalom. Ani rotzeh* Diet Cola *bevakasha.*"

Shopkeeper: "Where you from? You from America? I been America. New York, Chicago, very good."

Me: "*Lo. Ani mi* London. Diet Cola, *bevakasha*?"

Shopkeeper: "England. London. Manchester. Very good. You like Tottenham Hat Spirs?"

Me: "No. I don't like football. Can I have a Diet Coke please?"

Shopkeeper: "*Lama ata me deber Ivrit*? You should learn Hebrew."

One Friday afternoon I popped out to get some fruit from the local stall before the Sabbath started. I chose what I needed and soon had several paper bags of fruit on the counter. When I had paid I casually asked for a plastic bag in Hebrew so pure that the national poet Bialik would have been moved to tears of knuckle-biting-tear-welling ecstasy.

"No" answered the owner.

"Sorry?" I asked.

"No bag for you. You don't need a bag."

I was horrified and furious and immediately asked for my money back. He threw the coins back into my hand, and I stormed off feeling sick with frustration. I was pleased to see that the oaf had accidentally given me too much money back however. I boycotted his shop thereafter. This was just one of several encounters with petty racism. Another occurred weeks later when I was travelling on a bus. I was sat in the window seat and became aware that a passenger had sat down next to me and was elbowing me. I shifted a bit and carried on looking out the window but became irritated at another elbowing. This time I elbowed back.

"Your eyes are too blue" hissed the man, an elderly secular man.

"Oh, I'm sorry" I replied. "Let me nip home and pop another pair in."

"*Ma?*" replied the man. On another occasion, this time on a bus travelling down Allenby Street in Tel Aviv, I witnessed an elderly European-looking man stare at an African woman.

"Why you not go home?" he asked loudly. The woman stared hard out of the window and ignored him. Thankfully the other passengers didn't, and an Israeli woman retorted with that classic Israeli put down of *"ata lo beseder"* which literally means 'you are out of order.' There followed an animated discussion around the issue of immigration with a wide variety of passengers joining in, by which time the unfortunate woman had got off the bus.

Buses in Israel are a fascinating microcosm of life in the country. I encountered every variety of Israeli on them, and the interaction between passengers was also interesting. Ultra-Orthodox men preferred to stand rather than sit next to a woman. Heavens! The insatiable vixens might not be able to keep their wandering hands of those shiny-black-completely-inappropriate-in-a-hot-climate trousers. Who on earth could resist a pallid, emaciated bookworm with a four foot beard when the only alternative was a bus full of bronzed, muscular man-totty in olive green uniform? I know I couldn't. There were some privately owned buses in the town of Bnei Brak where women got on at the back and sat in the rear with a curtain down the middle. Elderly passengers often stood up for soldiers who looked shagged out and laden. No-one ever spoke, or engaged in eye contact. The only exception to this rule was if the driver closed the doors too soon, in which case every single passenger on the bus would join in an ear-drum perforating collective shout of *"Nahag!"* meaning "Driver, could you open the doors please?" Once the slow-off-the-mark passenger was safely off the bus everyone went back to ignoring each other, or engaging in some harmless just-kidding racist abuse. One sight which used to shock me every single time I saw it was the spidery, black tattoos of concentration camp survivors, which I often saw when they put up their arms to ring the bell. Another common sight was of course the dozens of young soldiers, both male and female in their olive uniforms, carrying kit bags and guns. I often had to squeeze past them, rubbing myself accidentally on the butt of an Uzi.

I continued to supplement my income with private students, fitting them in around my lessons at Berlitz. One of my least favourite students lived on the fourth floor of a block of 1970s flats in North Tel Aviv. The lady was a great dog lover, and was the proud owner of a large

Jack Russell. I am a great fan of dogs. I love them to bits; indeed I am never happier than when I am tickling one of the little fellows under the chin, provided they've been washed. However I don't love them in *that* way if you get my drift. This chap decided that he quite liked *me* though. In *that* way. As soon as I arrived, he was up and ready, panting and rising himself onto his hind legs, his raging canine erection there to greet me.

"Mushi *shev*" said the owner, busying herself in the kitchen, making teacher's tea.

"Erm, hello boy!" I said, giving him a friendly but firmly platonic rub on the head.

"Ooooh yeah!" said the dog. At least I assume that was the drift of his doggy speech. He began to mount my leg. This was Israel. It was hot. I was wearing shorts.

"Mushi! *Shev!*" repeated the woman, not bothering to cast so much as a look in our direction. She searched in the fridge for milk, knowing my quirky English ways.

"You like that don't you?" panted Mushi, his doggy breath, short and fast. He grunted and thrust, a firm but gentle lover it seemed.

"Down boy!" There's a good doggy!" I urged him, pushing his forehead away.

"You want it rough? Woof, oooh yeah. I can give it to you *real* rough, baby" he seemed to say. I was becoming alarmed, and was concerned the dog might be, erm, *close*. In the nick of time my tea arrived and Mushi ran off to find himself another leg to mount.

During April a particularly vicious terror attack took place in the north of the country when a booby-trapped car exploded next to a school bus. Images of badly burned school girls haunted me for days afterwards, but it was just an appetiser for more to come. Days later a suicide bomber targeted yet another bus.

One night Avi woke me on his return from late shift. "*Dai*, Miss Reid!" he shouted gently, considerately shaking me awake and emptying a bucket of cold water over me.

"It's one o'clock in the morning" I replied gruffly, pushing away the electric cattle prod. Avi then dragged me out to the communal area of the flats where someone had left a sofa for the bin men. Still groggy with sleep I helped carry the sofa up the communal stairs, our tempers flaring as we attempted to negotiate corners. Lights went on in neighbouring flats.

"*Allo! Allo! Ma kara?*" yelled an irate neighbour. In the end it was worth the effort however, and we had a perfectly good faux leather sofa to show for our labours. This process was repeated over the months, earning us a new wardrobe, bed side table, kitchen table with matching chairs, and an arm chair. It also earned us the undying enmity of our neighbours, many of whom moved out or received counselling.

Apart from *Erev Shabbat,* my favourite evening was Thursday. I only taught until 7 that day and then Avi would meet me from work and drive to the Kanyon. This may sound like an exotic miracle of nature, a deep geological rift. It is in fact an Israeli term for shopping centre. We pulled up in the vast car park and I was always struck by something vaguely biblical about the surroundings with tall date trees looming over the car. Eucalyptus trees grew by a small brook, next to the car park. The air was always sweet and tropical and in winter there was a sharp fresh smell from the nearby orange groves. The whole area was given over to a sprawl of shopping complexes that stretched from the brook and the single track railway to the borders of Bnei Brak and to Ramat Gan. Huge neon signs in Hebrew advertised the supermarket chain of Super Sol, whilst others flashed in a variety of colours over Home Center, Toys'R'Us and an electrical outlet. I often felt unsure where I was. I could almost imagine myself in America at times. We needed to be searched before entering the mall and then we separated for half an hour or so. Avi went to look for CDs whilst I was free to browse the bookshop which sold a wide range of English titles, admittedly at much higher prices than in England. There was an upmarket Kapulsky café in the central court of the mall, and I looked hungrily at the fresh fruit and cream cakes, the chocolate pastries and pieces of savoury quiche in the glass cabinets. We then went through to Super Sol, an enormous hypermarket. There was something uniquely Israeli about the experience. The fruit counter was stocked with boxes of Israeli produce only. There were very few imports and therefore there was the joy of eating fruit in season. I savoured the smell of ripe pungent guava, as well as melon, banana and mango. There were crates of enormous water melons, so heavy they were hard to lift into the trolleys. It was common practice to help yourself to fresh yellow dates in order to sample them, and I often 'sampled' quite a few. This was also the case at the chocolate counter, where the shoppers shamelessly helped themselves to fistfuls of sweets, bringing the goodies to their germ-laden lips before thrusting their fingers back in for another 'sample.' They even encouraged their children to do this. People were sometimes sick, wiping the bile from their lips with the back of their hands, before rejoining the fray.

At the dairy counter were dozens of white cheese in tubs, but there was little in the way of harder cheese. Those which were on offer were usually yer-'avin'-a-larf-aintcha expensive, apart from the rubbery *gvina Americanit* or American processed cheese. On Thursday night the bakery began selling sweet braided *cholla* bread for the Sabbath as well as a square cholla which was more like traditional white bread. There were dozens of pastries, cakes and biscuits in tubs and on shelves. There were of course packaged biscuits and these were nearly all Israeli made. I missed English biscuits such as Digestives, Nice, Rich Tea or even Malted Milks. There was a long and unpleasant smelling delicatessen counter, with rubbery and jellified things on it which we both eschewed. There was no shellfish of course; it was entirely kosher.

I enjoyed browsing the dry good shelves and looking at the strangely retro range of Israeli toiletries. These included kosher soaps and various hand and face creams, all featuring drawn pictures of very old fashioned looking women. It reminded me of Bewitched. I felt I was in the 1950s and the eight gore skirt was back in fashion. After we had paid and loaded the car we often treated ourselves to chips at McDonalds, or else we drove straight home to prepare some of the delicious food we had bought.

April saw the arrival of the first *Chamsin*, a heat wave with high humidity and close grey skies. I hated this weather. My brain felt like it was boiling and I was sluggish and tired from lack of sleep. "It must break soon" grumbled locals at the bus stop. But it didn't. It dragged on and on. It was so hot people were putting their heads under the grill to cool off. When it did eventually break it was in the form of a dry thunder storm, followed by a light shower. Despite the 'break', the weather remained nauseatingly hot and muggy.

In May there was an historic agreement between the PLO and the Israeli government signed in Cairo. This had all the hallmarks of a stage managed gimmick, and was not a genuine peace between peoples. I hoped and prayed that it would lead to a true peace. I doubted it. Peace would only come when the Israelis and the Palestinians each had a state of their own, and when their interests were separated. I believed strongly in a two-state solution. Peace would not come by Balkanising Israel into a power-sharing hell. It would never work. Israel was fractured enough as it was; each group, whether religious or national was more concerned with the power it could secure for its own, rather than for the good of the nation. I did not believe that many Palestinians would wish to have Israeli style secularism forced on them either, and that they would prefer to forge their own identity in their own state. Peace would only come when everyone realised that fact. Attempts by the West to mediate a multi-cultural, cosy power-sharing Israel-Palestine were not appropriate to this conflict. This was a conflict about land and who owned what. Peace would come when both sides agreed on borders that were fair and viable, and agreed about resources for those states. This was already summed up in UN Resolution 242.

One issue that was being glossed over was that of the several million Palestinians in exile. The refugees maintained their right to return not only to the West Bank and Gaza but also to Israel under Resolution 194. This needed to be addressed early on in talks. I was tired of the softly softly approach, the let's wait and see attitude that was termed 'confidence building.' All this did was make both parties edgy and store up trouble for the future, as well as giving extremists a chance to derail the process through violence. Both peoples wanted to be nation states; both wanted to live with their own people, to feel safe together and to feel that their culture and way of life would be preserved. For the Jews, there was a need to never again be a minority in a hostile land. This was what Zionism was all about, and despite a wave of left-wing hatred, it remains a valid ideology. This is why Israel could not implement Resolution 194 and survive as a Jewish state. Without a state where they are a majority, the Jews would never be safe. Once the Palestinians grew to be a majority in Israel, the Israeli Jews would lose the power to control their own destiny. Jews outside Israel would loose their fall-back guarantee and their enemies would know it. If every Palestinian refugee were to return to the places where their grandparents had once lived then Israel as a Jewish state would die. I wanted those who supported UN Resolution 194 to come out and honestly say that. When the Resolution was passed in 1948 the number of refugees was but a fraction of the present number. An influx of up to 3 million Palestinian refugees into Israel-proper would bring a horrible civil war. Anyone with a grasp of basic Middle Eastern politics would agree. This was the reason Israelis opposed the right of Palestinian return. To force a one-state model on Palestinians and Israeli Jews would be to deny a basic reality about the nature of the two nations. The only hope was to share the land and to divorce, an ideology succinctly put forward by the Israeli peace activist and writer Amos Oz. The Palestinians would need to settle for a right of return to the Palestinian state only, just as the Jews must renounce Judea and Samaria.

Another source of concern for secular Israelis was the rise of Jewish fundamentalism. This was expressed in two distinct forms, the so-called *Haredim*, and the settler movement. The *Haredim* are split into pro-Zionist and anti-Zionist camps. *Haredim* are ultra-Orthodox Jews. They usually wear black suits, white shirts and homburg hats. Women usually wear ankle length skirts and have their hair in a net. They don't usually live in secular, or *chiloni*, communities so Israeli towns are divided into religious and secular areas. Most of Tel Aviv was secular, as was Ramat Gan. The settlers are similar to the *Haredim* but are often a bit freer in their clothing, and more political. Some of the very pious Jewish sects reject the state of Israel altogether and recognise the PLO as their legitimate government. Israel, they believe, will only be created with the arrival of the Messiah. In addition to the *Haredim* are the Modern Orthodox, whom Israelis describe as 'knitted kippa' referring to their more modern taste in skullcaps. These live all over Israel and are much more integrated.

The political landscape was horribly fractured. Each minority had a political party to represent its, and only its, needs rather than the needs of the nation as a whole. In order to create a viable majority in the Knesset either the Labour Party (*Avoda*) or the Likud needed to do some serious butt-worshipping, getting their tongues well and truly up the holy cracks of a range of extreme and repulsive parties. Simple acts like passing a budget required generous, disproportionate grants to religious communities, or agreeing to the religious coercion of the secular majority. As the Arab parties were never involved in the coalitions the rules of the game dictated that their communities got the short end of the straw when it came to grants. The Arab voters also made the error of always backing Labour, who took their votes for granted. The same was true of the Progressive Jewish community.

On the southern side of our housing estate or *Shikun* was a *Haredi* area. I enjoyed walking here on a Friday afternoon, when the whole place went slightly nuts preparing for the Sabbath. Rugs were hung and beaten over balconies; small boys with socks up to their knees and long *payot* ran riot as hysterical mothers yelled from windows. Men returned with last minute groceries, and bunches of wilted flowers and there was a distinct meaty smell hanging over the area. Here were small synagogues the size of living rooms with bright strip lighting. Bearded men were assembled and I could hear their prayers from the street.

Our own Sabbaths were slightly different and involved me going for a swim at the country-club-my-arse Leisure Centre on Friday afternoon. I loved the pool with its icy and oh so refreshing water. Occasionally a rather Androgynous and beefy Russian lady decided she would like to swim in straight lines very quickly and ploughed everyone else out of the water. I took a *Rumpole of the Bailey* out into the thick grass and lay on a lounger. A few feet away was the perimeter fence of the club and beyond that the orange groves. There was a stall selling ice creams, lollies and cheese rolls as well as drinks. After my swim I returned home and did my chores which involved mopping the tiled floors and mixing an *Angel Delight* which was our pudding. Sometimes I ate thick tuna sandwiches for lunch, the oil mixing with the white bread, then I enjoyed an episode of the *Brady Bunch* or the *Streets of San Francisco* before Avi came home.

Often I needed to nip down to the *Mecholet* or corner shop, which was located in a 1960s shopping precinct of run-down shops. These included a ghastly butcher that reeked of death and was always full of chicken feathers and bins of chicken feet and offal. There was also a couple of derelict shops which would have made ideal shooting galleries back home. Inside, the *Mecholet* was gloomy and cluttered. Industrial-style fridges with glass doors were full of flimsy yoghurt cartons so thin they bent to the slightest touch. The wine bottles were often dusty and the canned produced looked dated. It was like popping down to a *How-They-Lived-Yesterday* style of museum for some groceries. I half expected a woman in an ankle-length dress and Shaker headscarf to charge me admission.

Whilst I enjoyed Friday night, Saturday could drag. I devoted the morning to reading and perhaps a walk if it wasn't too hot. When Avi woke up we had a much bigger breakfast than usual, often on our crumbling balcony. This consisted of scrambled eggs, white cheese and cucumber salad. After, we had white bread with butter and *Silan*. Our coffee came from a huge tin and was extremely thin and powdery, more like floor-sweepings than coffee granules. If Avi was free we sometimes drove to the beach or to old Jaffa. Otherwise I was at the mercy of the TV and whatever was on. This was often very bad.

"That woman has just bitten the head off a snake" I thought, casually glancing up at the TV one Saturday afternoon, a cup of tea perched on my knee, and Jane Austen's *Pride and Prejudice* resting on the other. I almost dropped my sandwich. "Oh my God!" she really had just bitten the head off a snake. Horrified I looked more carefully. It was a documentary called *Assad's Women Soldiers*, a notorious exposé into the Syrian army and some of their less orthodox training methods. I had heard Avi talk about such a scene before but had never believed him. The cruelty of the Syrian army was legendary in Israel and I was terrified of anything to do with that country. During the Yom Kippur War there were just too many accounts of mutilations, eye gouging and other atrocities to dismiss out of hand. I shuddered with horror at the idea of being taken alive by them and pitied the tiny Jewish community left behind in Syria. It was against them that the fury of the humiliated regime was directed with Jewish families being forced to billet members of various Palestinian guerrilla movements in their homes. Syrian Jews were forbidden from leaving and if one family member needed to travel the others had to stay behind as a 'guarantee.' I changed stations.

One morning in June 1995 my new passport arrived. I looked at my details written in Hebrew and at the words *Israeli Citizen* in small print. On the front was the symbol of the state of Israel. I spent the rest of the day opening and closing it with pride. Despite the debacle of *Schlav Bet* perhaps I was Israeli after all. In my own peripheral way.

I was at work one morning in June 1995 when I heard the tell-tale sirens of police vehicles and my heart sank. I asked myself the usual questions of where, when, how many and turned on the radio. I was horrified when I heard the name Neveh Sharet, which was of course our housing estate. Dear God, it was getting closer all the time I exclaimed to myself. Then it became clear that we were not dealing with a bombing at all but rather a violent bank robbery at my own bank. Shots had been fired and one woman was hurt whilst drinking coffee on her *mirpesset* or balcony. I was shocked by this. I always enjoyed going to the bank here. For a start it was air-conditioned but more than that it felt normal and calm.

Although there had been no terrorist attack in Neveh Sharet the tentacles of violence came ever closer with a bomb on the number 20 bus in July 1995. There were two bus routes out of Neveh Sharet, the 20 and the 23. The 23 was the quickest as the 20 went round the estate for a good quarter of an hour. Both buses stopped at the Kanyon shopping mall and then continued to Ramat Gan and the Diamond Exchange where Berlitz was. That morning I was on time and caught the 23, and as I was teaching at another site I stayed on as far as the Central Bus Station. I didn't hear the news till I got home. A terrorist, (sorry a *militant*, force of habit) had tried to board the number 23 at the Kanyon but had just missed it, and as Israeli bus drivers take a perverse pleasure in not letting passengers on if they are a nanosecond late, the bomber boarded the number 20 just behind it. When the bus arrived at the Diamond Exchange, which was my usual stop, he had detonated himself at the centre of the bus, killing 5 and injuring many, many more. One of the victims had survived the Holocaust. I was now so freaked out by the attacks that I had taken to sitting either at the very front of the bus or at the rear as I figured I had a slightly better chance of survival that way. I had also written my ID card number on the inside of my shoe.

Shortly after the attack Prime Minister Yitzak Rabin arrived at the scene and was jeered by a large crowd of demonstrators. Israelis were sick and tired of seeing him make concessions to Arafat, despite the man's double dealing and tacit support of terrorism as a bargaining tool. It was clear that the slowly-slowly approach of the Oslo Accords was doomed. One big wrench was needed. The current approach was like a dentist trying to extract a wisdom tooth over a series of weekly appointments. The following month two more horrible attacks on buses occurred, provoking outrage. Anger was welling up in Israel. One morning at work I came into my classroom to discover that someone had written *Welcome ToThe Piece Process*, deliberately replacing *piece* for *peace*. Most of us felt strongly that the government should be protecting its citizens, and there was growing evidence that the attacks were happening with the support of Yassir Arafat, who was talking peace with one face and terror with the other. It was in such a climate the Israeli Right could reap rewards and play on people's fears. One night Avi suggested we go to a rally organised by the right wing parties to protest at the bombings. I decided to go, partly out of interest and partly out of genuine anger. By the time we arrived, Dizengoff Square was a sea of people. Hundreds and hundreds of flags were being waved and still more and more people were arriving from all over the country, in specially chartered coaches. Many, but not all of the protestors, were Orthodox Jews and many headscarfed women were pushing pushchairs with one hand and trying to carry placards with the other. As the march moved slowly off there was chanting. With so many people, progress was slow and the entire boulevard was crowded from pavement to pavement. I became aware of something unsavoury in the protest. It wasn't like the protest in Madrid after the bombing there. It wasn't an outpouring of grief. It was rather more a surge of anger against the left-wing government of Yitzak Rabin. Many of the placards contained pictures of Rabin with red, evil eyes. Some depicted a blend of Rabin with Arafat and Hitler. Then I heard a chant that was becoming both familiar and oddly catchy.

"*Ba dam va esh, Rabin nagaresh!*" they shouted again and again, the noise echoing off the Bauhaus buildings. This means "in blood and fire Rabin will be driven out." Many of the younger protestors were Yeshiva students and one of their favourite chants was *mavet le Aravim* (death to Arabs) or *Rotzim nekama* (we want revenge.) I began to feel very uncomfortable around these people and decided to leave, which was easier said than done, given the density of the crowd. The mood in Israel was turning very sour. People were sullen and seething. Protest was rife. A headline in a national daily revealed that the secret service or *Shabak* were concerned that there could be an assassination attempt on the Prime Minister. I dismissed this as nonsense and life carried on as normal despite the bombing and threats.

The grim domestic news was pushed aside briefly in September 1995 by the hijacking of an Iranian passenger plane to Israel. This was forced to land at the desert airport of Uvda near Eilat where the siege ended with the surrender of the hijacker, a rather desperate airline steward. The passengers were offloaded into the terminal and fed, oblivious to the fact that they were deep in the heart of evil, Zionist Israel. The steward was taken into custody. The plane was allowed to take off but only after the authorities spray painted a message asking for the whereabouts of missing Israeli airman Ron Arad. Arad had gone missing over Lebanon in the 1980s, was captured alive and then apparently 'sold' to Iran by Hizbollah. Iran Air ultimately decided not to renew the steward's contract.

"They've shot Rabin!"

In September the government signed Oslo 2, agreeing to more withdrawals from the occupied territories, and throwing fat on the fire. There were huge waves of protest and brooding talk of assassination and civil war. If the government wanted to evacuate settlements they needed to do so and to stop farting around, seeking approval. One evening in November 1995 I decided to go to bed early and Avi left for his night shift. There was nothing on TV except a rally celebrating a peace that hadn't materialised and which was, in my opinion, utterly premature. I curled up in bed with the cat at my side and began reading the latest Jeeves and Wooster story, which my mother had sent me. I sat still. I could feel something was wrong. After several years in Israel I had developed a freakily accurate sixth sense. I listened carefully. The TVs were on too loud. Then I heard car horns and, oddly, cheering. Had Israel been playing a football match somewhere I wondered. The phone rang. It was late, around 11.30. I starred at it for a moment. Then I picked it up. It was Avi.

"Andrew, it's me. They've shot Rabin." I was stunned and ran to turn on the TV. A tearful government official was standing outside Ichilov Hospital in Tel Aviv. Rabin was dead.

"Oh God! Oh God! Oh God!" I mumbled, feeling confused and disgusted. I flicked from channel to channel, with coverage on every TV station. Soon the events became clearer. Rabin had been on the stage with other members of the Israeli left and had sung the famous song *Shir HaShalom*, or song of peace, followed by the Israeli national anthem. He had then gone down some steps where a young man had been waiting for him, shooting him three times at point blank range. The following day

I took the bus to Kikar Malchei Israel where small groups of stunned Israelis had gathered. Many of them were sat around small mourning candles on the concrete. Some were weeping, others just looked empty. I went to the steps where Rabin had died and looked bleakly at the site. At work the atmosphere was heavy but I continued with lessons, making an effort to avoid discussing the killing with the students. Soon afterwards arrangements were made for a state funeral, and heads of states began to arrive from all over the world, resulting in the airport being closed down. TV was dominated by the news. Yet amongst the Right there was almost undisguised glee at the killing with Yigal Amir, the assassin, being lauded as a folk hero by some. Although as a rule of thumb I avoided discussing politics with Israelis I once asked Avi why Amir's family home wasn't going to be demolished. This was the standard response of the army after a Palestinian suicide bombing. If you've ever thrown a bottle of Vodka at a chip pan fire you can get a rough idea of the reaction this received. The Deputy Prime Minister Shimon Peres formed a temporary government but the forces of the Right were massing under Bibi Natanyahu, the charismatic youthful leader of the Likud. I quite fancied Bibi. I imagined being told to come into his office for a stern telling off. Meanwhile the Hizbollah in southern Lebanon began to bombard the north of the country, sensing weakness.

Whilst the violence and turmoil raged around me I knuckled down to my correspondence course in teaching English. This course would lead me to a Diploma, the next step in my career. Every month large folders arrived with assignments for me to complete, and I was required to begin some serious reading in the fields of linguistics, phonology and teaching.

One November morning Lola woke me up. She was behaving oddly, running and meowing. I drifted back to sleep but then awoke minutes later with the strangest sensation that I was vibrating. My initial reaction was that a heavy goods vehicle was reversing and was making the flat shake. The windows were rattling strongly and I noticed a glass of water sloshing gently.

"What the fuck?" I exclaimed suddenly leaping out of bed. I felt myself sway slightly. And then it stopped as suddenly as it had started. Later that morning I heard the word *re-adat adama* or earthquake repeated several times on the radio. It had been severe in the south, wrecking some hotels in Eilat and measuring 6.2 on the Richter Scale. I found this alarming. Israel has experienced some severe earthquakes in its history, notably when the entire town of Tiberias was destroyed hundreds of years ago. When I walked outside the flat it became clear how vulnerable it was, being built on stilts. I never slept quite as easily again after that.

Towards the end of the month the Israel army began fairly wide pullouts from the West Bank, provoking widespread protest on the Israeli Right and a volley of missiles from Lebanon. However one image I recall from that winter is that of Yigal Amir, Rabin's killer smiling sweetly from the dock during his trial. The man had no sense of shame but rather displayed the serenity of a martyr. This attitude was not helped by the creepy and widespread support he had received from some rabbis who were treating his murderous act as a *Mitzvah*, or religious obligation. There were sinister rumours and conspiracy theories about Rabin's death. Was it sanctioned by the secret service asked some newspapers? I think this was just the talk of journalists seeking to keep a story alive.

Israel felt like it was tearing itself apart, as the left-wing government forged ahead with widely unpopular peace talks with a duplicitous Syria. Meanwhile the forces of the religious Right were marshalling their forces, and engaging in some very, very unpleasant tactics. It was with relief that I flew home that Christmas and enjoyed a full two weeks away.

Shortly after my return to Israel in January 1996 I heard the news that a leading terrorist with the snazzy name of Yihyeh Ayash, or the 'engineer' as his mates called him, had been blown up. This had been done by the Israeli secret service using a call on his mobile. I wondered if his last words had been 'hello?' He was behind the deaths of nearly 70 Israelis and the maiming of hundreds more. He was a legitimate military target, but I was worried that, like Medusa, there was plenty more where he came from. The attitude of some in the West annoyed me. I imagined fuming armchair liberals in Hampstead saying "Hey, terrorists have rights too!" The British media complained that he should have been tried. The hypocrisy of this was breathtaking and for once I did not argue when Avi denounced Britain. The words 'Shoot to kill' and 'Internment' sprang to mind. It seemed the *Guardian* and *Independent* were stuck in some idealised fair-play naïve fantasy. The Jewish people had every right to take military action to defend themselves. It was ridiculous to expect the Israeli police to produce an arrest warrant for the man. Any attempt at an arrest would have resulted in the death of Israeli troops, a needless sacrifice for the sake of a legitimate target. The government would have been criminally negligent if they had not fought back. However my concern was justified when a dual suicide bombing occurred soon after, on the number 18 bus in Jerusalem and at Ashkelon killing 27. A week later a second bomber chose the same bus route at the same place and at the same time. A few days later I was sat on the bus on my way to work. At the Diamond Exchange a group of female soldiers boarded with a sniffer dog. They walked the length of the bus, allowing the dog to sniff the passengers and under the seats before getting off. Not a word was said. No one looked at each other. I did feel reassured by this but I am not sure how effective it would be if they had actually rumbled a suicide bomber.

Soldier: "Excuse me sir, what do you have under your jacket?"

Suicide Bomber: "Cor blimey officer you've got me banged to rights. I'm a human bomb."

Soldier: "Yes, well I am afraid I am going to have to place you under arrest."

Suicide Bomber: "Yes officer. I understand officer. I'll come quietly."

No, if I had been a suicide bomber I think I might have decided that the arrival of sniffer dogs and some nubile girl soldiers was as good a time as any. During this period a ghastly set of urban myths began to circulate. One of the most grotesque was that of the smiling bomber. I heard this from a few sources and therefore began to believe it. According to the story, the suicide bomber would open up his jacket to reveal his bomb, and for a split second smile at the victims before blowing himself up. Another story was that the bomber would whisper a warning to any Arabs a few seconds before. Surely a bomber would be too nervous and crazed to bother with such social niceties, I thought.

Incredibly the government agreed to a mass release of prisoners in an attempt to kick start the peace process, not only releasing less risky prisoners but also men convicted of violent acts. Meanwhile Israelis responded to the bombings by donating blood by the tanker-load. One story that intrigued me was the issue of Ethiopian blood. One of the largest waves of immigration to arrive in Israel were the black Jews of Ethiopia. Their integration was proving difficult and for many of the older generation it was profoundly traumatic. Suicide was common. The new immigrants were housed in trailer parks in the desert to preserve some feeling of community. Nevertheless the Ethiopian Jews were loyal and devoted citizens and the younger ones were earning a name for themselves in the army. The government was anxious not to cause any offence, but it was leaked that the Ministry of Heath was throwing Ethiopian blood away. This was because of the high incidence of HIV. The Ethiopian community, furious at the cover up, demanded to know why they were not simply asked to stop donating blood.

In March a suicide bomber blew himself up near the Dizengoff Centre, on a pedestrian crossing, killing 13 and wounding hundreds. The bombing was timed to spoil the festival of Purim and the aim had been to kill as many children in fancy dress as possible. This sickened me to the core.

I think there was a great deal of hypocrisy in the European judgement of Israel. America and Britain reacted strongly after the 9/11 and 7/7 bombings, but in 1995 neither of those countries had ever experienced terrorism on the scale that Israel was suffering. Per capita Israel was experiencing worse than July 7th every single week. The weekly death toll was sickening. What was the point of having a free Jewish nation if we were to die like dogs every Sunday morning asked many Israelis. Soon it was only too easy to find those who knew someone who had been killed. There was growing rage and anger as the attacks were happening almost at will. Meanwhile the BBC refused to use the word terrorist when reporting the attacks. They used the word *militant* instead, unless of course it was Britain who was the victim. I don't remember talk of IRA militants.

There was a sickening routine to the attacks. I first became aware of louder than usual radios, usually around 8 in the morning. Then there was a spate of phone calls to check if anyone I knew had been harmed, followed by hours of sickening TV footage. This became utterly distressing. Israeli TV doesn't hold back. I would see an aerial view of a blown-up bus with dozens of sheets around it, many with shoes or bare feet sticking out. This distressed me more than anything; the shoes. Posh high heel shoes, tatty trainers, children's shoes, sandals, all strewn on the ground. Often there were people hanging limp from blown out windows or bags of shopping strewn on the tarmac. If it was a market bombing most of the victims would be middle aged or elderly women, and there was always the ghastly, blood-curdling screams of the wounded and shocked. Young paramedics with their Magen David Adom high-visibility jackets were scattered around the scene of carnage, patching up wounds and loading victims into fleets of large American ambulances. There was a constant yak-yak of sirens and horns, and shouted commands in Hebrew. Later came the Orthodox Jews, also in high-visibility jackets, but this time crawling along the road or inside the shell of the bus with paint scrapers and plastic bags. Their concern was to make sure that every scrap of human flesh was given a decent burial. If the bombing was in Tel Aviv the news crews would switch to a place called Abu Kabir, a name which still makes me shudder. Here distraught relatives crowded around the doors of the forensic laboratory waiting for news. By the time it was evening the news was very much focused on the political impact of the attacks and news of any leads or action to be taken. All comedy programmes were cancelled and the radio would play sad or at least subdued music for a few days. As the attacks continued this was reduced to a day or so, otherwise there would be nothing cheerful on TV at all.

In total 60 people had died in terror attacks in two months. Israel had been created to prevent the slaughter of Jews. It seemed as though the government was betraying that basic principle by not taking the action needed to eliminate the terrorists. It was clear that action could be taken to clear the terror bases and wipe out the various cells but such action would lead to a rupture in relations with the new 'Peace Partners' and would incur the wrath of the Americans. For this reason the public were starting to hold the government very much responsible. In a clumsy attempt to deflect this, the government launched operations against *Hizbolla* in Lebanon rather than *Islamic Jihad* and *Hammas* who were operating from the Palestinian areas and in Syria. One tragic result of this was the slaughter of innocent civilians at Kana in Lebanon when the army struck the wrong target.

To relax, Avi and I started watching a new American TV comedy called *The Nanny* staring Fran Drescher. Every day before Avi left for his late shift, and before I went to Berlitz for evening classes, we made coffee and pastries and sat down to watch Fran. Fran was the zany nanny to the terribly stuffy and English Mr Sheffield and his three children. Watching *The Nanny* was serious business; we took the phone off the hook, pulled the *trissim* down and let ourselves be transported to a magical world without violence. Here there was just joy and sex and hilarious misunderstandings about what happened when American Jews fell in love with English gentiles.

In May elections were held to replace the government of Yitzak Rabin. Everyone knew it would be bitter and close. The main opposition contender was the suave former war hero Bibi bend-over-for-a-vigorous-spanking Natanyahu for the Likud. The Left was represented by the dovish Shimon please-be-nice Peres. Whilst Rabin had been seen as a strong leader, Peres was seen as weak and naïve. For the first time in Israeli history electors would vote directly for the Prime Minister, and then cast a second vote for a party. And for the first time in Israeli history I voted.

In the weeks before the elections we were bombarded with party political broadcasts and there were posters and leaflets on every tree and lamp post. The TV commercials made Avi scream and rant, especially when he heard the jingle *Israel chazaka im Peres*, meaning *Israel is strong with Peres*. There was a huge range of parties to choose from including *Chadash*, a Jewish-Arab Communist party, *Tzommet* who proposed the 'transfer' of Arabs, and the religious and populist *Shas* who were standing on the give-us-all-your-money-and-we'll-tell-you how-to-behave platform. There was a wide range of creepy religious parties who reminded me of political whores, selling themselves to the highest bidder. *Meretz* promised to rid Israel of religious coercion, presumably by jumping straight back into bed with *Shas*. On the morning of the election Avi drove us both to Neveh Sharet, where we registered to vote, and my name was crossed off the list. I selected a little piece of paper with my choice of candidate's name and dropped it in the box. Then I went to give my mad Turkish student a lesson. Bibi squeezed in by

30,000 votes. One of them was mine. Despite the jingle I did *not* think Israel was strong with Peres.

In June I returned to Edinburgh. On the way back I stopped in London for a few days, dropping into an *Erev Shabbat* service at West London Synagogue. It was wonderful to be back in the cool, reverential sanctuary, listening to the soothing organ music. Oh the style! The decorum! An incredibly so-posh-the-Queen-would-feel-like-a-bag-lady-in-her-company woman came up to light the Sabbath candles. After she had lit them a huge blast of organ and a deafening *amen* from the choir almost blew the Ascot-races hat off her head. I had the distinct feeling that I was not Their Kind Of Person in my trainers and jeans. I was always going to be on the fringes of Anglo-Jewry but it took me a long time to realise that fact. I was a convert. I was gay. It was going to take a lot of hard work.

Back in Israel I saw a very different face of Judaism, when *Haredi* protestors in Jerusalem began once again to stone cars driving on the Sabbath. Why didn't the police stop them, I screamed at the TV? I felt like I was living in *The Life of Brian*.

One news story which dominated that summer was the issue of foreign workers living in Israel illegally. I had been aware of this issue for a long time but the extent of it surprised me, with the number estimated at nearly quarter of a million. Many of the workers lived in the unpleasant and poor areas of south Tel Aviv. I had always hated this area, with its poorly paved streets, depressing and shabby flats and concrete houses. It was dirty, with the *trissim* or plastic blinds caked in soot. The houses and flats were densely built up, and a forest of aerials, water tanks and rusty air-conditioning devices stabbed into the skyline. Here I saw dozens of Chinese and African men, walking aimlessly on Shabbat. Sometimes the men brought their families with them, but despite their numbers, the children had little access to education or health care. The government was playing a disingenuous game by turning a blind eye to the problem, preferring a bank of non-Arab labour to fall back on when it decided to seal the West Bank. It is virtually impossible to get in and out of Israel undetected. The government therefore had precise statistics about who was in the country and why.

The illegal immigrants lived completely separate to the rest of society, remaining unseen and uncounted.

Behind the wheel of a car Israelis can be lethal, a fact which became soberingly clear in 1996, with record traffic accident fatalities. I had many arguments with Israeli drivers about the dangers of speeding. Avi responded by citing the dangers slow drivers posed, 'forcing' fast ones to overtake. The carnage got so extreme, and the culture of death-defying driving so entrenched, that a new two-pronged campaign of tough policing and graphic warnings was launched. This was about as popular as dog shit on an Axminster yet the number of Israelis dying on the roads far outstripped the numbers killed in terrorism or even all out war. No-one took the slightest bit of notice. I saw a huge poster bill-board with the slogan *ima mechaka babayit* (mum is waiting at home). This was supposed to guilt-trip drivers into slowing down. Wrapped around the support of the billboard were the crushed remains of a Fiat Punto. There is a joke about an American tourist who takes a taxi in Israel. To her horror, the driver speeds through every red light. Suddenly he brakes at a green one. "Why did you stop?" she finally asks the driver. "What, are you crazy? The other driver had a red light. We could have been killed!"

One way of ensuring I could have a bit of alone time abroad was by scheduling my return trips to Scotland with airlines other than El Al. It was often as cheap to fly to Scotland via Paris or Prague as it was through London. For this reason I found myself on a KLM flight to Amsterdam very, very late one rainy December night. I was going to spend two whole days in Amsterdam with my friend Andrew and was relishing the fun time to come. We were soon airborne and as it was just after 3 a.m. the normally boisterous Israeli passengers were falling asleep like dopey bees in a beehive, giving me some peace. This flight was beginning to drag I decided, half an hour after take off. I tried a variety of positions in order to get comfortable in my aisle seat. The cabin crew were just beginning the coffee service, and I was just enjoying a pleasant stretch, when I heard a gasp. I looked up to see, in slow-motion, a turquoise uniform containing a stewardess stagger forward, a huge pot of coffee flaying in each hand. She broke her trip by skilfully, crash landing with both elbows onto the front of the seat in front of me. She slowly turned. She wasn't any old stewardess but rather the Chief Purser and she wasn't looking happy.

"Dat vosh very, very dangerous shir" she hissed, her wide face flushed. "Put your feet away dit minute!" Cringing with shame I complied and tried to watch the in-flight entertainment. This consisted of pictures of large swans splashing into water and a repetitive documentary about diamonds. There was a little display showing the flight's progress and we were just over the south of Italy. I was too tired to read. I was sure I detected a smirk when one of the crew said "For coffee?" quickly every time she walked past. In fact *was* that what she was saying? By the time the little plane on the screen was over Cologne I was bored senseless, but we were soon below the clouds and I got my first glimpse of the flat Dutch countryside. I felt a pang. I wished with all my heart that this was the end of my journey, that I was coming home here and not just passing through. As the passengers disembarked into the bitterly cold dawn our passports were checked on the tarmac by a group of no-nonsense Dutch immigration officers. There had been a spate of asylum seekers destroying their documents in the short distance between plane and passport desk. This meant they could refuse to say where they were from and therefore not get sent back there. With the new system anyone who didn't measure up would go straight back onto the plane. At immigration we needed to present our passports again. I proudly took out my spanking new Israeli passport for the first time, and joined the non-EU passport queue. As EU citizens were waved through with little more than a glance, I savoured my extra minutes of martyrdom as the immigration officer ran the details through her computer.

I took one of the yellow double decker trains to the city centre, shivering from fatigue and cold. I drank in the sight of my favourite city as the train approached Amsterdam, admiring the neatness and cosiness of the modern flats. At Centraal Station I caught a tram to the Rembrantsplein, smiling to myself at the noises and sights around me. The journey brought back a flood of memories of happier holidays. I felt at home. Everything inside me begged to stay forever. I checked into the smart hotel and was told the room would be ready at midday, giving me the whole morning to kill before I could have a red hot shower and a delicious snooze in crisp clean sheets. It was still half dark as I wandered reverentially along the canals, soaking in the atmosphere of the medieval buildings. I went to the pleasant museum café of the former church on Dam Square and sipped creamy, strong coffee and nibbled a spicy ginger biscuit. At lunch time I returned to the hotel to meet Andrew and freshen up. He was on top form and greeted me with a bitchy put-down. Soon we were wandering around the Red Light District, tittering like school girls. We had lunch at a café near the Stock Exchange and Andrew ordered a large plate of shell fish. It looked delicious. I mentioned I was tempted and Andrew asked why I didn't eat some. I explained about Kashrut, to which he tutted scornfully. "Eat what you want. Life's too short." I was tempted but didn't, the taboo feeling too strong to break yet.

After a rest in the hotel, and a restorative cup of Dutch coffee, we were ready for more sightseeing. In the evening we enjoyed a slap-up Indonesian meal with bottles of beer and we then went to a cheerful Hash Coffee shop. Andrew ordered a big spliff to take away and I took a deep puff. Just to be sociable. I coughed like a man of eighty and then tried another draw. Nothing; I felt nothing. The beer however had made us both giggly, and we staggered up and down the Damrak, finding everything inexplicably funny, especially the look of alarm on tram drivers' faces as we veered onto the tracks. The following morning we both felt repentant and ill but we travelled to Haarlem by train, enjoying the bright, frosty weather. In the evening we once again got pissed, this time on wine. All too soon our holiday was over and the following morning I travelled alone to Schipol airport, catching the first tram of the morning from the hotel.

I had a pleasant Christmas as usual. After New Year it was time to return to Israel once again via Amsterdam. Although I had a long gap between flights the brief visit felt strange. Andrew was not there, I had no cheery hotel to rest in and the weather was bitterly cold. The canals had frozen in the centre of Amsterdam and I walked the gloomy streets feeling cold to my core and profoundly depressed. I wanted to stay here. I felt so much at home. I paid a visit to the gay and lesbian bookshop to stock up on postcards and souvenirs, mementos to remind me of this place when I went back to my life in Israel. I ate a sandwich of strong, ripe *Oude Kaas* cheese and had a couple of coffees to warm me up at a canal side café, before deciding to head back to the airport. It was late and the airport was harshly lit. I was tired. I was fed up. I heard the clamour of Hebrew. I saw the security staff asking passengers questions. I toyed with a little rainbow flag I had in my pocket, then I went into the waiting area. Beyond the window a huge Iran Air flight to Tehran was waiting to take off. How odd travel was I thought. You can be in Amsterdam, with its gay bars and liberal laws and democracy and yet within seven or eight hours you could be in Iran with its beheadings, floggings and hangings for homosexuality. I shuddered. Five hours later Avi greeted me at the gate in Tel Aviv. It felt kind of nice to be home.

"Rivka, Mrs Slocombe's Pussy is soaking wet!"

One day our rent went up and Avi went puce. It did seem a tad excessive for what we were renting. As Avi had been promoted and I was bringing in money from Berlitz we decided to move away from Neve Sharet to the posher and more central Ramat Gan. We went to see a ground floor flat, at the top of our budget. I loved it as soon as the tall, young women opened the door. The ground floor flat was roomy and open plan with a huge kitchen and a balcony about a foot off the ground. The lush garden provided shade and an exotic scent pervaded the rooms, a mixture of rain and guava. I half imagined Tattoo from *Fantasy Island* to appear from behind a rose bush, muttering something about a 'plane' and calling me 'boss.'

We signed the lease and a few weeks later we were stacking boxes next to the car for the first of several drives across town. My body was aching, when four hours later we paused for a very kosher falafel at the outdoor stand in Bnei Brak, the Ultra Orthodox town adjoining Ramat Gan and Tel Aviv. Around 1 a.m. we locked the door of our flat in Neve Sharet for the last time and loaded a very nervous Lola into her basket.

I loved the new flat. I also loved the area. When I had free time I went on long night-time walks along the well-to-do streets, admiring the huge detached villas and gardens with their marble pathways, palm trees and red roofs. I became a flaneur again. As spring came the nights were scented with pollen and blossom and I relished the gentle evening warmth on my skin. After an hour, or even two, of walking, I returned home and sank into the sofa for some TV. If I was lucky I got to see some British programmes, which became a window on home; they served as a reminder that England was still there waiting for me. I found this a great comfort. I enjoyed the refined manners and gentle humour of *Keeping Up Appearances* and the monstrous Hyacinth Bucket. It may sound incredibly sad but that programme helped to keep me sane. For 30 minutes I was transported to Middle England. Another favourite was *Are You Being Served?* which became "*Mishu Metapel Bach*" in Hebrew. Avi also loved this, and often we watched it together. I enjoyed sharing part of my own culture with him, and he told me how it was shown repeatedly during the 1973 Yom Kippur War, to cheer people up. This seemed a bit weird. The largest tank battle since El Alamein was raging a few miles away, and Golda Meir was seriously considering using nuclear weapons but meanwhile everyone was chuckling over Mrs Slocomb's Pussy, which isn't even rude in Hebrew. They just translated it as "cat" in the subtitles.

Elderly Israeli TV viewer in 1973: "Rivka, Rivka, put that gas mask down a second. The hairs on Mrs Slocomb's cat are standing on end because it's cold. What strange pets these English have. Chortle."

I enjoyed Avi's tales of growing up in the seventies, as it was a form of living history. He told me about eating satsumas with his brothers on the balcony on Yom Kippur, whilst everyone was listening to the news of the joint Egyptian and Syrian attacks and all able-bodied men ran to the bus stops. When he was older he remembered brothers coming home on leave and his sister going AWOL from the army. His dad had to drive her to the police station.

I soon discovered two more favourite places in Ramat Gan. One was Givat Napoleon, an odd hill with a flat table top surface, covered some olive trees and gorse bushes. At dusk I came here to watch the sky turn first pink and then purple. There were beautiful views over Tel Aviv and Ramat Gan. The Yarkon river was visible below. My other favourite place was the usually deserted riverside walk. Here there were tall reeds, Eucalyptus trees and cacti. There were huge Aloe Vera plants and, in spring, wild flowers. I often walked at dusk although it was not advisable to walk there at night. At one point the river forked and it was here where the deserted remains of some Arab houses stood, little more than ruined shells. A student told me how he had once seen an elderly Arab man walking around the area, looking for the remains of the home he had left in 1948. The river calmed down in the spring. In the winter however, it became a truly frightening torrent, rising so high that it engulfed both ends of an arched pedestrian bridge, leaving a bow in the middle of the bubbling brown water. One morning I was jogging by the river when I saw a particularly peckish-looking snake slither across my path. It was at least four foot long. I never frolicked bare foot in the grass again after that. Time permitting I would cross the Ayalon and enter the expansive public park beyond. This stretched for miles and was a pleasant place to stroll. Often large Arab families came here to eat picnics, and it was a pleasant reminder that coexistence was possible.

Soon after we moved, Berlitz announced that they were opening a new school in Ramat Gan and I jumped at the chance to transfer. The new school was even swisher than the first and was located in a smart shopping mall next to the Diamond Exchange. Here we had a pleasant teacher's room with a kitchenette, and there was a large reception area with leather sofas. The rooms were airy and all of them had windows overlooking the Ayalon motorway and beyond that, Tel Aviv. I was now able to walk to work, which was a treat. It was great not to dice with death on the bus. However, the walk to work was often unbearably hot, and I had to pace myself. I felt like I was in one of those Foreign Legion films and would arrive at work gasping for water and seeing visions. One day I passed a cyclist who was shouting and repeatedly smashing his bike against the windscreen of the 23 bus; I think there had been a slight difference of opinion vis-à-vis lane discipline. No-one seemed the slightest bit bothered. I often worked till nine or even ten at night so by then the walk home was a delight, especially as I could stop off at the all-night Iraqi bakery. Huge trays of freshly baked *Bourekas* were laid out, giving off a heavenly scent. There were doughnuts and mini pizzas and larger cheese filled pasties, made with sour Arab cheese rather than yellow, so-called American cheese. I usually had a couple of small *Bourekas* and ate them as I walked, hot from the paper bag, which became almost see-through from the grease.

I was fascinated by the rusty and dusty *Elite* Chocolate and Coffee factory, near the Diamond Exchange. I often passed it on my way to and from the bus stop, and was always struck by the sweet smell of melted chocolate. The industrial architecture hinted at danger and mystery. Behind the huge, rusty iron gates were rows of tankers, and huge round cylinders full of milk or cacao. There was a sense of nostalgia for the idealism and creativity of the 1950s and 1960s when the factory was built. It reminded me strongly of Socialist Realism art. For a while this was popular in Israel during the 1950s and early 1960s. Bank notes, stamps and public buildings featured pictures of proud, muscular workers and farmers. Nearer home I cut through a little park, smelling strongly of catnip and hibiscus and piss. Here stray cats watched me, their eyes glinting in the darkness. Soon I was home and it was time to have a milky coffee and hear how Mrs Slocomb's cat had ended up sopping wet again. A wet cat? What's funny about that?

I enjoyed my rest period in the afternoons, between the morning and the evening class. If Avi was resting before work we had lunch together, often avocado and cheese and some of his mother's rice. We then had lemon tea, made from powder, some of Avi's mum's homemade date pastry and then we settled down to watch *The Bold and The Beautiful* in Italian on cable TV. This was a camp treat, as we enjoyed laughing at the terrible acting and at the unbelievable story lines. It invariably involved either one of us impersonating the big-haired, massive shoulder-padded women, and screeching with laughter. However our favourite programme was *Sappir,* an awful Israeli soap opera that really did deserve cult status. In each fifteen minute episode the tragic, female heroine was double-crossed, cheated, dumped, bitch-slapped and informed that she was adopted, terminally ill and/or the incestuous product of a previously unknown relative. During the whole fifteen minutes the unfortunate woman, wailed, screamed, sobbed and shouted and my Hebrew improved noticeably. I wasn't able to read the newspaper or to translate the news but I certainly knew the Hebrew for "your sister is actually your mother and she's pregnant with your child. Oh and by the way I opened this letter from the doctor and you should have actually died last week." This helped my integration into Israeli life enormously.

When Avi was on his nightshift I often walked to a tiny, dusty, cluttered shop on the main road. Here the owner used to smile and greet me with a cheery shalom, which made a change, and I used to engage in my favourite vice. I would spend some of my secret money on a huge water melon and go home and eat the whole thing. I then spent the following twelve hours urinating. I loved that little shop with its dusty tins and peeling adverts; it was like a time warp. I came home just in time to watch *Drop The Dead Donkey*, another British sitcom, set in a TV news station. I enjoyed its liberal, left-wing humour.

Sometimes I walked a bit further and got to Rechov Jabotinsky. Here the atmosphere was more urban and there was a strong Iraqi feel. Ramat Gan had become home to thousands of Iraqi Jewish refugees in the 1950s when they had been expelled by the *Ba'ath* party, with their property stolen by the regime. One shop was filled with sacks, overflowing with bright-coloured spices and powders, the air thick with the smell of curry and turmeric. Next door was a falafel bar with metal tubs of fried aubergine, grated cabbage and jars of wickedly spicy sauce. The falafel was always crispy to bite and moist inside, and I always made numerous trips to top up from the salad bar. There was a small sex shop in Ramat Gan, located in a deserted mall next to a cinema. This fascinated me, and it was weird to see the word Sex Shop written in Hebrew. This was one shop I never went in, as it looked unwelcoming and I didn't really need any vibrators or over-priced knee high leather boots. They were so last season.

Ramat Gan means *Garden Heights* in Hebrew, and the original 1920s settlement was built on the gentle hills, just beyond the town centre. When the town was first built the residents refused to have any shops, as they felt it would let the tone down. What a silly, snooty thing to do. I can just see a bunch of Zionist pioneers sitting around in splendid isolation, cursing themselves because they had forgotten to get the milk.

Zionist Pioneer 1: "I think we should review the no-shops rule comrades!"

Zionist Pioneer 2: "No, shops represent the bourgeois Ghetto Jew life we came here to escape. No shops!"

Zionist Pioneer 1: "We're out of loo paper as well comrades."

Zionist Pioneer 2: "OK. But just one *socialist* and Zionist shop."

The week had its highlights. Three or four nights a week we would eat together at the table and had our regular favourite dishes. Sometimes

Avi prepared *Malawach*, which were mouth-watering-gut-busting puff pastry pancakes served with a spicy tomato coulis and a hardboiled egg. We also had homemade chips and Israeli fishfingers at least once a week.

My favourite day was of course Friday, when I only worked a half-day. There was a pleasant relaxed feeling, with most people already off work and a purposeful bustle in the air. Supermarkets were busy with pre-Sabbath shoppers and car radios played chilled out Hebrew classics. Berlitz closed at 12 o'clock and I then went home to prepare for the Sabbath, washing the tiled living room floor and tidying up. I often experimented with my cooking on this day, referring to my cherished English cookery books. I also made up a pudding from my carefully counted packets of Angel Delight or Crème Caramel, which I brought back in bulk after holidays home. After this I spent some time relaxing over lunch and watching American cop shows. I often lay on my bed and read or else went for a walk by the river or to the park. I missed the Country Club in Neveh Sharet. I always lit the candles at dusk and we drank some cheap wine with our meal. After dinner Avi made a cocktail, and we would eat some crisps and watch the evening film. In the morning I stretched and enjoyed my only lie in of the week, listening to the chorus of birds and crickets from the semi-tropical garden. We lingered over breakfast, enjoying our cholla and cheese, or eggs. Sometimes we went for trips in the car, sometimes we went to the beach at Tel Aviv, and sometimes we stayed at home.

One Friday evening when I went for a late afternoon pre-Sabbath dinner walk, I noted a small synagogue that was emptying out. What struck me was the presence of women and men socialising together and that some people were getting into cars. The following evening I walked back and noted the name of the congregation. It was called *Emet va Ahava*, Truth and Love, and to my joy I read that it was *Mitkademet* or Progressive. I was surprised by this as I had never heard of it before. The following Friday I gingerly decided to go along. It was a lovely congregation. Almost immediately people came to chat with me and the service was lively, a Jewish version of "happy clappy" with the rabbi strumming a guitar. Afterwards there was a *Kiddush* with some delicious *bourekas* and *cholla*, and small cups of sickly grimace-inducingly sweet *Palwin* wine. I came home to a very grumpy Avi, waiting for his dinner so I got into the habit of bringing him home some *bourekas* or a slice of cake. I returned to the synagogue fairly often, sometimes on a Saturday morning but usually on a Friday night, which was softer and less Torah based. I have never really enjoyed Shabbat morning services which, as Rabbi Lionel Blue once so rightly said, stretch like bubble gum.

There is a joke about this. Three rabbis all discovered they had an infestation of rats in their synagogues. The first rabbi said he had managed to get all of the rats into a trap, had put them in his car and had driven them a hundred miles away. When he returned the rats were there again. The second rabbi said that he had the same problem, had also managed to trap them into a container and had driven them a hundred and fifty miles away. When he returned the same rats were there in the synagogue. The third rabbi told them his solution. He invited each of the rats up to say a blessing over the torah reading. Four hours later all of them had fled and he hadn't seen any of them since. After three or four Shabbat morning services, entirely in Hebrew, I had had enough. There were only so many hours of watching spotty nervous teenagers stumbling over a scroll reading I could take. On one occasion we even had to say prayers for a member who was about to go to California on holiday.

When we went on an excursion we always left early. I enjoyed being driven through Israel. I loved watching the passing countryside and cityscapes. It was good to see parts of the country that I had never visited before. On one trip we drove to a place called the *Muchraka*, a shrine to the prophet Elijah, looking down over the valley below. Sometimes we visited Druze villages in the Galilee. On these occasions we had lunch in local cafes where we were served huge *mezzes* of dips and pitta. We always came back eye-wateringly late from these outings and I became worn out by the lack of sleep. Insomnia was becoming a problem again. Israeli nights are muggy and close. I often lay on a crumpled sheet in the double bed with Avi's dulcet snoring in my ear, unable to sleep. The more I tried the hotter and stickier I became. Most Israelis have a very laid back attitude to sleep, a result of their army years. Part of their training is sleep deprivation, and it is common for recruits to sleep less than five hours a night for up to a week. They then spend their entire Sabbath leave asleep. This is all very well if you are in a crack commando unit. Personally I didn't want to incorporate this pattern into my own life, needing my 7-8 hours, especially as lessons at Berlitz often usually began early on Sunday morning. I felt like an extra in the 1999 adventure horror classic, *The Mummy*. My eyes were becoming so sunken and black that I looked like a panda after a particularly nasty pub fight.

I gave mostly private lessons in the morning and I found this exhausting. As usual it involved being closeted in a small classroom with an ego-inflated business man. I needed to at least try to get some coherent response to my questions, in order to correct them. What was unpleasant about some businessmen was their openly prejudiced attitudes and their willingness to act on their prejudices. Some candidly told me they never promoted women because they got pregnant; the women that is, not the businessmen. Another student managed an Orthodox run bank; he didn't employ men who weren't married because they were 'more liable to move on.' He also told me he had sacked someone for being camp. "It's a family business" he shrugged, smiling. I was still unsure about how "out" I could be. I was working for a company that cared about its profit margin and not the sensibilities of its teaching staff. I gritted my teeth and mercilessly corrected his use of the Present Perfect tense.

At 10.00 I usually taught classes made up mostly of women. Once I had a class of only Ultra Orthodox women. I loved teaching them, enjoying their zest for learning and getting a buzz from their sense of fun. I think they were mostly there in order to get out of the house but at Berlitz prices it may have been cheaper to meet up for a coffee or twenty, or even to buy a café. All of them wore wigs and part of the deal was that the doors in the school were made of glass. This was in case I got any funny ideas and made a gotta-get-me-a-feel-of-that lunge for their breasts or pinched their comely buttocks. This was also the case for lessons given by female teachers to Orthodox men, although I do think there is an element of self-flattery by ageing, obese, bearded men who think that a pert young female teacher would for one moment feel anything akin to sexual attraction for them.

Nubile Gentile Teacher 1: "Cor cop a load of that Susan."

Nubile Gentile Teacher 2: "Phoar bloody hells bells, it's that Rabbi Mendele Schneerson of Brooklyn."

Nubile Gentile Teacher 1: "Here isn't that him with the twelve inch beard?"

Nubile Gentile Teacher 2: "I don't know about that but he can come and bless my mezuzahs any day I can tell you."

Avi and I were starting to fight more and more. I spent most of my time in my room, my haven. On one wall I attached all my postcards of Amsterdam. I had decided that one day I would live there, alone if I needed, as Avi was dragging his feet. Amsterdam became my symbol of a new life and new hope. One day, somehow, I would leave here and get there. One postcard showed a sharp corner at a junction of three canals. It was dark and frosty and the canals were lit by a magical collection of lights. I meditated on that corner, willing myself to be there, to float away. My room also contained my books, things which Avi hated because he felt they were dusty. I love books. I love seeing them lined upon shelves, their titles resonating throughout the room. Avi wanted me to put them in a drawer. It was getting petty.

To keep out the heat and light I closed the typical Israeli blinds, known as *velonim*. These became incredibly dirty very quickly. Outside were bushes and palm trees that provided more shade and I heard birds singing in the lazy heat. Every day I threw bread soaked in milk to the dozens of feral cats which lived between the houses and which made a pitiful sight. On a few occasions I discovered dead kittens by the roadside, and contacted the *Tza'al Ba'alay Chaim* or Israeli RSPCA.

"If they are dead, what can I do?" asked the lady at the other end of the phone, pragmatically.

Our lease stipulated that we keep the garden tidy, a task I usually enjoyed. However, next door lived the elderly, and batty, owner's mother. The owner himself lived in California, funded in part by our rent money. The old lady often peered out of the window at me when I was in the garden. She had an endearing habit of watching me work, then telling what I was doing wrong. She ingratiated herself further by ending each sentence with "it's not your house you know, it doesn't belong to you." Everytime I went outside I could see her werewolf eyes glinting in the gloom through her *velonim*.

I liked our street with its well kept gardens, palm trees and highly individual houses. It was quiet and located off a much busier main road known as Abba Hillel. One day I was washing our car when I heard a sound which froze me to my core. Rigid, the hairs on my neck on end, I listened as a woman's screams filled the air. "*Lo! Lo! Lo!*" she screamed. "No! Please God no!" I heard other voices, followed by broken sobbing that seemed to go on for hours. I didn't know what had happened or what to do. I imagined it was probably the news of a bereavement. As she sounded young I wondered if it may have been a military casualty. Violence and death lurked beneath the surface but were real in Israel. On the main road was a modern block of flats. Every time I passed it on the way to work I was reminded that this was where a Scud missile had destroyed a residential block in 1991.

Beneath my bed was my gas mask. I had received my Chemical Warfare kit about a year earlier; it was a spooky experience. I had a list of things to do that day. A) get washing up liquid B) wash kitchen floor C) get a chemical warfare kit. The distribution centre was in a local school and it reminded me of going to vote. Female soldiers sat behind desks ticking off names from huge lists. For once it was quite jolly and the soldiers were drinking *café afuch*, a kind of Israeli *latte* made with instant coffee. I had to go to another room where I was given a mask to try on. The soldier, who looked as though she should be playing with dolls or colouring in, put her hand over the filter and asked if I could breathe. I couldn't. This meant it was good to use. I was then given a kit with an antidote serum and a syringe. Afterwards I went round the local supermarket, carrying it in a box in my trolley. It was surreal. Occasionally I saw people walking around with them, although most Israelis considered this decidedly uncool. In the bowels of every modern Israeli building, whether residential or commercial, is a *cheder atum* or sealed room. This serves as an air raid shelter and as a refuge from chemical or biological attack. Some people use their shelters for storage or even as a spare room. Those without such a room in their buildings always know where the nearest public ones are. Obviously they don't use the public ones as spare rooms. I shuddered when I saw signs to these rooms, with their massive, reinforced doors that resembled a ship's engine rooms.

Despite the lack of money and the threat of chemical warfare I did manage to go out with my friend Tzafi and this was a lovely experience. I enjoyed being able to talk and have other people listen. I often talked to Tzaffi about Avi and got comfort from having my feelings validated.

I sat in her room as she got ready, thinking "wow, some people are allowed to be messy and that's OK!" We then walked and talked until we got to Shenkin Street, the centre of Tel Aviv's secular intelligentsia and cool crowd. Here there were dozens of trendy cafes and bars. There were also shops selling incense, little Buddhas and African artefacts, along with foreign magazines and books. Every lamp post and telegraph pole was covered in photocopied papers advertising things for sale with little strips of paper giving the vendor's phone number. These could be ripped off and taken home. There were adverts for flat shares, for cars, for social groups and political groups. I loved the buzz of Shenkin Street. It pulsated with energy and life.

"Why don't you just leave?"

About a year before I finally left Israel I received the wonderful news that my friend Bruce was coming to spend a year in Jerusalem, as a volunteer at the Church of Scotland. I was delighted, and immediately began planning all the nice things we'd do together. I also had mixed feelings. I imagined how I would feel when it was time for him to leave. I understood very clearly that I did not want to be still living here when that time came. But how would it end? I couldn't just walk out on my home, job, relationship, cat etc. Or could I?

Soon enough I got a call from Bruce. He had arrived and had settled into his new room at the church. We arranged to meet in Tel Aviv the following day, and I enjoyed the role of tour guide, showing him the beach and café Nordau. It felt good to be speaking English with a native speaker, and I relished the subtle humour and shared cultural references. Bruce's presence calmed me. He was kind and understanding and reasonable. I often discussed religion with Bruce and had done so for many years. He never once preached at me. Bruce's Christian faith was deep and spiritual but tempered with huge amounts of humour and a wonderful sex-positive attitude.

It was around this time that Avi 'found' a friend for me. This was a South African, who was a similar age to me. Avi had 'bumped' into him whilst 'going for a walk.' I really didn't care what 'bumping' and 'walking' had been going on; I liked Bengy. He was fun to be with and it was good that Avi liked him too, which meant we could socialise and go trips together. On one occasion the three of us drove up to Jerusalem to meet Bruce. It was fun to be able to hop into the car, have dinner in Jerusalem and come home. The trip there took just under an hour and we drew up outside the Scottish church at dusk. Bruce showed us round the pilgrim's hostel, and I was struck at how Scottish it was. Obviously there were no kilted men in sporrans eating haggis and neeps, saying "hoots mon, whit'syer problem yerunglish bastard." Nor were there any teenagers nibbling on deep fried Mars Bars and crack cocaine, but nevertheless it felt like Scotland. There were heavy, frayed sofas and arm chairs, nests of teak coffee tables and a wonderful life-size portrait of General Allenby above the fire place. A Scottish Saltire flag fluttered in the evening breeze from the church tower, and there was a peaceful herb garden. The dining room had a simple B&B feel to it, with about ten tables and a slightly fusty smell. I absorbed the peace of the hostel, its familiarity and its spirituality.

We went for an after dinner walk down some quiet back streets before driving back home to Ramat Gan. However I was soon back, this time by myself and I stayed overnight for a thoroughly bizarre and enjoyable evening. It was the annual Scottish folk dancing night and ex-pat Scots from all over Israel had converged on the hub of Scottishness in the Holy Land, for a night of Highland Reels, Gay Gordons and shortbread. The furniture was pushed back to create space and soon the room was pulsating to the sound of fiddles, and hoots of joy. The minister rolled up his sleeves and joined in and I had to remind myself that I was in Jerusalem and not Inverness or Edinburgh. There were several Palestinians there, and it was the first time I had really spoken to any since arriving in Israel. Between dances I sat on the terrace and chatted to various people including an Israeli Scottish woman from Haifa. She told me she'd lived in Israel for over thirty years. A voice whispered in my heart "Andrew, it's time to go home." "I know" I answered. In the morning Bruce showed me the church and we had some Arabic cardamon coffee with the cook, sitting on a step in the sunny herb garden. Bruce and he were talking about the incredible difficulties the man faced coming to work, due to the *Seger* or closure of the Occupied Territories. Despite this, the cook, a devout Christian, was cheerful and resigned. He topped up my cup and brought out some pastries to eat with it. I was fairly confident he was not trying to poison me; block an artery possibly.

Despite Bruce's presence in the country I often felt lonely and my arguments with Avi were reaching ridiculous new heights. We were like two drugged up, psychotic drag queens. I fantasised about leaving and I was thinking of ways I could do this. Avi's line had always been that we would stay in Israel until there was a change in law in England or another European country and then we would move. I had agreed to this. I valiantly wrote letter after letter to the British Home Office and to newspapers, pointing out how unfair the law was and each time I received a polite but firm rejection. One day I came across a group called the Stonewall Immigration Group, a support and pressure group for British gays and lesbians and their non-EU partners. I wrote to them and received an information pack. I noted with rising excitement that the Netherlands often allowed the foreign partners of EU citizens to settle there and before the leaflet had time to hit the floor I was on the phone to the Dutch Embassy. The clerk confirmed that under certain circumstances my gay partner might be allowed to settle in the Netherlands, providing I was earning enough to support the two of us and that I had registered on the population register. Avi was dubious and asked for more details about when he would be allowed to stay in his own right etc. I soon began learning Dutch and made serious enquiries about transferring to Berlitz in Maastricht. A few weeks later I got the answer that this would indeed be possible. It was beginning to fall together, and I imagined my new life. We would live in a canalside flat, or maybe even a canal boat. We would have a little car, driving to Belgium or Germany for the weekend. I would dye my hair blond and change my name to Fi Fi Van der Valk. Every evening I went for long walks by the river with my personal stereo, picturing our new lives. I applied for a new British passport, curious to see the new European Union passports. Although I had a year to run on the old passport I felt I wanted to make a new beginning. I enjoyed making the visit to the British Embassy in Ben Yehuda Street, as it was a small link with Britain and I felt I was standing on British territory even if it was just for a few minutes. "You can go sir!" ordered the well-spoken but unpleasant clerk after I picked up my passport.

"I know but I don't want to" I felt like replying.

I continued working on my Diploma course in TESOL which involved completing assignments in large folders and reading dozens of teaching books. There was a great emphasis on teaching communication skills and on pronunciation and obviously this impacted on my work at Berlitz, where I began trying to enlighten my Israeli students to the critical importance of politeness conventions and appropriate register, along with solid pronunciation. As you can imagine this went down a storm and I soon went back to teaching them how to ask if pens were pencils in heavily accented, rude English, manfully accepting defeat.

We were approaching Passover and soon the street was alive to the sounds of carpets being beaten over balconies (had no-one heard of a little invention called the Hoover?) and buckets of soapy water being thrown into the path. Shops began stocking enormous packets of Matzot and heavily discounting certain items deemed unkosher for Passover. Avi had recently come out to his parents and it had not gone down well, with dark threats of early deaths and evenings spent alone in the dark. It was therefore unthinkable for me to go round to his parents for the Seder. For this reason I spent the Seder night alone with a tin of tuna and some Matzah. This was not how I had imagined my Jewish life to be. Fed up and lonely I went to my room and forged ahead with my Diploma assignment.

One November morning I woke up, aware of an agonising, almost electric, feeling in my back tooth. It felt as though the tooth fairy was doing bungee jumps on my dental nerve. Trying not to cry out I ran to the bathroom and took a fistful of painkillers. The following morning I was the first in the queue at the local dentist in Ramat Gan. I was used to the soft Scottish accents of my dental team in Edinburgh. I had always made a point of avoiding the dentist in Israel. Now it seemed I might not have a choice. I am, I admit, a highly strung punch-people-in-the-mouth-if-they-go-near-my-sensitive-teeth kind of patient. I am sure I have secret markers on my dental record which may explain why the dental nurse handcuffs me. I was not naïve enough to think that the nurse would coo over me whilst the dentist uttered soothing messages in my ear. It was a dingy, small, horrible surgery, and not all that clean. It was the kind of place where you would step on a used syringe and need to sweep extracted teeth off the dental chair before sitting down. I was ushered in and saw a young woman pulling on some rubber gloves. "Ah, a woman dentist" I thought. That was good, she might be more sensitive and I was also pleased to see women breaking into the male bastion of dentistry. As I was sitting down the real dentist came in, dour and unsmiling. And male. Without so much as a grunt by way of greeting he told me to open my mouth and within seconds told me I needed a staggering ten fillings. Horrified and deeply suspicious I told him I would think about it and he looked quizzical. Was I not going to sign up there and then? I am sure he was mouthing something about my mother as I left, but I might be wrong. I went to the pharmacy and bought a bottle of clove oil for the pain and phoned my mother to book the dentist at home for me. I was due to come home about ten days later for Christmas so I managed to dull the pain with a cocktail of aspirin, clove oil and warm water till then. It was a relief to see the slush around the runway of Edinburgh airport as my flight from London touched down. With the briefest of hellos at home I went straight to my own dentist in a taxi.

"Am gooinuneedtenhillins" I tried to say my mouth full of rubbery fingers and cotton wool.

"What was that Mr Reid?" asked my dentist, removing his hand.

"The Israeli dentist says I need ten fillings" I repeated.

"Well, I think that's quite frankly rubbish" he replied. I thought with fury at how the man had wanted to cheat me. Not only did he want to cheat me out of money; he wanted to cause me unnecessary pain and fill good teeth with useless fillings. I did need one root canal however, and I sat patiently for an hour or so whilst the dentist put little sticks into the crater in my back tooth. I was relieved I was having the treatment at home. This done, I was free to enjoy Christmas and New Year as always. At New Year I met my friends and went to see the fireworks in Princes Street before going on to a party. I loved being with normal people, people I could relate to and who respected me. All too soon it was time to go back to Israel. The night before before going back, I lay awake in my bed wishing I could stay.

In February 1997 I heard Avi shout in the living room, and rushed through to see what was wrong. On the news was the image of a wrecked aircraft of some kind and the newscaster was talking about an horrific helicopter collision in the north of the country. Two military personnel carriers had crashed, killing 73 Israeli troops. I returned to the kitchen area, feeling shocked at the scale of the tragedy. Later I came out in time to watch *Seinfeld* my favourite TV programme at that time. However instead of seeing Jerry, George and Elaine laughing at Kramer's wacky antics there was news on every station.

"Let's watch something funny" I suggested. I was unprepared for Avi's anger.

"Fucking hell. How can you watch comedy at a time like this!" he shouted.

"But people die horribly every day. As we speak kids are dying somewhere in the world!"

"There has never been an accident like this, with so many of our soldiers killed." He was furious and I just couldn't see how someone could live in Israel and absorb the trauma of every tragedy and stay sane. I went to my room to read *Rumpole of the Bailey*. Of course there wasn't long to wait for the next tragedy which occurred in March of that year when seven Israeli school girls were shot and killed by a Jordanian border guard from the other side of the frontier fence. I tried to imagine what was going through the man's head. Had he woken up that morning and decided 'that's it. I am going to shoot some kids'? Had he thought it through? And if he had thought it through, what did he hope to achieve by it? Would his action bring an end to the Palestine-Israel conflict? How could a man hate a group of Jewish school girls so much?

In early spring Avi and I had planned to spend a holiday with my parents, meeting them in Prague. Shortly before we were due to leave Avi announced he was not coming. Truthfully, I was not disappointed and I knew that the relationship was dying. If I had been happier I might have tried to keep it alive but I wanted the relationship to die so I could leave Israel with a clear conscience. I flew to Prague alone, using my Israeli passport, on board a dated and crowded Czech Airlines flight. The cabin crew consisted of ex-shot putters and made El Al cabin crew look like butlers to the Royal Family. A cup of tepid, weak coffee was quite literally snatched out of my hand as we began nose diving into Prague airport to the strains of Smetana's *Ma Vlast* on the intercom. As usual I drank in the sight of greenery and freshness and this time there was even a touch of snow. I was struck by how dated and poor everything seemed, compared to Israel. After having my passport stamped, I boarded a special shared taxi into the centre.

My first impressions were confirmed by the long, dreary drive along potholed roads. On both sides of the road were block after block of depressing 1970s flats, streaks of damp oozing from the walls. As we approached the centre the shared taxi began calling at hotels, dropping off passengers. Fortunately I had a pre-paid voucher but I noticed that one Israeli couple was becoming agitated. It was becoming apparent that the people leaving the taxi were not paying and that the unfortunate couple feared they might be saddled with the entire bill.

Our hotel was simple but it was pure luxury to have a whole room to myself, to feel cool, to open a window and smell the air. I bounced up and down on the soft bed, feeling a thick duvet beneath me. I went downstairs to see if my parents had arrived and after lots of greetings and hugs we took a taxi into the centre. We walked around the Old Town Square and then over the Charles Bridge. We returned to the Square to hear the Glockenspiel at the old town hall. It was a pleasure to be treated as a valued family member again. That evening my parents took me for a delicious dinner in the hotel, where we got slightly drunk on Schnapps. The following day was spent on an organised coach tour to the mysterious and misty *Karlstejn* Castle. This was perched on a rocky hill and surrounded by deep pine forests. I felt so refreshed and happy to be there.

In the evening, after dinner I snuck out by myself, and caught the spacious and dated underground train a few stops. Then I walked along a badly cobbled street, passing a relic of Communist rule, a giant space needle made of ugly concrete. Just beyond was a small gay bar, notorious for its rougher clientele. I ordered a beer, went through to the next room and took in my surroundings. I had never seen anything like it. There was a cage, some stocks and a sling suspended from the ceiling and, unlike the London Dungeon, they were all being used. I heard a man moaning what I assume was Czech for "Please sir, I've been really bad sir." He might of course have been asking if anyone fancied another beer but there was no misunderstanding the internationally recognised "ow!" following the sound of leather hitting buttock. Horrified and deeply traumatised, I gingerly crept passed the night porter of the hotel and crawled into my cool, soft bed, snuggling up under the duvet.

My parents were staying one day less than me and after seeing them off in a taxi, I took a tram to the ugly coach station where I struggled to find information on my bus to Terezin. After extracting the information from a clerk, using a pair of pliers and an electronic cattle prod, I eventually boarded a bus that would have been old-fashioned even when I was a child. We creaked and rattled through the suburbs of Prague and were eventually heading down a thin country road with fields on both sides.

When I got off I found myself at the edge of Terezin, better known to the world as Theresienstadt. I crossed a moat and entered the town through a thick, brick gate built into a grassy mound. The walls circled the entire town. It was utterly bleak and depressing. Tenement flats were arranged in rows along deserted cobbled streets and I couldn't see any shops, cafés or places for a cheery toasted cheese sandwich. After a brief exploration of the town I walked to the former prison, the site of one of Nazidom's most notorious concentration camps.

It was here that the Germans had introduced a so-called model camp, and had stage-managed the entire production, even making a film called *The Führer gives the Jews a Town*. The Swiss Red Cross were invited here and shown how the inhabitants had their own currency, their own shops and civil administration. Suitably duped they left and the town's unfortunate inmates were entrained for their journey to the gas chambers. There were still traces of the real Nazi prison which had been a brutal and secret hell. I walked through a gate under the notorious slogan *Arbeit Macht Frei*, which was painted in fading colour. What was so awful about the prison was that years of Communist neglect had ensured it had stayed exactly how it was; there was no renovation or sanitation. Inside the cells were rotting bunk beds, three or four high. A rusty metal desk and chair remained in the doctor's office, with wooden cabinets behind it. The doors of the cabinet had been left open as if the doctor had popped out and had just never returned. What horrific events had this room seen? What prayers had been uttered in those bunks and tears shed? I shuddered as the spirit of place entered me and chilled me. I was, it seemed, the only visitor that day. I wandered outside to a yard and froze at the sight of a gallows, a noose still swaying in the wind. After taking just about as much as I could of Terezin I walked to the bus stop and waited patiently for the hourly service back to Prague.

The following day I took a taxi to Prague Airport for my Czech Airlines flight to Stansted. Here I took a connecting flight to Edinburgh. It was a pleasure to be back home and I spent a lot of time at the bookshops, delighting in the enormous range of ideas and political thoughts. I was tired of Avi's relentless tirades and of the fundamentalism that I encountered in some sections of Israeli society. I was tired of the never-ending conflict and the intercommunal bickering. I wanted to read about other things now. I took pleasure in philosophy, in comparative religion and in gay and lesbian liberation.

As usual, on my visits home, I stocked up on supplies of favourite foods, such as Marmite, Angel Delight and decent tea, along with new clothes and some gay reading material. At the end of the holidays I spent a couple of days with my sister in Wimbledon. It was lovely to be surrounded by family. My niece proudly brought me her pets and my nephew had just been born, filling me with a sense of wonder. I spent a day alone in the city centre, visiting Soho and having a coffee at the *First Out Café* near Tottenham Court Road. I enjoyed sitting over my coffee, watching other gay people enjoying life. Two lesbians were holding hands. At another table an older man was reading a free gay newspaper. I picked up a copy and browsed through it, looking in amazement at the variety of groups and activities on offer. The older man smiled at me and I returned his greeting. It was a quick moment of shared camaraderie. There was no agenda. I promised myself that I would return home, and it would be sooner rather than later. I prayed briefly and silently that God would find me a way out. Above all I wanted to meet someone who would love me and respect me.

Later, when I was walking with my sister I confided my feelings for the first time. Instantly she was on my side and was discussing ways of helping, both practically and emotionally. On the day I was due to leave we all went to a local Asian supermarket and I was reminded of how varied and colourful London could be. I wanted more than anything to buy food for a meal I would cook myself in my own home, in my own country. This was not going to happen that night. A few hours later I was on my way back to Prague. The first leg of the journey was just about bearable but at Prague there was a four hour gap. This was not long enough to return to the city but it was a long time to kill in an airport that could have been the set for *Raid on Entebbe*. There was one stall selling weak, Czech coffee, a tiny souvenir shop filled with Mozart-themed rubbish and a few rows of benches. Feeling like a bear in a Swiss zoo I started walking around in circles before deciding to go through security, just for something to do. As usual all the passengers for Israel had been herded into a small holding pen but this time there was nothing at all in the way of facilities except a single toilet. The noise was deafening as the other passengers competed with each other in the who-can-speak-loudest-about-their-holiday competition. Hebrew is a beautiful language but I was tired of hearing it. On board, I sat miserably in my seat reading a gay romance about someone who went to live in London and actually had a life they enjoyed. I did not want to go back. Avi was too busy to meet me and I caught the 222 back home.

It was shortly after Pesach. I was just finishing the washing up when I noticed I felt unusually sluggish and slightly sick. I sat down for a while, burping gently but then settled down to watch the *African Queen* on TV. By the time Katharine Hepburn had washed her hair in the river I had been violently sick five times. In the background I heard Avi turning up the volume and pouring himself a drink. I sat panting on the bathroom floor and then realised I had pressing business at the other end too. The following morning I tried to go to work but simply couldn't. This meant a significant loss of income. I sat miserably at home flicking between channels and cursing the energy-sapping heat which pervaded the flat, despite the closed shutters. The following day I did go to work and noticed that the receptionist was looking at me strangely. By lunchtime I was so ill I had to go home, staggering in the heat of the afternoon sun. I hadn't eaten anything for 48 hours.

Reluctantly I made an appointment with the doctor, although I have an abiding fear of the medical profession. This was worse in Israel as Israeli doctors always refer you for *b'dikot* or tests everytime you so much as sneeze. They also have a severe I-think-it-might-be-cancer-but-I-need-to-have-it-confirmed look as they silently fill in their chits, not giving anything away. Back in Scotland it had been a different story with Doctor Chakrabarty prescribing me aspirin for every ailment. The following day, weak from lack of food and thoroughly dehydrated, I sat on the hard wooden bench of the waiting room. The practice was in a 1930s house and I was reminded of the early days of the state of Israel, and also of the Kibbutz. Indeed I half expected Paula Ben Gurion to stride in fresh from the fields to see about her bunions/incurablenastydeathitis.

This feeling continued when an impatient bark indicated I should go through. A small, elderly woman with a grey crewcut sat unsmiling behind a teak desk. Her mouth was so puckered and sour it looked like someone had stuck a very powerful vacuum cleaner up her arse and left it on. A curt nod indicated I should speak and I told what had been happening. She then shone a light in my face and stood up, drawing herself to her full four feet.

"*Yesh lecha Hepatitis*" she pronounced flatly. I reeled with shock and horror, not really knowing what that was. She asked me who I lived with, as we tried to narrow down how I'd caught it. When she registered that I was living with a man she took out a note book and began writing.

"What are you writing?" I asked.

"You're having an AIDS test" she replied flatly.

"I don't want one" I replied. She seemed nonplussed, like she could see my lips move but couldn't grasp the concept of a patient having a choice or opinion.

"9.15 next Tuesday" she went on, shaken but not deterred.

"No. I told you. I don't want one." This was too much. Ever since I had come to Israel I had been prodded and tested more than a particularly hard working lab bunny. It had happened on the kibbutz and in the army and now I was tired of it. I was sick and weak and low and I didn't want anymore. Eventually she crossed out the AIDS test request with a I-don't-believe-I-am-doing-this-you-diseased-little-faggot look in her eyes before handing me the slip for the other blood tests. I arrived early at the clinic the following day and waited on another wooden bench. A selection of miserable looking people sat on the other benches, some nursing sticking plasters, others waiting to get tests. All of them had one thing in common; they were all staring at me. In the surgery a much more pleasant medic sat me down and asked me four little words that I hadn't heard since I had got ill, namely *how are you feeling*? She took some of my blood, using a syringe the size of a bicycle pump and she glanced in horror at my eyes, which were bright yellow.

As soon as the blood was on its way to the lab, she was on the phone to my GP.

"Doctor, listen to me….listen. The man is SERIOUSLY ILL. He should be in hospital" she shouted in frustration.

"I think you should go to hospital Andrew" she said when she came off the phone and I resorted to my usual stoic response in these situations, I burst into tears.

"Noooooooooooo" I wailed at the very idea. She then agreed I could go home if I promised to take care of myself and was told to make myself lemonade with lots of sugar and nothing else. It was actually the only thing I could face. I simply could not drink tea or coffee nor eat anything. After a few more days I decided to go work, worried at the loss of income and bored at home. I staggered slowly and yellowly up the main road, pausing to wheeze and rest. Passers-by stared at me in all my banana-glory and I felt like the Elephant Man in the scene where he arrives at Liverpool Street and someone pulls his mask off and everyone chases him and he pants that he's a human being not an elephant man. I managed to struggle though one lesson, with the students nodding politely, backed against a wall with hankies over their noses. I then walked home and noticed that I had a hankering for some cheese. Over the next few days my appetite returned and it was time to go back to the doctor's for the results. The doctor confirmed that I had Hepatitis A, probably from food prepared by a cook with a strong aversion to toilet paper and soap. She then gleeful announced I was also suffering from acute anaemia. I really didn't know what it was. It sounded serious. Oh my God, I was going to die here and be buried in a pit and dogs would come and shit on my pauper's grave and Avi would put my books in a mincing machine! The doctor explained that my iron levels were actually lower than a woman who had just given birth. As I hadn't noticed any babies passing my way recently, she wanted to know what I ate.

"You need meat, chicken, beef. Meat. Stew? You like eat stew? Chicken salad?" I explained I was vegetarian and that bemused look returned to her sun dried face.

"*Ma?*" she gasped, translated as "I'm sorry my dear chap. Not quite with you there. Would you mind awfully elucidating me on that one."

"*Ma?*" she grunted again. "*Vegi-tari?* You no eat meat?"

"That's the general idea. Yes." After a little chat about sources of iron which was only slightly less threatening than an afternoon at the Lubianka Jail courtesy of the KGB, I was persuaded to eat a tin of tuna everyday and then I was dismissed. After penning a letter to Amnesty International, enclosing photographs of the doctor, I went to the supermarket to stock up on tuna.

"I think I just spat a piece of quiche onto that woman's dress."

An English friend of mine was visiting me, staying in Ramat Gan for a few nights before moving on to Jerusalem. Avi was not happy about this and there was an 'atmosphere', a fact which was not unusual anymore. I spent a few pleasant days with my friend, chatting, and discussing the woeful state of my relationship. One night we went to a branch of a new chain of smart coffee shops in Ramat Gan, called *Apropos*. I had passed it a few times, thinking how nice it would be to go in, but not having anyone to go with I hadn't tried it. It was good to sit in the air conditioned coolness, sipping a large glass of *Mitz Tut* or (supposedly) fresh strawberry juice, and sharing a slice of incredibly rich cheese cake.

"Why don't you just leave?" my friend suggested. I had struggled with this question many times. I had longed to leave. I basically lacked the moral courage to walk out. I was afraid of the guilt I would feel, leaving Avi alone.

"Oh for heavens sake!" my friend exclaimed hotly. "He's not a child. This is his country. I am sure he'll cope." I mulled this over, a strange excitement growing inside me. I felt change was coming. I was still feeling weak after my bout of hepatitis and therefore didn't have a lot of energy to take my friend around so we spent a lot of time at home. In order to avoid Avi, we stayed in my room, quietly gossiping. It was early in the afternoon. Suddenly we both heard a loud, dull crack. We looked at each other.

"What the fuck was that?" exclaimed my friend. As if to answer him a wail of sirens erupted on all sides, coming from both Jabotinsky

Street and from Abba Hillel Street. I turned on the radio but there was nothing out of the ordinary. I went into the garden, where the sun was shining and a couple of feral cats were lounging around. Every minute or so I heard the urgent honking of emergency vehicles passing along the main roads. A neighbour was leaning out of her window.

"*Ma kara?*" I asked her. She shrugged.

"*Ani lo yodat*" she replied. I went back in. By now the news was reporting a bomb at the *Apropos* Café in Tel Aviv. This was the first time I had ever heard a bomb explode and although we were over two miles away it was loud enough to hear indoors. The fact that the target was an *Apropos* Café also shook me. We had been to another branch of that chain the day before. Life was beginning to feel like a lottery of death. Shaken by the bomb at *Apropos*, and still analysing Avi's strange behaviour, including his newly acquired taste for aftershave and smart shirts, we took the bus into central Tel Aviv for the Berlitz Purim party which was being held at a large, modern hotel on the seafront. I loathe fancy dress and refused point blank to wear it. I have a fear of being involved in a serious accident and being rushed into intensive care dressed as a bunny rabbit. Paramedics would giggle uncontrollably as they tried to restart my heart and stick a drip into my arm. We were pretty sure therefore that we wouldn't be winning the free bottle of Champagne for the best dressed couple but this was a small price to pay for keeping my dignity. Many of my colleagues had less inhibitions than I did and many were dressed as, amongst other things, a giant glass of Guinness, a *Chassidic* kangeroo, and Teyve from *Fiddler on the Roof*. One of the very religious women from Berlitz Jerusalem was dressed as a female clown, but retaining her tight headscarf. At least I think she was dressed as a clown. Perhaps she was just dressing down. I am panicking now as I write this because I laughed in her face. She was having a great time in a pious and holy way, refusing all manner of food and drink and smiling in that way that American religious fundamentalists do before they say they'll pray for you. My boss had taken the unfortunate decision to dress up as a witch. By the end of the first hour she was glowering realistically and threatening to sack the next person who told her she suited her costume. The drink was flowing and was free and I was getting a little silly. My friend was seriously drunk but in a dangerous, mischievous way, laughing discreetly at the antics of a distraught American woman who had been promised a lift home and wasn't getting one.

"I need to go home now" she roared aggressively. "You said we'd leave by ten!" she accused a colleague dressed as a fairy who was trying to turn her back on the demented party pooper. I felt uncharitable bubbles of mirth come uncontrollably to the surface. "Don't make me laugh" please I begged.

"I was promised a lift home!" The woman had now made her way to the centre of the party and was now shouting at no-one in particular.

"Oh let's have a fucking whip-round" suggested a cross and drunk Irish leprechaun.

"I think I just accidentally spat a piece of quiche onto that woman's dress when I laughed" hissed my friend. Trying not to laugh I purposefully walked across to where the lady in question was standing. Sure enough about two inches from the woman's neck was a small piece of masticated quiche.

"What shall we do I?" I laughed, my voice slurred and strangulated.

"Oops!" replied my friend, looking pleased with his handiwork. It was around this point that I cornered a particularly attractive, and completely straight, French colleague and confessed that I thought I fancied him. I mumbled something incoherent about 'shy bairns getting nae sweeties.' He smiled politely, and displaying impeccable manners he thanked me for my interest. In the early hours of the morning we staggered into a taxi and made our way back to the house of gloom where Avi was waiting up in his curlers, a rolling-pin under his armpit. The following day I said goodbye to my sour and hung-over friend and went back to the flat. By now the rows with Avi were intense, exhausting and routine. All I wanted to do was go home and start a new life. I wanted to go back to college and get diplomas and an MA. I wanted to buy a flat and make friends. I was getting too old for this life. Until now I had tried to minimise conflict, preferring a quiet life but now I actively sought chances to assert myself, conflict or no conflict. I just didn't care any more. One hot Saturday afternoon the atmosphere was heavy and explosive. A row erupted when Avi wanted me to turn off that 'fucking Captain Morse' and I refused. Moments later we were at each other's throats and Avi spat out his favourite line of "Dai! Stop making your shows!" He then followed this up with the by-now familiar "You're playing with fire!" I felt years of rage and frustration bubble up inside me and lashed out at the nearest thing to hand which was a porcelain duck with a blue ribbon around its neck. I had always hated them and decided, quite reasonably I felt, to smash it. Avi looked stunned as the ceramic mallard flew floorwards at speeds previously unknown to man. I gasped with satisfaction as the little fellow disintegrated into a thousand pieces. Avi turned a deeper shade of purple before looking for something of mine he could smash. As we were in the living room this involved going to my room in order to find something suitable and he began to rip up some of my postcards. After a brief scuffle I slammed the door and lay on the spare bed weeping. I felt so alone and I had no-one nearby who could support me, take my side or validate my feelings. As soon as Avi had left for his nightshift I went to Independence Park for a 'walk.' After a week of silence and tension we decided to talk about the situation. It was time for this to end. We decided I would go home. Avi agreed to a basic financial settlement, and as soon as he had left for work, I phoned my mother to tell her I was coming home. Events began moving fast. Luckily the decision to break up coincided with a visit by some of Avi's friends who acted as a buffer-zone. Now that I was free I relaxed in their company. I felt excited to be going home. I made arrangements for a haulage company to take my things back to England but came across a problem.

"If you are leaving the country you need to take your duty free fridge with you" the haulier told me over the phone. It sounded as though he were either chewing seeds or performing a sex act of some kind.

"But I don't want to take it!" What would I do with a massive Israeli fridge freezer at my sister's house?

"The problem is you can't sell it. You bought it duty free as a new immigrant." He spat something out, either a seed or a pubic hair. Or both. I really don't know what was going on there but it was noisy. Eventually we found a legal solution, with the fridge remaining in Israel. I still had some notice to work out at Berlitz and the haulage company needed a few weeks, so I bought a single ticket for early May.

"What about the cat?" I asked fearfully.

"I'll find a solution" Avi reassured me.

"What kind of solution? A trip-to-the-canal solution or a nice-new-home solution?" After some enquiries Avi informed me that the cat would be going to live with a family in Petach Tikva. I really hoped this wasn't some kind of Hebrew euphemism for euthanasia.

Israeli vet: "I am very sorry Mrs Goldfarb. He was really very old. We decided the best thing to do was to find him a nice family in Petach Tikva."

Distraught owner: "Sniff. I understand doctor. Thank you. And what about the cat?"

In order to have some time out of the flat and to gather my thoughts I arranged to go to the north of the country with Bruce. I met him early one morning at the train station in Tel Aviv. I liked travelling by train in Israel. The station was dated and functional and women soldiers were conducting a bag search at the door. The train was a relic from the 1950s when Germany, feeling a tinsy winsy bit guilty about the Holocaust, kindly donated some of its rolling stock. I find the concept of countries giving each other gifts a bit odd.

Germany: "Just a little somfink to say sorry. Ve hope you like zem."

Israel: "Oh that's OK. I'll put them on a track in the kitchen."

Germany: "So are ve OK now? No hart veelings?"

It's like when Norway gives the UK a Christmas tree every year but we never get them anything.

Finland: "Hello Sweden, are you sending El Salvador a card this year?"

Sweden: "Oh Hi there, Finland. I don't think we're bothering this year, to be honest."

The train trundled along slowly and noisily, a bit like in one of those old Basil Rathbone *Sherlock Holmes* films. I found the trip exciting, as it went through places I had never been before, often stopping for long pauses at remote stations. The heat was becoming unpleasant as we were experiencing a *Chamsin,* one of those periods of intense, humid heat when the sky turns grey and Israelis become even more irritable than usual. My lips were cracked and chaffed, a bit like a survivor of a desert plane crash with a particular weakness for salt licks and anchovies. Nevertheless I was determined to enjoy myself. Slowly but surely the train made its way north and eventually we got to the ancient crusader city of Akko, or Acre. We headed for the Old Arab part of town which is the heart of Akko. It was pleasant, exotic and laid back and I browsed souvenir shops and drank a couple of cups of thick, syrupy mint tea. We sat on the old town walls and ate pitta bread, watching Arab boys diving into the sea, which looked very dangerous but they seemed to be having fun. We wondered around the court yard of a quiet, peaceful mosque and then returned to the station. We broke our journey in Haifa, Israel's third biggest city. Some compare it to San Francisco but apart from the fact that they are both by the sea and that Haifa has a steep road up a hill, I can't see the similarity. Some Israelis compare their cities with American ones, unfortunately with no good reason. Tel Aviv becomes the Miami of the Middle East, and whilst they both do have sizeable populations of geriatric Jews and some Art Deco buildings, the similarity ends there. Eilat is the Las Vegas of the Middle East because there is a poker game on the first Tuesday of every month. However, this is not as bad as the Lebanese habit of referring to Beirut as the Paris of the Middle East. Now, it is true I did once have a slightly unfortunate mini-break to Paris, but I would need to have several dozen glasses of *vin de table* before I started to believe I was in Beirut. On the one hand you have the Louvre, the Eiffel Tower, Montmatre, and on the other you have erm, *Hizbollah*. Where will it end? Will Ramat Gan become the Windsor of the Middle East because they both have parks? Perhaps Karmiel New Town would like to put itself forward as Israel's answer to Oxford because they both have schools. Many Israeli cities like to twin themselves with more glamorous European ones; it's sweet but misleading. Nice, on the French Cote d'Azur, is twinned with Natanya. Bless.

Meanwhile back in Haifa, Bruce and I decided to try Israel's only underground system which is a cable car in a tunnel. This took us to the upper town, the Beverly Hills of the Middle East presumably. Apart from a rather posh hotel and a promenade overlooking a Bahai temple (Kyoto of the Middle East?) there was little to sustain our interest so we quickly rejoined the train. It was dark as we approached Tel Aviv and I was sad that our day was ending. I did not want to leave the calm Christian comfort of Bruce and return to that strife-torn flat. The fights were growing worse daily so it was to Bruce and the Church of Scotland in Jerusalem that I fled one weekend. Here I could reflect and have some time out from the cauldron of feelings at home. His room was located in a small tower and was only accessible from the church roof.

It felt peaceful and monk-like and I began to unwind. From the roof we could gaze out over Jerusalem and in the evening cool we would sit and talk things through.

We ate our dinner in the hospice dining room, prepared by the same smiling Palestinian cook.

The next morning I asked Bruce to show me some of the Christian places in the Old City. We began with the Lutheran Church, where I smashed my head as we wound our way up the spire.

"Och my, are you OK?" asked Bruce.

"I'm fine thanks" I replied, discreetly whipping out a sewing kit and an emergency supply of blood. We made our way through some depressing and threatening streets in East Jerusalem on our way to St George's Anglican Cathedral. Here the shutters of shops were firmly drawn and covered with Arabic graffiti. I felt edgy but Bruce seemed to know where we were going and soon we arrived at the gates. A wave of homesickness engulfed me at the sight of the quaint English church and I felt like singing a rousing chorus of *Jerusalem* before popping into the vicarage for Victoria sponge. In the grounds were beds of flowers and fragrant herbs. As we went inside I was struck by the cool, and by the cosy familiarity of England. I looked at the kneelers, the hymn books and the pulpit and every fibre of my body screamed "I want to go home." We spent the rest of the day in the Old City, exploring more holy places and the Arab souk. For most of the afternoon we'd been having an on-off discussion about Arab feelings towards Israel. I was of the opinion that most people in the Arab world would like to see Israel destroyed. Bruce admonished me and suggested I was projecting. A few minutes later we passed a small barber's shop in the souk. In its window was a picture of a Star of David with a huge bloody dagger shoved through. Around it was Arabic writing and, whilst not professing to be proficient in the language, I'd be prepared to bet it wasn't a Likud Party election poster. We visited the Western Wall, a place which was leaving me increasingly cold, with the fervent, fundamentalist prayers of the Ultra Orthodox all around me. Why was I praying at a wall to a temple I would personally hate to see rebuilt? It was stark and masculine and, as far as I was concerned, deeply unspiritual.

We walked back through the market and made for my favourite place in the Old City; the Church of the Holy Sepulchre. This was not my first visit, I had been many times before, but I knew it would be my last for many years. Inside the church was gloomy and reeked of frankincense and myrrh and the smell of thousands of candles. We passed the shrine marking the place where Christ's body was anointed, and made for the tomb itself, the focal point of the vast, crazy church. In the background I could hear a party of pilgrims chanting and I waved away the cloud of thick incense in order to see.

"Bruce? Where are you?" I called out, running my hand along a wall trying to see.

"Here I am" he replied, crawling on all fours. The smell was so strong and pungent that it was making me slightly high. I am sure it was addictive.

Israeli drug dealer: "Pssst. D'ja wanna score some myrrh? It's Moroccan."

Israeli drug user: "Naaa. Myrrh's for mugs. I'm sticking to heroin."

A Greek Orthodox priest beckoned me into the cave-like tomb of Christ but I declined. This was not a place for a nice Jewish boy. We wandered around the vast church, chatting and then I asked Bruce to wait while I went to the loo. Now, I am aware that there is a very complex *modus vivendi* amongst the different denominations in the church. For example there are rules about burning incense and candles in various places or about saying Mass out of turn. This agreement obviously did not extend to a cleaning rota for the loos. These were bile-swallowingly-hand-clapsed-over-the-mouth awful. Flies, sated and lazy on goodness knows what floated slowly in the air saying "Oooh that really hit the spot that did" in fly-language. I came out feeling shaken by the humanity of it all, and was glad to get back to the sweet smell of incense and interdenominational strife. I have always found the reports of conflict in the church disillusioning but at the same time, funny. During the Ottoman period the clerics actually came to blows, and whilst there was no evidence of violence now, there were clear areas of control with the poor Ethiopian Copts being stuck up on the roof. What would the fights actually be about, I wondered.

Greek Orthodox priest: "Hey you! Yes you. Catholic nuns. Shut up with your bloody Hail Mary's and Mass. Some of us are trying to worship God in *His* way down here."

Catholic Sister Superior: "Ah, feck off. Look at ya, wit ya big feckin' beards and yer foncy oycons."
Greek Orthodox priest: "In the name of Christ I repel you."
Catholic Sister Superior: "No, just a minute pal, oy repel *you*."
Would someone call the police, I wondered?
Local police: "Ah, bloody 'ell. Anuver bleedin' domestic down the Sepulchre Fred."

It was time to go back to Ramat Gan to begin the painful process of packing up five years of life and memories, five years of loving and arguing. During that time we had travelled around Europe, opened a café, I had converted to Judaism, become a citizen; we had adopted a cat; I had made and lost friends; we had laughed and cried together; I had learned Hebrew, served two days in the army, and now it was over. There would be no more Friday nights, no more trips to Eilat; no more Super Sol on Thursdays or Turkish coffee, watching *Nanny*. Crying, I began packing up piles of books into boxes and I carefully removed my postcards from the wall.

"Please don't look at me like that" I said to the cat.

"Mummy, mummy, please don't leave me!" her little eyes seemed to say. I broke down, sobbing and squeezed her. I left a few things unpacked in a rucksack and a few hours later the haulage van arrived. For the next few days I lived out of a suitcase, but I still had to go to work. On my last Friday morning my colleagues arranged lunch at the smart dairy restaurant in the D-Mall shopping arcade, below Berlitz. Here they presented me with a lovely gift and card, and we had a lazy, boozy lunch. It was both a happy and a sad occasion. I was determined to spend as much time as I could out of the house for my last day and night, so I went for a last walk by the river and then wandered around the suburban streets of Ramat Gan, envying the families their Sabbath peace. Avi was more relaxed than I had feared and we spent our last night watching a film on TV. It was the last *Erev Shabbat*, the last Angel Delight, the last cocktail and crisps. The following evening we drove in silence to the airport where we both sat awkwardly over our pastries and Latte. Avi pretended to be one of the many characters we had invented together and I quickly told him to stop; I couldn't bear it. There was a death row feeling of unreality as the minutes ticked by and the boarding of El Al flight LY 218 to Stansted became imminent.

Outside it was dark and I could see the taillights of an El Al jumbo jet taking off silently. And then it was time. Avi's eyes turned red and watery and his voice cracked. I tried not to look him in the eye. We hugged for the last time, both of us shaking and sniffing.

"*Dai, Putchy*" he said, using a pet name he hadn't used for years.

I curled into my window seat on the half-empty plane and let myself cry quietly as we climbed steeply, flying over Tel Aviv. Below I could make out the curves of Old Jaffa and the neon of the sea front bars and hotels. Then it grew pitch black and I couldn't see Israel anymore. In five hours I would be back in England and I would begin the next stage of my life. But I would be back I promised. There would be holidays, and soon it wouldn't hurt anymore.

"Goodbye Israel" I whispered.

Epilogue:
"Is cancelled until there is a cease fire!"
August 2006

"Will the day trip to Nazareth be running?" I asked the nice man from *United Tours*. I was sitting in my kitchen in Loughton, my diary in one hand and an industrial-sized spray of *Bach Flower Remedy* in the other.

"Is cancelled until there is a cease fire!" shouted the man pleasantly, over the phone from the office in Tel Aviv. "We have nice tour, Massada and Dead Sea. You want?" For some reason I imagined him to be in a bunker, wearing a helmet with the tour company logo on it. On the TV screen in front of me hillsides in Lebanon were exploding like volcanoes. A rather hunky reported from SKY News was stood on Mount Carmel in Haifa, wearing a flak jacket. "Yeah, not bloody San Francisco of the Middle East now, is it?" I muttered to no one in particular.

It was nearly a decade since I had left Israel and moved back to England. Life had not stood still. Soon after settling back in London I met Carl, my life partner. After a few years Carl and I moved up the property ladder together, eventually settling in the peaceful Essex town of Loughton on the eastern edge of London. On a rainy morning in February 2006 we became Civil Partners at Brighton Registry Office.

My proposed trip back to Israel had been prompted by my niece's decision to visit Israel. Rachel was five when I had my Kibbutz experience. Now she was nineteen, and on a kibbutz herself. A few phone calls and a trip to the Israeli Embassy passport office in Kensington later, and I was ready to go. And then a war broke out.

I was feeling trepidacious as the date approached for me to fly to Israel and collect Rachel. Much of the north of Israel had become a no-go area, with missiles raining down indiscriminately. The crisis had begun in Gaza, had spread to Lebanon, and was now threatening to draw in Syria and perhaps even Iran.

My nerves were frayed and I felt I was going to die when I eventually took my seat at Heathrow's gate 56. I had spent most of the day travelling to and from Stansted Airport, where I had discovered my flight had been cancelled, and then to Heathrow for an overnight flight. For some reason I had aroused the suspicion of the security staff and went through a swab-taking-toothpaste-tube-squeezing forty-minute ordeal. I felt I would never see Loughton again! I imagined the front page of the Loughton and Epping Guardian. 'Local Man Dies In Israel Plane Missile Tragedy' the headlines would scream. As the incoming passengers disembarked I envied them. They had just landed safely in London and I was just about to leave. 'It isn't too late to turn back' whispered a bad angel on my shoulder. Feeling bruised by the suspicion of the security staff, I shuffled onto the waiting plane. I took my seat next to an older man who was munching his way through a sack of celery. Would he ever stop, I wondered in distress? There was so much of the stuff that even a brontosaurus would have politely shaken its head saying, "not for me mate, I'm stuffed. " Luckily he was friendly and the flight passed quickly. Like me, my fellow passenger had dual citizenship, and soon I was helping him finish off the celery. Around five in the morning I saw the familiar shape of Tel Aviv in the grey dawn.

We thumped onto the runway. "Welcome to Israel!" boomed a very posh pre-recorded voice. The woman sounded terribly English and she was bursting with wonder and rapture. "We have just landed in Tel Aviv" she gushed. I felt the message was slightly obvious. Presumably most, if indeed not all, the passengers had realised they were boarding a flight to Tel Aviv. The abundance of heavily armed police marksmen at check-in may have been a clue. And presumably most of the passengers would have been aware that once the plane had stopped flying and hit the ground it meant that we had arrived. Maybe I am assuming too much. Perhaps there were passengers who needed to be told.

Posh woman on pre-recorded announcement: "Ladies and Gentleman. We have just arrived at Tel Aviv's Ben Gurion Airport. (And I am so excited about it I think I am about to cum.)"
Passenger One: Here! Philip! That woman says we've just landed in Tel Aviv.
Passenger Two: Naa! Don't be daft. This is Doncaster you silly mare."

I was pant-soilingly nervous as I handed over my spanking new Israeli passport to the peroxide blonde Slavic immigration officer. For some paranoid reason I expected her to press a secret button and have me whisked away and sent back to the army or some such horror. I sighed with relief as I heard her crunch a stamp onto my passport. The new airport terminal amazed me. It gleamed and shone like a sergeant major's boots. The huge bricks reminded me of the Western Wall. Outside I took a taxi straight to Rachel's Kibbutz, relishing the new sights and sounds. I had never driven this route before and we past the outskirts of Lod and Ramle, both with significant Arab populations. Mosques punctuated the skyline.

"*Yesh harbe aravim ka'an!*" said the taxi driver conversationally. "Many Arabs here." I agreed. It was true. There were. However I sensed the driver wanted to talk politics and I was keen to reactivate my Hebrew and soon we were discussing the crisis in Lebanon and Gaza.

"We are too nice with them, that's our problem!" fulminated the driver, steering the speeding car with his elbows and trying to dial a number on his mobile phone using his chin, whilst simultaneously changing gears, fiddling with the radio, eating his breakfast and sewing buttons onto his shirt. I wasn't sure I would subscribe to the statement that we were 'being too nice to them' but I didn't really want to get into a heavy discussion and perhaps find myself hitchhiking the rest of the way.

"*Eze maniak!*" he cursed, swerving past a petrol tanker. "Where is the kibbutz?" he asked me in Hebrew, tying his shoe laces and scratching his arse.

"I was kind of hoping *you* might know that" I replied as we sliced through junction after junction on the approach to Be'ersheva. God, it was depressing around here I thought, looking at the semi-desert with low quality housing estates and factories. Moreover I had forgotten to buy any water and my tongue was furry. The driver rolled down his window, screaming at passers-by. Eventually a solider pointed the direction to the kibbutz and with relief with drew up at the checkpoint, where Rachel was waiting patiently with her case, looking as fresh as a cucumber. After a quick hug we jumped back in and headed towards Tel Aviv.

We checked in at the pleasant City Hotel, thankfully receiving our rooms immediately. We then descended like ravenous beasts on the groaning buffet table. Surfeit, we explored Tel Aviv. I had grown into one of those boring geriatrics who said things like "'ere this were all trees when I were a lad." I pointed out memory after memory. It felt different. People seemed politer, friendlier. I had changed too. I was more confident, mature and settled. I was less touchy. Suddenly I felt at home. I was enjoying being here. I also felt safe.

The day was spent trying to stay awake and strolling around the city. I took Rachel to the top of the Shalom Tower and memories flooded back; memories of the Ministry of Interior and trips to extend tourist visas, and then of the final visit when I had become a citizen. How far I had come since those bad old days, I thought happily. We sat in a café on Nachalat Benjamin Street, enjoying a creamy *café afuch*. It tasted delicious. There was a buzz, an energy to the city that I had forgotten. There was now even an edition of *Time Out Magazine* dedicated to Tel Aviv. That evening we strolled around Old Jaffa, sharing a pasty stuffed with white cheese from the Arab bakery. I was taken aback by the deeply hostile attitude of the man who served me. What was that all about, I wondered, pocketing my change. We then stood, transfixed, beneath the minaret of a mosque as the muezzin began his call to prayer. The red sun was sinking into the sea. It was magical.

At an ungodly hour the next morning we were collected by a minibus and driven to the Dead Sea via Jerusalem. Tourists were thin on the ground, it seemed. We were alone till Jerusalem, where we were joined by a couple from a land without soap or deodorant. Eyes streaming, I greeted a more fragrant American mother and daughter, and a couple from the Caribbean. On our way to the Dead Sea we past the newly built Security Wall, snaking its way across hilltops. I sadly, and I am sure controversially, welcomed it. It was as an admission that this land needed to be divided into two states and that there needed to be a border. And as it was never going to be the friendly just-nipping-over-for-a-pint-of-milk kind of border, I felt a wall might be a good idea, at least for a few years. I just did not want the wall to become an excuse to grab land. I also felt pleased at how the Jewish settlers were now on the wrong side of the wall and panicking.

There had been a delay to our tour, caused by a mix up with the pick up point. Two guests were wondering where their bus was. The result was a U-turn on the desert highway and a return to Jerusalem. The two dopey guests boarded the bus to the icy stares of their fellow passengers. We had to wait for ten minutes at an army checkpoint and then a further twenty minutes in traffic. Furious, the driver-guide sped back towards the Dead Sea, trying to make up lost time. For the next hour and a quarter we drove at the speed of a plane just before take off. With one hand the driver pointed out the caves where the Dead Sea Scrolls had been found and with the other he steered the rattling minibus past an army jeep. The passengers gasped with fear. The guide interpreted this as rapture. "Is beautiful, yes?" We nodded in terror.

At the top of Massada I felt unexpectedly moved. I felt a tremendous sense of Jewish history. I snuck away from the guide. He was talking too much and I just needed a moment alone. I breathed deeply. The light was blinding and the heat was making me heavy. I could feel the spirit of the Jewish people. This desert was alive with our tragic, heroic history. Strange birds landed near me. For miles around was rocky desert. I picked up a stone to take home. It would sit on my desk and remind me of this moment. Later, at the Ein Gedi Spa I sank into the warm sulphurous water, feeling it sting my rashes and cuts. I laughed with joy as I smeared my body in hot mud and then floated in the Dead Sea.

It was *Erev Shabbat* and I paused to light two candles in a sandbox in the hotel lobby. That evening we took a taxi to Ramat Gan to visit Avi and his partner of ten years, Joseph. Before going to their flat I showed Rachel my old haunts. Every street brought back memories, both good and bad. I felt like Barbara Streisland singing 'Memories.' When we got to the riverside park I was sad to see the wildness had disappeared and a landscaped park had risen in its place. I felt as if something had been stolen from me. The old Arab village was still there. Except it had never been an old Arab village. It was in fact a deserted outpost from the British Army. A small plaque explained the history.

We arrived at Avi and Joseph's flat and heard their husky, Sky, barking and slobbering. And, if my last visit was anything to go by, he was getting himself all stiffed up for a good old bit of leg rubbing action. Inside Joseph and Avi had set a festive table and prepared a cocktail with enough Rum to keep a Christmas pudding on fire for a month. The flat was lit with soft candlelight, and the smell of baking, cucumber and guava scented the air. We then demolished Joseph's mouth-watering shouldn't-have-anymore-but-my-hand-can't-stop cauliflower cheese and mushroom risotto. I was glad to see Avi and Joseph looking relaxed and happy together. In the background was the news. Hizbollah had launched an unprecedented number of rockets. Haifa was reeling from the assault, and missiles had reached as far as Hadera, a short drive from Tel Aviv. And despite this, I felt calm. I was a Jew and an Israeli and this was still my country. It was less scary to be in Israel than to be watching the one-sided news in England. Israel felt united. Flags hung defiantly from balconies. People were pulling together. This was not a war we had sought out. It was going to be an unpleasant war, a war for which Iran and Hizbollah had been preparing for six years. Hizbollah strategy was clever and cruel. Their tactic was to fire missiles from densely populated civilian areas, using their own people as human shields. Israel would need to make a diabolical choice between allowing its own people to be killed or to fight back, inflicting massive civilian casualties on Lebanon. Would the missiles soon have chemical warheads? No country could allow such a threat to continue unchallenged. And yet every action by Israel was described by the western media as a war crime, or as disproportionate. Camera crews were on hand to take full advantage of the civilian casualties but nearly all Western TV channels refused to show Israeli army videos of rockets leaving the buildings which were then destroyed by Israeli fire. Meanwhile Syria was supplying Hizbollah with fresh missiles, using the roads and bridges from Syria into Lebanon. I shook my head in resignation. Once again we were going to have to do what we needed to stay safe and world opinion would turn against us.

Meanwhile Iran, Syria and Hizbollah escaped international scorn. In England there were demonstrations demonising Israel. The far left continued their odd alliance with Islamic fundamentalists and rallied public opinion against Israel. Socialists, including some Jews, marched happily alongside protesters with banners which called for the destruction of Israel. Hizbollah was succeeding in its war aim of becoming the new heroes. The Scottish MP George Galloway stated in public that "we are *all* Hizbollah now" and I seethed with anger. According to Jewish lore, in every generation arises an implacable foe called Amalek. As far as I was concerned, Iran was the new Amalek and Hizbollah were their henchmen. Like the gullible appeasers of Nazi Germany, most of Western Europe preferred not to see the truth. Only the odd maverick such as columnist Julie Burchill broke the trend. Yet Iran was clamouring for genocide against Israel, and against the Jews, and was developing the ability to carry out its threat. The entire Middle East was now facing the threat of Islamo-fascism. Only days before I had seen photographs of two lovely sixteen year old boys being publicly hanged in Iran for being gay. I had felt sick as I saw them blindfolded on the gallows. A man was tightening the rope around their necks, wearing the now familiar *kafiya* head-dress. Next to him another man was calmly talking into a mobile phone, grinning. I had also seen photographs of a woman buried up to her waist, her head covered in a white sheet. Next to her was a pile of stones. This was Iran in 2006, and Hizbollah was their puppet. This was a government which promoted a dangerous, anti-Semitic ideology and with whom no dialogue was possible. This was a country which revelled in Hitlerian propaganda, which was hosting an exhibition of Holocaust cartoons and which revived long-dead anti-Semitic mythology.

Life never used to be this scary. Back home a plot had recently been uncovered for a wave of devastating attacks on synagogues. Attacks on Jews were on the increase and the delegitimization of Israel was becoming increasingly acceptable. Israel had become the liberal west's new whipping boy. I was increasingly frustrated at the tirades and the energy of the campaign against Israel, and appalled by the double standards and hypocrisy, which let the barbaric regimes of Saudi Arabia, Iran and China off virtually scot-free. The result of this was a world opinion which was becoming dangerously hostile to Zionism, Israel and the Jews. I sighed. There was no point talking anymore. Dialogue seemed futile. The media portrayal of Israel and the absurd positions taken by otherwise rational people left me feeling profoundly weary. I had no strength. I would leave the task to those better connected and more patiently articulate than I.

The next day, after breakfast, we relaxed on the beach. I enjoyed the luxury of a sun lounger and umbrella, and ordered Turkish coffee from a baby-faced Russian waiter with a body that even Greek gods would envy. I suddenly realised I was a middle-aged man. Everyone seemed young. People who were kids when I lived here were now soldiers. I went for a swim in the warm sea, trying to ignore the sinister and constant cackle of news bulletins and the drone of army helicopters that past every few minutes.

Early on Sunday morning we discovered that there would only be three of us on the tour to Jerusalem. "You here on 'oliday? There is a war!" shouted the guide by way of greeting, giving the only other guest the front seat. Our driver guide took us on a route I had never taken. We climbed through the Judean Hills, past the new city of Modiin, which had not even existed when I lived here, and into the West Bank. I felt uneasy. Was this such a good idea? The landscape became biblical and rough. Beyond a high wire fence were the outskirts of Ramallah. 'Please don't get a puncture!' I prayed to myself. Once more my mind saw the front page of the local newspaper. "Local Man And Niece Hacked To Pieces In Israel Guided Tour Carnage Horror." To my relief we soon arrived at the northern outskirts of Jerusalem. It was a wonderful trip. I saw places I had never seen and the guide had a knack of surprising me. The place names evoked memories of reading my first ever Jewish book. I had read *O Jerusalem* nearly quarter of a century earlier when I was in my mid-teens. The impact of it made me long to live in Israel. We past the spot where 73 Jewish nurses and doctors had been butchered on Mount Scopus in 1948. We past the British First World War cemetery and the Hebrew University. Then our minibus trundled down into the Kidron Valley, passing the beautiful Russian Orthodox church and the Garden of Gethsemane. We disembarked into the heat and made our way to the Tomb of King David. I could not genuinely believe that King David was buried here but the place felt holy. We walked through the Arab market. The tourists had all fled but the stallholders were busy selling fragrant spices from huge tins. There were stacks of clothes and plastic sandals and packets of soap. Arab music filtered through radios and I sniffed the aromas of coffee, leather, turmeric and smoke. We arrived at the Holy Sepulchre. It was wonderfully quiet and atmospheric. Candles flickered, and the sounds of a Catholic Mass floated over. The worshippers seemed to be mainly Russian women, immigrants who were Jewish according to the Law of Return yet Christian in faith. We were then taken to an Arab shop in the Old City where the guide had contacts and we emerged carrying armfuls of overpriced souvenirs, with our wallets depleted and our faces stunned. It was however heartening to see the Jewish Israeli guide being greeted by Palestinian Arabs all over the Old City.

All too soon we left the Arab market which I found fascinating and exhilarating and soon we were back in the modern Jewish Quarter which lacked the buzz, thrills and smells. We saw an interesting exhibition of photographs about the fate of the Jewish residents of the Jewish Quarter taken prisoner by the Jordanians in 1948. The photographs showed the grim internment camp deep in the Jordanian desert and the utter devastation wrought on the ancient synagogues and homes in the Old City. Gravestones from the Jewish cemetery on the Mount of Olives had been used to pave the road to Jericho. Soon it was time to visit the Western Wall. I had hoped that the visit would feel like a pilgrimage and that I would leave with a feeling of spiritual wholeness. I was wrong. The plaza felt alien. I looked at the men in black fedoras and knee-length socks. They barely glanced back at me. Our visions of Judaism were so different I wondered whether we were part of the same religion.

We rejoined the now stifling bus and gasped as we waited for the air conditioning to kick in. We drove through the German Colony, an nineteenth century suburb with a lively high street and then continued to the urban kibbutz of Ramat Rachel, overlooking Bethlehem which was now in the control of Hamas and out of bounds. The guide explained how the once thriving Christian community had been driven out by Hamas. Nearly all of the town's Christians had joined the Palestinian Diaspora overseas; their homes were used for firing missiles at Jerusalem's Jewish neighbourhoods. At the kibbutz we had a buffet lunch though I made do with some roast potatoes and a strawberry and banana juice. We had arrived just in time, as a huge party of African Christians starting forming a vast queue out the door and halfway back to Jerusalem.

Our final stop was Yad VaShem, the Holocaust Shrine and museum.

"Zer are some Germans over there!" our guide indicated gleefully. "Interesting to see zer reaction." I was not entirely sure what he expected them to do. Perhaps there would be some sackcloth and ashes for them to buy at the Yad VaShem gift shop.

"Hello, ve vould like some sackcloth unt ashes unt ein hair shirt please" they would say, adding "mein grantvarther woz only followink orders you know." I found the concept of being personally guilty for one's country's history ludicrous but I was having a good day and could not be bothered arguing. As I entered middle age I found I had less and less appetite for confrontation with people who had strong opinions.

I noticed the changes to Yad VaShem immediately. A new exhibition snaked around an airy hall, where photographs and exhibits built slowly up to the gas chambers. I was transfixed by a huge screen showing footage of Jewish life in the *Shtetls* of Eastern Europe before the war. I was glad to see that the exhibition now mentioned other groups. I watched out of the corner of my eye as a very devout Jewish man read an explanation of the pink triangles and the systematic murder of gays. His face was not giving much away. We visited the dark room commemorating the children. It was not my first visit here, yet this time it really got to me. "Oh God! I'm going to cry," I thought, panicking. This was so uncool. I brushed my eyes vigorously and emerged into the brilliant sunlight, breathing the scent of the pine forest. I told my niece I had had enough Holocaust for one day and she agreed. I grabbed a deliciously rich *café afuch* for the bus and soon we were on our way home. We past the village of Ein Kerem, and the famous Hadassah Hospital and finally Kasteel, a vitally strategic point in the 1948 War of Independence and the site of an epic battle.

It was our last night and we celebrated at *Aladdin* in Old Jaffa, with a meal of *labaneh* or Arab white cheese with hyssop, warm pitta, hummus and falafel. The green neon light of the mosque came on as night fell and once more the haunting cry of the *muezzin* called the faithful to prayer. I remembered being at this restaurant a decade earlier with my mother and Avi. Then I remembered my first visit to Jaffa in 1990, looking at this restaurant and wishing I could afford it. The view had changed slightly. New skyscrapers punctured the horizon in Ramat Gan. Tomorrow we would both go home. But just for tonight I was an Israeli in Israel once more.

The End

About the Author

Andrew Reid lives in Loughton in Essex, along with his civil partner and two cats. He teaches English at a busy East London college. The book is based on his experiences of living as a new immigrant in Israel and as a Jew by choice.

Printed in the United Kingdom
by Lightning Source UK Ltd.
117747UKS00001BA/274-288